Paradigms in Progress
Life Beyond Economics

Also by Hazel Henderson:
CREATING ALTERNATIVE FUTURES: THE END OF ECONOMICS
POLITICS OF THE SOLAR AGE: ALTERNATIVES TO ECONOMICS
REDEFINING WEALTH AND PROGRESS (contributor)

HAZEL HENDERSON is an internationally-published futurist, lecturer and consultant to organizations in over thirty countries. She is also an activist and founder of many public service groups and has authored over two hundred articles. She is a Director of Worldwatch Institute and a Trustee of Appropriate Technology International; an advisor to The Cousteau Society and the Calvert Social Investment Fund; a member of the World Futures Studies Federation (Turku, Finland), and the World Social Prospects Study Association (Geneva); a Fellow of the Lindisfarne Association (Berne) and the Elmwood Institute (Berkeley). She serves on the Editorial Boards of *World Paper* (Boston), *Technological Forecasting and Social Change* (New York), *The Journal of Humanistic Psychology* (San Fransisco), *Futures Research Quarterly* (Washington, DC), *Resurgence* and *The Journal of Inter-disciplinary Economics* (both of Britain). She holds an honorary doctorate from Worcester Polytechnic Institute, Massachusetts, for her work in alternative economics and technology, was a Visiting Lecturer at the University of California, Santa Barbara (1979) and held the Horace Albright Chair in the Department of Forestry, University of California, Berkeley in 1982. She is a Senior Research Fellow at the Research Center for Economic, Technological and Social Development of the State Council of the People's Republic of China (Shanghai) and served on the Speaker's Advisory Committee on the Future, of the Florida State Legislature. From 1974 to 1980, she served as a member of the U.S. Congress Office of Technology Assessment Advisory Council and on advisory committees of the National Science Foundation and the National Academy of Engineering. Henderson, who was born in Britain, lives in St. Augustine, Florida, and is associated with the Center for Governmental Responsibility and the Division of Continuing Education at the University of Florida in Gainesville and has founded the non-profit Center for Sustainable Development and Alternative World Futures in St. Augustine.

Paradigms in Progress
Life Beyond Economics

Hazel Henderson

133 lines
Berrett-Koehler Publishers
San Francisco

Acknowledgments

Portions of this work, of which the author retains original copyrights, have appeared previously in different form, as follows: parts of Chapter One in *Gaia: A Way of Knowing,* Ed. William Irwin Thompson, The Lindesfarne Association, New York, 1987; parts of Chapter Two, in *Futures,* September, London, 1990, and in *The Green Fuse: The Schumacher Lectures,* 1983-1988, Quartet Books, London, 1990; parts of Chapter Three, in *Business Ethics and the Environment,* Eds. W. Michael Hoffman, Robert Frederick and Edward S. Petry, Quorum Books, Westport, CT, 1990, and in *Technological Forecasting and Social Change,* Elsevier, New York, June 1990; and Pecos River in *What I Have Learned: Thinking About the Future Then and Now,* Eds. Michael Marien and Lane Jennings, Greenwood Press, New York, 1987. Brief passages in Chapter Seven appeared in some of the author's editorials in the *Christian Science Monitor.* The author acknowledges the courtesy of all these publications in respecting all of her original copyrights on all of the above material for the purpose of inclusion in this book. A final acknowledgment is to Knowledge Systems, Inc. for their persistence in urging me to write this work, and to my editor, Margaret Helen, who played an indispensable role and who supported me far beyond the call of duty during the whole process.

Berrett-Koehler Publishers, Inc.
155 Montgomery Street
San Francisco, CA 94104-4109
Tel: (415) 288-0260 Fax: (415) 362-2512

Orders for college textbook/course adoption use
Please contact Berrett-Koehler Publishers at the address above.

Orders by U.S. trade bookstores and wholesalers
Please contact Publishers Group West, 4065 Hollis Street, Box 8843, Emeryville, CA 94662
Tel: (510) 658-3453; 1-800-788-3123 Fax: (510) 658-1834

Printed in the United States of America

 Printed on acid-free and recycled paper that is composed of 85% recovered fiber, including 15% post-consumer waste.

Library of Congress Cataloging-in-Publication Data
Henderson, Hazel, 1933-
    Paradigms in progress: life beyond economics / Hazel Henderson p. cm.
    Includes bibliographical references and index.
    ISBN 1-881052-74-5
    1. Economic development—Environmental aspects. 2. Democracy.
I. Title
HD75.6.H46 1991
363.7—dc20   91-37215
CIP   iv

First edition published in 1991 by Knowledge Systems.
This edition published by Berrett-Koehler Publishers, Inc., San Francisco.
First Berrett-Koehler Edition May 1995
    99 98 97 96 95   10 9 8 7 6 5 4 3 2 1

For Brendan
Alexander Cassidy
with love

Dedicated to all the members
of the Human Family who are . . .

Nourishing OUR BODIES

Enriching OUR MINDS

Sharpening OUR SKILLS

Empowering OUR ACTIONS

Inventing NEW TOOLS

Building OUR COMMUNITIES

Mediating OUR CONFLICTS

Feeding OUR HUNGRY

Planning FAMILIES

Planting TREES

Enhancing OUR LIFESTYLES

Developing NEW BUSINESSES

Pioneering IN SPACE

Converting WEAPONS TO CIVILIAN GOODS

Aiding OUR NEEDY

Living LIGHTLY

Protecting THE EARTH

Defending ALL WILDLIFE

Cleaning UP OUR AIR AND WATER

Greening DESERTS

Investing FOR A HEALTHY PLANET

Rearing CHILDREN

Helping NEIGHBORS

Being CITIZEN DIPLOMATS

Volunteering SERVICES

Sharing SUCCESSES

Learning FROM MISTAKES

Creating ALTERNATIVE FUTURES

Alerting US TO DANGERS

Cooperating FOR COMMON GOALS

Making OUR MUSIC

Singing OUR SONGS

Envisioning POSITIVE GOALS

Designing HARMONIOUS COMMUNITIES

Encouraging OUR ARTS

Weaving OUR NETWORKS

Sheltering OUR HOMELESS

Teaching OUR YOUNG ONES

Giving OUR GIFTS

Dancing OUR DREAMS

Fostering OUR HOPES

Serving THE PEOPLE

Exploring THE WONDERS OF NATURE

Leading US TOWARD WHOLENESS

Loving EACH OTHER

Communing TOGETHER . . .

AND *Celebrating* LIFE!

Contents

List of Illustrations

In its established usage,* a paradigm is an accepted model or pattern. . . . In a science, a paradigm is rarely an object for further articulation and specification under new or more stringent conditions. . . . Paradigms gain their status because they are more successful than their competitors in solving a few problems that a group of practitioners has come to recognize as acute.

—Thomas S. Kuhn, *The Structure of Scientific Revolutions*
(University of Chicago Press, 1962)

In spite of Thomas Kuhn's many cautions to me not to over-generalize or to use his definition of paradigm in a social context, I believe a paradigm is a pair of different spectacles which can reveal a new view of reality, allowing us to re-conceive our situation, re-frame old problems and find new pathways for evolutionary change.

—Hazel Henderson, *Paradigms in Progress*
(Knowledge Systems, 1991)

A social paradigm, for me, is a constellation of concepts, values, perceptions and practices, shared by a community that forms a particular vision of reality that is the basis of the way the community organizes itself. It's necessary for a paradigm to be shared by a community. A single person can have a worldview, but a paradigm is shared by a community.

—Fritjof Capra, *Belonging to the Universe*
(HarperCollins, 1991)

---

* "Established usage" refers to the limited sense of application to models of scientific enquiry. —*H.H.*

Pecos River Meditation

Lovers of learning
And all life
Ponder meaning, over steaming cappuccino
Wafting cinnamon
And smooth cream.
Chill snow
Dusting the bright spring morning
In ancient pueblo country
Heart of the Land
Of the Eagle.

What high purpose
Gives deepest meaning to their lives?
Teacher? Learner? Enabler?
Just helping others along?
Lover! Why not say it plain!
Perhaps such candor might offend,
Misconstrued by those in cultures
Which blind people
To their own divinity.

All life is sacred.
Truth that loses its meaning
In a welter of high-tech toys,
Trendy tricks and
Counterfeit spirituality.
Yet each one of us is sacred still,
Holy children of Gaia's love
And teeming plenitude.
How deep, deep we now must reach
To find our
Inner glory.

Blest are those who find special ones
With whom to share the search.
Even as we see the love in
Every one we meet
In every stone and flower
Of the great creation
Still the warmth and comfort
Of each other,
Communing together
In awe and celebration,
Loving the magic, the dreams, the faith,
Is pure benediction.

How best to communicate these meanings?
And the essence of the journey?
"The Hero's Journey," we are told.
Sounds a pompous note?
Separating us from mother's blood,
Soil, trees,
Pots and blankets,
Toys, and
Sacred babies' diapers.

"The Lover's Journey"
Feels better for life's daily round
Of Holiness,
Each task performed
With mindfulness
Each encounter with friend, lover,
Vendor, passer-by,
A pious opportunity.
This loving impulse,
Born anew each day, each generation,
Is the sacred core
Of all sects and cults.
The Golden Rule, Mythic wisdom,
Cultural DNA encoding all our learning,
Distilling all our prayers.

Life's Lovers
Glean the images of history
For universal themes.
Archetypes that can symbolize
The sacred understandings in
Friendly garb and metaphor.
What deeply-known roles
Can the players don
To help reduce the strife,

Re-weave the patterns that bind us all
Within the wheel of life?

Trader, builder, host,
Juggler, jester, scribe,
Artist, musician, hunter,
Poet, farmer, weaver, or gypsy-nomad,
Bearer of strange treasures from afar?
All can bring messages of light
More palatable than those in haughty masks.
King, guru, sage,
Orator, emperor, warrior chief
In horns and antlers
All lead by power and fear,
Dimming each soul's sacred flame,
Creating only dependency and shame.

Lovers lead gently, by attraction
No longer to capture females or DNA,
No longer to give birth to many young,
But to nurture each other,
To make a difference with their sacred lives,
To weigh in on evolution's side.
No longer impaled on sad crosses
Of guilt,
But singing and dancing the songs within
Their souls
And celebrating art!

Lovers always recognize each other
And all who share such meanings.
Beyond all roles, garbs, and many-hued
Disguises.
Lovers with high purposes
May also choose kingly roles,
Accepting karmic risks of leadership,
Some pure souls may don the mask of "success.'
Others prefer to flit as butterflies,
Tuning, blending, sharing energies,
All keeping faith mid unlikely scenes,
Honeycombed industrial hives,
Corporate ranches mushrooming
In holy snow-capped wilderness.

When all remember they are lovers
Then all places are sacred once again,
Each red pepper drying in the sun,
Each seed of corn,
Sweet smelling cedars flanking

The peaceful stream.
The spirit of all things is in the brisk, chill wind,
The untidy, boisterous dogs,
The winter-coated, sweating horses.

Sacredness is everywhere,
From the lonely pueblo ruins,
To mysterious dugouts, black pots
Lost on sandy isles,
Amid tangled seagrape and diving waterbirds.
Neither is sacredness the province
Of antiquity, or any age,
Each time and culture offers us its gems
Even in our own "post-industrial era."
It is for us to see the beauty in this too,
Amid the strutting "Information Age,"
The nuclear nightmare.

Lovers always seek and find the grail
Anew in every time and place
To show the truth that art is everywhere.
In beads and shells,
Weavings, pots and purses,
In all the subtle rituals and little things,
In healthy meals,
In warm-fleshed human intimacy,
The highs and lows of daily lives.
No rose without the sacred shit
On which it thrives,
The chaos out of which
All forms are born.

The grail is in ourselves.
Verbs are truth,
Nouns sometimes mislead.
If all things are sacred,
Then, at last,
Each lover's inner light
And reverence
Shine forth.

—Hazel Henderson
Pecos River Conference Center
Santa Fe, New Mexico, March 1985

Introduction

Now that the terminology of alternative thinkers has been adopted by heads of state, corporate executives and their speechwriters, it is time to move on.

Phrases such as *the new paradigm, empowerment, the new world order, partnership, networking, organic, bio-diversity* and *planetary ecosystem,* now show up in official documents and press releases. However narrowly conceived and interpreted, they indicate new opening to a fuller comprehension of larger realities and, at least, the possibility of a saner, more enlightened political debate in many countries.

How best can alternative thinkers use these opportunities to expand the "policy envelopes" of business and government decision-makers and prevent further homogenization, trivialization and devaluing of the transformational power of such alternative worldviews? How can we seize the rhetorical moment and help "step down" these new paradigms into practical form?

A case in point is the metaphor of "transformation" itself. In 1975, I remember testifying before the Joint Economic Committee of the United States Congress concerning my views of "The Great Economic Transition" then occurring in mature industrial societies, as they bogged down in the results of their "success": urban crises, crime, drugs, pollution and the growing imbalances between rich and poor. I recall that I was almost laughed out of the hearing room, with protestations that there was no evidence of any such economic transition. In 1991, I was invited to a meeting in London of the Inter-Action Council (a group of thirty-five former heads of state) as an expert on the subject of the meeting: Economies in Transformation: Limitations and Potential of the Transition Process.

Meanwhile, of course, economic transitions, restructuring, perestroika, and other such terms are the stuff of daily headlines. Yet these stories are still told, too often, within the old paradigms: the celestial mechanics of Isaac Newton, the reductionist legacy of René Descartes and worst of all, the left-right, communism vs. capitalism dogmas of traditional economics still evoking the specters of the Cold War era and entrapping these dynamic changes in static assumptions of general equilibrium.

In April, 1964, two farsighted American scholars, Warren G. Bennis and Philip E. Slater co-authored an article in the *Harvard Business Review* entitled "Democracy is Inevitable," followed in 1968 by *The Temporary Society* (Harper & Row). The nub of their stunning thesis (at the height of the Cold War) was that as societies, corporations, and other institutions became larger and more complex, they would become *unmanageable* with top-down chains of command. The necessary information and feedback from the shop floor, the branch offices and ultimately, the grassroots of whole societies, would be suppressed and distorted by the layers of bureaucracy in such pyramids of power and the leaders would become out of touch—ignorant of changing realities.

Bennis and Slater, in predicting the crumbling of such pyramidal structures, asserted that flattening hierarchies, decentralizing organizations and democratizing societies would be inevitable in the 20th century, simply because it would be more *efficient*. When there is just too much information, too many variables to digest, the executive suite, the junta or dictator, becomes in effect, the dinosaur's brain: a bottleneck, too slow and rigid to manage change.

Under today's conditions of accelerating change—driven by globalizing forces unleashed by human activities creating such interacting complexities—*only* devolving toward self-managing, smaller, more cellular units in much deeper communication with each other, can lead to functioning organizations and the body politic, i.e., democracy is *necessary*.

The stunning events of August, 1991, and the breakup of the Soviet Union represented only the largest and most dramatic example of this new necessity. The trend in so many places toward devolution, decentralization, *Small is Beautiful* principles as outlined by E.F. Schumacher in his book in 1973; the local "town meeting" revival, grassroots movements of citizens for greater accountability of governments and corporations, academic, professional and religious institutions; expresses this necessity, as do demands for the protection of human rights, consumers' and workers' safety and of our endangered Planet itself.

Today, we see the old political and economic paradigms shifting before our eyes. Democracy itself is on the march all over the world.

Soviet "hardliners" in their old-style, militaristic coup attempt are referred to by all as "right-wing." In the United States, those on "the right" are generally deemed to be for individual liberty and economic laissez-faire, i.e., the "freedom" of the market. But as Philip Slater points out in his latest book, *A Dream Deferred* (Beacon, 1991), the American right-wing is, at heart, authoritarian and seeks order in hierarchical institutions. While still believing that democracy is an unstoppable "mega-culture" rising everywhere to meet the needs for self-organization and feedback, Slater examines the deep roots of authoritarianism in the United States itself, of which our own "right wing" is only the iceberg's tip. When we dissect the authoritarian personality, family, corporation, as feminist theoretician Riane Eisler also points out in *The Chalice and the Blade* (Harper & Collins, 1989), we find deep fears that exist to prevent even Americans from fulfilling their own democratic dream.

Authoritarians, whether in the United States, the Soviet old-guard patriarchs, militaristic dictators or the hierarchies of mega-scale corporations have much in common: they fear and distrust "human nature" and any rule "of the people, by the people and for the people," because they perceive them to be as power and ego-driven as themselves. Revealingly, as the Soviet "Gang of Eight" disintegrated on August 21, 1991, (due to their misunderstanding of the people and the new conditions of glasnost and perestroika) an American media pundit "on the right" during a TV interview, criticized the coup in typical authoritarian terms: for not being tough, smart and ruthless *enough*, as "the gang who couldn't shoot straight!"

Thus we need to recognize that the march of democracy will be resisted in many ways—particularly when it threatens authoritarians or those opposed to *economic* democracy. Economists, particularly in the West, often equate democracy and human rights with the freedom of the marketplace, rugged individualism and the frontier. Huge corporations have operated comfortably behind such theories which hold them as "individuals" before the law—whatever the costs of their activities to society and the environment.

The economic and social transformations in the Soviet Union and Eastern Europe are helping illuminate such theories and rewrite the scripts of many Western think tanks and advisors "on the right" now swarming all over Eastern Europe and the Soviet Union. They are still trying to straightjacket the many-faceted movements toward democratization with capitalism and equate these movements with "free" markets. Yet in many countries, for example Chile, Singapore, South Korea and South Africa, free markets co-exist comfortably with repression.

Rather the new democracy movements need to be understood in the multi-disciplinary terms of living systems theory: as the spontaneous rising—chaotic as it will be—of self-management, autonomy, the expression of human rights and potentials, aspirations for political and economic democracy. These processes are the most efficient and necessary way to operate complex societies riding the tiger of change in the 1990s.

Today, at least, some adventurous economists are broadening their minds, trying to find chaos theorists to take to lunch, or tiptoeing off to such hangouts as the Santa Fe Institute, where old-paradigm physicists and superannuated cold warriors seek to recycle themselves. The Santa Fe Institute is another case in point, illustrating the issues involved in actually changing paradigms. The Institute seeks to explore these changes using the new non-equilibrium tools and chaos models (see Plate 3-16, Emerging Change Models) described in 1981 in Chapter 11 of my book, *Politics of the Solar Age* and in such popular books as James Gleick's *Chaos* (Viking, 1987) and David Peat's *The Philosopher's Stone* (Doubleday, 1990). Yet the Santa Fe Institute is largely funded from conservative sources, including Citibank, which obviously wants to use this research to become a more efficient global profit maximizer and play its electronic financial markets with its own "rocket scientists" or "quants" (Wall Street's term for the new wizards of high-tech information systems and mathematics). These new wizards arbitrage currencies and create risk-hedging strategies such as program trading of stock index futures and derivatives: options, puts, calls and, ominously, "virtual securities." *Plus ça change, plus c'est même chose!* as our French friends say, since all these wonderful new chaos models are being co-opted into old paradigm pursuits. Similarly, the Santa Fe Institute, while seeking to study uncertainty, diversity and change, is peopled predominantly by white, Northern Hemisphere men of late middle age schooled in the "hard" sciences and classical physics and math.

Another case is point is George Bush's view of the new paradigm: "empowering" the poor to take care of themselves; fostering voluntarism and expanding the 1000 points of light, while protecting the Federal Budget Agreement's priorities and beneficiaries (the Departments of Defense, Energy, and Transportation, et al.) and their corporate contractors. Only as the U.S. economy visibly weakened did Democrats sharpen their focus on this decline and Bush began shifting budget priorities from military to domestic security concerns. Neither party, however is working with a functional paradigm and unemployment worsened in September 1991. The battle over budget priorities as well as the collapse of the Soviet empire led to Bush's historic unilateral disarmament initiatives.

They focussed, correctly, on cutting nuclear weapons, for which opinion research had already identified strong public support, according to Americans Talk Issues Foundation (ATIF) Survey #16, June 1991. In this rhetorical cloud cuckooland, Bush's New World Order looks to many, particularly in the Southern Hemisphere, as "Might Is Right." This view was expounded in a *South* editorial in their February 1991 issue entitled "The Sleek Shall Inherit the Earth" which saw a new era of American hegemony, with the United States seeking to consolidate its Gulf War victory, paid for by its "burden-sharing" partners and well on its way to becoming a mercenary economy and the world's first "rent-a-super power"—a term echoed by the London-based *The Economist*.

This book summarizes my own paradigms in progress and my efforts over the past three years to intercept policy debates anywhere in the world that I could—offering new directions, expanded contexts, connections, and possibilities for creating "win-win" solutions in our ever-shrinking, more crowded, polluted Planet. I hope that this sampler— conceptually incomplete (as required by the new paradigm itself) serves as an invitation to every reader to get involved, to act, try new avenues toward building a saner, more equitable, gender-balanced, ecologically-conscious future.

As physicist David Peat notes in *The Philosopher's Stone*, there are all kinds of novel connections in the universe. "What we call the past is really a creation, a projection from the present." For me, this truly means that I can choose to see each new day as the dawn of creation. All of the wonderful alternative thinkers and doers with whom I work and dialogue intuitively grasp this daily cosmic dance of realities. It is this kind of embracing of the potentials and possibilities on our living Planet that brought down the Berlin Wall, ended the Cold War and the hardliners coup in Moscow. If we all work hard enough and are inspired enough, we, the people, in all countries can still reclaim the peace dividend and restore the Earth.

The global transition to the Solar Age

The premise of my work over the past fifteen years was studying the transition of industrial societies from their nonrenewable resource base as they shifted toward a new base of renewable resources. This transition is both inevitable and evolutionarily necessary, and the only question is whether industrial leaders will recognize this shift and **work with it** or continue to try to override its signals, as the United States did in the Gulf War.

In fact, the wrenching shifts to sustainable and ecologically-viable forms of productivity have been manifesting themselves in many ways since the 1960s. But the overall pattern of this great industrial transition, until recently, has been obscured and misdiagnosed by obsolete analytical and policy tools. These events and changes have ranged from new forms of social pathology such as domestic resource-based inequities (permitting old and poor people to die from lack of heat) to international conflicts and the spiralling arms race. They have included the appearance of new "post-materialist" values in industrial societies, shifting geopolitical power and terms of trade to the new Gordian knot of oil prices, Third World debt and the continuing threats they pose to the global banking system.[1] In 1991, world demand for oil (around 66 million barrels a day) is growing by 1.5 percent per year. Americans, now 5 percent of the world's population, consume 25 percent of the world's energy. The underlying pattern in all these events has been concealed by the myopia of traditional economics (whether market oriented or socialistic) and by industrialism's fragmented, Cartesian worldview which, in turn, allowed its singleminded pursuit of mass production, undifferentiated growth of Gross National Product (GNP), its overemphasis on supply of energy and models and its narrow definitions of efficiency, growth and human welfare.[2]

Of course, the inevitability of this great transition of industrial societies to sustainable, renewable resources based productivity has been evident for decades to those trained in the life sciences, as well as many thermodynamicists, chemists, engineers, physicists and systems analysts, not to mention sociologists, anthropologists and psychologists and millions of well-rounded citizens and generalists. But as the great industrial societies reached their fossil-fueled zeniths in the 1950s and the "Soaring Sixties," signs of trouble were only publicized by a courageous few, such as Barbara Ward in *Spaceship Earth* (1966) and Rachel Carson, whose warning in *Silent Spring* was dismissed in 1962 by the celebrants of industrialism's success.

So great was the euphoria that ominous social costs, from polluted air and water to deteriorating cities, mass transit and infrastructure were ignored. But not only were the social and environmental *costs* of industrialism ignored, so were its many *subsidies* unaccounted for in economic models. These costs for the U.S. energy sector alone range from $100-$300 billion per year (depending on high and low estimates), and include tax credits, environmental degradation, increased health care expenditures and lost employment according to Harold M. Hubbard in "The Real Cost of Energy," *Scientific American*, April 1991.

The social subsidies hidden from analyses were based on a set of industrial values we now view as colonialism, racism and sexism. For example, the *colonial* value system was perpetuated in globally inequitable terms of trade which locked Third World countries into such deals as those by which Ghana sold its hydroelectricity for aluminum smelting at a fraction of world energy market prices[3] or misguided development advice and "assistance" which created today's external energy and technological dependencies on the North. The hidden subsidies to industrial economies by *domestic colonialism* (i.e., racism) included categorizing many lowly but indispensable maintenance jobs as "less productive," e.g., garbage collectors, cleaners and janitors, mass transit, road maintenance and other public service workers, hospital orderlies, domestics and farm workers, and as reserved for Blacks, Hispanics or other less powerful ethnic minorities. The subsidies provided by indigenous Native Americans were literally inestimable, as their lands and resources were plundered by force, and their peace treaties abrogated each time another energy or mineral resource became commercially attractive—all documented so well in Kirkpatrick Sale's *Conquest of Paradise* (1991).

Lastly, the subsidies provided to the monetarized GNP sector by *sexism* are only now coming into full view. The energy-profligate mushrooming of the "Suburban Lifestyle" was almost totally predicated on the unpaid labor of the American woman. She was relied upon to maintain the single family suburban home and backyard, parent the children, serve on school boards, volunteer for a host of community services and most of all to fill the key job of incessant chauffeuring of the automobilized population, on which the whole lifestyle depends. Not only was this huge subsidy (now estimated world wide as an uncounted additional average of some 30 percent to the GNP, as mentioned in Chapter Seven) unrecognized, but also the American woman's role as "heroic consumer," trained in millions of home economics courses and by advertising supported "service" magazines for her key role in "keeping up with the Jones" and thus maintaining Keynesian demand-led, economic growth.

A model challenged

As recently as a decade ago all of these linchpins of the industrial value system were accepted with little question. Today, all of it has changed. The advent of the Organization of Petroleum Exporting Countries (OPEC) in 1973 and subsequent private bank "recycling" of petro dollars altered the fundamental relationship between industrial and Third World countries. Formerly unacknowledged interdependencies are now crucial agenda items in economic summit meetings and will be in the foreseeable future. The old bankers' adage has entered the vernacular: "if the bank lends you $100, it's *your* problem; if it lends you $100 million, it's *the bank's* problem." Similarly, the subsidies of racism must increasingly be accounted for in the GNP. Black voters are proving this locally, in Chicago, Atlanta, Philadelphia and other cities, as well as in national politics, as they and Hispanic Americans change the economic rules as their clout increases. And political strategists ponder the growing "gender gap" in the voting patterns of women. While native American people battle in courts and legislatures for their land and resource rights, they are also trying to teach us how their value system protected resources and fostered sustained yield productivity,[4] making them almost "invisible farmers" of North America's natural ecosystem and wildlife.[5]

By the late 1960s, many of these formerly hidden environmental and social costs had become visible enough to produce citizen protest movements in most industrial societies, whether to fight pollution, or to lobby for civil rights, corporate and government accountability, better mass transit, housing and to reduce the dangers of nuclear proliferation and the arms race. But still the grand pattern of the industrial transition did not become fully clear until the onset of the "Stagflation 70s." Until then politicians had the comparatively simple task of maintaining GNP-growth, while keeping both inflation and unemployment at "politically acceptable" low levels. Resources were still readily available or could be cheaply imported from Third World countries; citizen movements had not gained sufficient political clout to enforce many of the new regulations on industries that dumped toxic wastes, discriminated against women and minorities or exposed their workers to hazardous materials.

Economists learned from OPEC

Right up until 1973, economists ignored the special role of fossil energy as the flywheel of traditional industrialism. Energy was still a vague, highly-aggregated input in most production modes—assumed to be inexhaustible and interchangeable as long as the price was right. So when OPEC flexed its muscles in 1973, thousands of biologists, ecologists, thermodynamicists and systems analysts discreetly rejoiced. At least OPEC would force economists to learn to respect the basic laws of physics and ground their abstractions in some baseline data from the natural world.

Economists were challenged to disaggregate their energy supply-demand models, to look at end-use efficiencies, to make net-energy analyses, and to adopt lifecycle costing comparisons for investment. A useful update of all these issues is provided by John P. Holdren, "Energy in Transition," *Scientific American*, September 1990, pages 157-163. Even more embarrassing, economists were forced to account for social impact, environmental costs and even acknowledge that "pollutants" and "wastes" were in reality often valuable resources misplaced and mislabeled—and sometimes even "profits" going up in smoke.[2] At the micro-level, all this was pretty obvious, but at the macroeconomic management level all these realities were still blurred by the heroic abstractions of national data-averaging.

National energy planners with their "supply side" models kept the general schizophrenic faith in the working of the "free market"—even as they poured well over a hundred billion of taxpayers money into subsidizing coal, nuclear, oil and gas. Rather than dis-aggregate these national models, economists continued to paper over the obvious symptoms of the transition to renewable resources. President Bush's National Energy Plan finally unveiled in 1991 still claimed to rely on the market, while ignoring the myriad subsidies to nuclear power and fossil fuels. The two surrogate variables for all the factors economists had left out became inflation and unemployment as they pursued the old capital/energy-intensive path at the expense of jobs and the environment. But no longer were inflation and unemployment the trade-offs familiar to economists in the past as the "Phillips curve"—both marched upward in "stagflation" and during the 1970s each recession left both inflation and unemployment higher than before. In the 1980s the Reagan administration pushed inflation down at the expense of ballooning the federal budget deficit.

Citizen's transformational movements

Even by the early 1970s citizens movements started responding with a positive agenda. They organized for safe, renewable energy development, emphasizing its labor-intensity; conservation and weatherization programs rather than new electric plant construction; smaller-scaled democratized technologies that decentralized economic and political power; retrofitting and renewing old center cities, revitalizing mass transit, local self-reliance and alternative economic development and enterprises. Their causes all began to flow together in their global agendas of transition to a planetary "solar age" which might reduce militaristic confrontations over nonrenewable resources; a saner, more equitable, ecologically-viable world order and a totally new path of "development" centered on human rights and basic unmet needs of grassroots populations, rather than continuing to chase undifferentiated, per capita-averaged economic growth.[2]

All these "transformational" movements in industrial countries came up with remarkable similar sets of agendas, and energy alternatives were basic to all of them: different mixes appropriate to each country of solar, wind, hydro, biomass, peat, biofuels, ocean-thermal wave or tidal power, solar ponds and a ubiquitous emphasis on organic agriculture, passive architecture, redesigning communities for safe walking and cycling and overall energy conservation, and efficiency ratings for cars, appliances, production processes and waste recycling. All these alternatives began to be seen as facets of the same transition, and while still derided by the central planners, politicians and corporate giants, generally captured much public imagination as more creative, innovative and viable than continuing the old centralized, standardized march to traditional industrial goals, now only producing an ever-more debt-inflated GNP and unemployment. Still the old paradigm persisted through the 1980s as President Reagan assured the nation that all was well. This "politics of denial" persisted, inevitably leading President Bush into the Mideast conflict of 1991.

The hoax of full employment

There was a dawning realization that the most basic promise of industrialism—full employment—was a cruel hoax. In 1978 the Organization for Economic Cooperation and Development (OECD) warned that due to continued capital-intensity and automation and the microprocessor revolution, the 1980s would be an "era of jobless economic growth." In 1983 there were some 35 million people unemployed in OECD's twenty-four member countries. Unemployment rose from 3 percent in the 1960s to 7.5 percent in the late 1980s. Today, there are 100 million people below the poverty line in these OECD countries. But minority groups and women began to point out an even more fundamental hoax in the promise of "full employment"—it was based on exclusion of many groups from the work force, from black teenagers to women. In fact, industrialism's definition of "full employment" assumed a (usually male) "head of household," and was actually predicated on excluding half the population from the workforce: the women—keeping the home fires burning and powering the suburban lifestyle. Today, not only is over half of the workforce women (mostly single breadwinners or supplementing their husband's inadequate income or unemployment checks) but only 12 percent of all U.S. families conform to the statistical norm of the nuclear male-earner headed household. Indeed, all over the world, the myth of the male breadwinner is being exposed.

New consumption habits

Further, as a result of the changing role of the American woman, who no longer has time to serve as the "heroic consumer," the world's economies can no longer look to the United States to be the consumption-led "locomotive" of world recovery, in spite of the brief debt-fueled consumption spree in the Yuppie 1980s. As Franz Schurmann, historian of the University of California at Berkeley points out, over 60 percent of U.S. women who are now in the workforce have drastically changed their consumption habits to basic needs, fewer goods and more services, e.g., education, day care, energy and shelter.[6] Already we see how such shifts have changed basic patterns of production and consumption. Daycare is one of our fastest growing industries as parenting became monetarized. Cooking is now in the money economy with fast food eateries, while all those other time consuming chores, from food shopping and cleaning to cooking and waiting for the appliance repairman, babysitting and home maintenance are shared by men. For example, one Madison Avenue survey leads to the conclusion that advertisers must now sell washing powders and toilet bowl cleaners with real respect, since almost 50 percent of their users are now men. The much vaunted job creation of the 1980s involved replacing free services of cooking, childcare and home making with paid jobs—together with the "part-timing" of millions of jobs. (i.e., What used to be counted as *one* 40-hour/week job is now counted as *two* 20-hour/week jobs.)

The energy-consumption shifts that are driving and being driven by such changes and major value-shifts now transform industrial cultures. Market surveys attest to these trends toward the do-it-yourself, home-centered consumption, the doubling-up and "downward mobility" in the housing market while incomes have remained flat since the mid-70s. Other studies from Yankelovich, Stanford Research Institute, Harris and Roper and John Naisbitt's Trend Reports underline these value shifts: away from traditional suburban materialism, to self-reliance and mutual aid in health care, bartering services, sharing and except for government (which has increased its energy-use since Mr. Reagan's supply-siders "revolution") the overall shift to energy-conservation as a way of life. *Business Week's* Harris poll (4 April 1982) found that over 35 percent of consumers said they would use *less* energy even if the price fell between 10 to 20 percent while an additional 25 percent said they would *not increase* their consumption. The biggest new energy market now up for grabs is that for energy-saving systems with current sales of $1.2 billion annually in building control systems alone. The Gulf War refocused attention on the energy-guzzling of Americans (which had resumed by the late 1980s as President Reagan renewed our faith that market forces alone could manage our energy sector). A survey in 1990 by the Americans Talk Issues Foundation found that Americans knew well the causes of the Gulf War. Large majorities thought the war might have been unnecessary:

if the United States had supported increased research and development of energy sources other than oil (85 percent); if there had been stepped-up energy conservation (75 percent); if we had continued improving the mileage of U.S. cars (75 percent); if we had levied a five-cent a year tax on gasoline for ten years (55 percent); and, if we had strengthened the United Nations (78 percent).

Meanwhile the increasing social costs of relying on traditional energy sources is clear: from the almost total unpredictability of oil supplies and prices, to the problems of cleaning up coal's sulphur emissions, acid rain, and while atmospheric CO_2 (carbon dioxide) levels and global warming rise to the level of international issues. In the United States, natural gas will probably be a basic transition fuel for power generation since it reduces CO_2 emissions by 50 percent over coal and oil and can readily be substituted. A 15-20 percent increase in natural gas use is forecast for the next 20 years, and it may also be used more in liquid form as auto fuel. While the Bush Administration claims that dealing with global warming would bankrupt the United States, views based on the end-use efficiency paradigm saw it as a profit opportunity. Amory Lovin's Rocky Mountain Institute's 1991 study "Least-Cost Climate Stabilization" demonstrated that by capturing synergies between agricultural, energy and foresting sectors and between industrial, developing and East European countries— all based on state-of-the-art energy-saving technologies, profits would outweigh costs. Such wildly different conclusions indicate different paradigms. For example, the Rocky Mountain Institute's calculation that if Americans were as energy efficient as West Europeans or Japanese, we would save $200 billion per year—enough to wipe out the Federal deficit or to give $800 back to every man, woman and child in the country.[7]

No wonder all the social movements for the transition to Solar Age societies are now linking across national borders, since the conditions they address are similar, whether in socialist France, Canada, "free market" oriented Britain and the United States or in the hybrids: Sweden, Norway, Denmark, the Netherlands, Japan. In such periods of massive change, politicians and institutions react in one of two ways: either they rigidify and redouble their efforts to apply the remedies that are failing, or they reconceptualize their whole situation.[2] The "politics of the last hurrah" is everywhere symptomatic of basic political watershed periods, where voters reject both Left and Right and begin to realign.

The nature of the transition

The transition of industrialism is multi-dimensional, non-linear, and practically unmodelable due to domestic and global interlinkages. Since energy and resource patterns form the very foundations of industrial societies, their multiplier effects cannot be mapped in simple economic terms but need new interdisciplinary policy models. Only change-models from biology and chaos theory (rather than mechanistic models) can capture these accelerating, interactive changes. Such multi-dimensional change processes are commonly known in all living systems as morphogenesis. The processes of morphogenesis are most familiar as the changes from caterpillar to chrysalis to butterfly. Morphogenetic systems are constantly evolving unanticipated new structure, because they are governed by positive feedback loops, which push many parts of the system over thresholds simultaneously. (See Plate 1-2: Two Cybernetic Systems.)

Once politicians begin seeing the nature of their industrial transitions they will come to see why the "politics of the last hurrah" and its simple economic remedies cannot work. They will see the vicious circles created by such remedies: for example, in the United States each additional 1 percent of unemployment *raises* the deficit by some $25 billion, and each additional percentage point of real interest rate *adds* another $10 billion to the deficit, while lowering federal taxes only increases state, local and property taxes. Policies focused on bailing out the past energy and resource patterns will only lead to higher inflation, higher unemployment *and* higher deficits *and* real interest rates, leading to an acceleration of world resource competition, the arms race and wars. Even though in the United States we are now hearing some political discussion of "transitions" taking place in our economy, there is little realistic description of their nature. Some call for "re-industrialization" (clearly a rearview mirror attempt to go back to the future). In the 1980s Democrats briefly flirted with a naive "high-tech transition scenario"—fatally calling themselves Atari Democrats—only to learn that the Atari Corporation, a "Silicon Valley" employer prototypical of future job creation, was moving offshore to Taiwan. Labor unions are now talking of an industrial policy to guide investment into the "sunrise industries"—but they are not talking of the transition to the Solar Age. Rather they envision some unspecified, high-tech version of industrialism, hoping that automation and robotics can be tamed to keep people at the scene of production, if not as employees then otherwise sharing the fruits of the per capita productivity increases via Employee Stock Ownership Plans (ESOPs).

Meanwhile, Japan continued to forge ahead on solar energy. Kansai Electric Power and Sharp Company are testing a new solar heater/air conditioner unit which can be mixed with conventional electricity— picking up enough load from a roof solar array to cool a two-story house in summer or heat it in winter (*Business Week*, July 15, 1991, page 131). In California, the Public Service Commission in 1991 requires utilities to account for costs of pollution. This has made wind energy more competitive since these pollution costs for coal are at least 2.3¢ per kilowatt hour (*Business Week*, July 15, 1991). Neither party in the United States is coming close to the more realistic transition to a sustainable Solar Age, of economic as well as political decentralization and a human-centered, skills-intensive, entrepreneurial path of development where investments are made in human development, resource conservation and developing renewable energy. Ironically, a May 1991 report of the Office of Technology Assessment (OTA) blasted the Federal Government, the largest user of energy, for its own waste.

But we should not be surprised that the dinosaurs' brains are the last place to get the message that conditions have changed and a grassroots revolution has already occurred, since half of the eligible U.S. voters are too turned off by money-corrupted elections, spin doctors and sound-bite campaigning to vote. Whether it is New York's Wall Street and broadcast network headquarters or Washington with its 18th century politics, or whether it is the Kremlin, London, Brussels, Paris, Bonn, or the head offices of ever-larger corporate conglomerates, leaders will seek to manipulate the new complexities with statistical illusions, often oblivious to the disastrous local impacts of their economic-based policies.

What we see emerging today in all the industrial societies are basic value and behavior shifts, new perceptions and an emerging paradigm, based on facing up to a new awareness of planetary realities and confirmed by a "post-Cartesian" scientific worldview based on biological and systemic life sciences, rather than inorganic, mechanistic models. Its principles involve: Interconnectedness, Redistribution, Heterarchy, Complementarity, Uncertainty, and Change. (See Plate 2-8: A Post-Cartesian Scientific Worldview and Plate 2-12: Social Implications of the Post-Cartesian Principles.)

The newly interlinked agendas of citizens

These new worldviews are already generating better policy tools and models, beyond economics: technology assessment, social and job impact studies, environmental impact statements, futures research, cross-impact studies, scenario-building, global modelling and forecasting no longer based on past trend extrapolation. At the grassroots level, in academia and all our institutions the politics of reconceptualization has begun.[7] We see it in the newly interlinked agendas of citizens converging on the June 1992 U.N. Earth Summit in Rio de Janiero and in the emergence of human rights and planetary citizenship. These movements all embrace a new world order based on renewable resources and energy, sustainable forms of productivity and per capita consumption, ecologically-based science and technologies and equitable sharing of resources within and between countries as the only path to peace-keeping and redirecting the billions spent on the global arms race.

Consistently the public is ahead of the politicians. A 1991 survey by ATIF found 86 percent of Americans support an international tax on arms sales and 93 percent favored the United States taking the lead in solving global environmental problems. Citizens feeling disenfranchised by special interest groups are doing "politics by other means" at the local level: solar and renewable resource politics, farmer's market and co-op politics, organic agriculture politics, holistic health care politics, worker-ownership and new entrepreneurial enterprise politics, environmental politics and so on. These people can already form a winning coalition, together with human rights, corporate accountability groups, peace activists, labor and the women's movements.

One of the most creative and responsible citizen initiatives in dealing with the growing crisis over where to store the U.S. backlog of nuclear powerplant wastes is the Nuclear Guardianship Project, which would create public corporations overseen by boards of citizens to provide vigilant monitoring of these radioactive wastes, and full public disclosure.[8] A survey by Americans Talk Issues in June 1991 found that Americans were 59 percent in favor of a 5 percent tax on imported oil. The new economy is now being born: a Solar Age economy[9] which can help assure the path to a peaceful, ecologically sane, more equitable world order for our children.[10]

In July, 1991, almost 100 of the leading solar and renewable energy specialists from all over the world, convened by physicist Niels Meyer at the Technical University of Denmark, issued a 300-page report on the feasibility of achieving the transition to a Solar Age entitled *Global Collaboration on Sustainable Energy Development*. It called for radical changes in energy policies, a new U.N. agency to promote the transitions, immediate carbon taxes on industrial countries and greater North-South equity. Citizen groups throughout the United States and elsewhere are promoting Sun Day 1992 to organize grassroots support for the shift to the Solar Age.[11]

Introduction Footnotes

1. *The Economist,* "Oil's New World Order," July 13, 1991.

2. Hazel Henderson, *Creating Alternative Futures: The End of Economics,* Putnam & Sons, NY, 1978.

3. Daniel Deudney and Christopher Flavin, *Renewable Energy, The Power to Choose,* Worldwatch Institute, Washington, DC, 1983.

4. *Basic Call to Consciousness,* Akwesasne Notes, Mohawk Nation, via Rooseveldtown, NY, 1978.

5. Garry Paul Nabhan, *The Desert Smells Like Rain,* North Point Press, San Francisco, 1982.

6. Franz Schurmann, "No Longer Spending Machines: The Habits of American Women have Remade the Global Economy," May 1983.

7. Such research and citizen action and legal battles are covered in detail in the Newsletter of the Rocky Mountain Institute, 1739 Snowmass Creek Road, Snowmass, CO 81654-9199.

8. The Nuclear Guardianship Project was co-founded by ecologist Joanna Macy in 1989 in Berkeley, CA.

9. See for example, *Consumer Guide to Solar Energy* (1991) and *Solar Today,* the magazine of the American Solar Energy Society, Boulder, CO.

10. Americans Talk Issues Foundation (ATIF) opinion surveys can be obtained from 907 Sixth Street SW, Suite 602C, Washington, DC 20024.

11. For further information contact Public Citizen, Attn: SUN DAY, 215 Pennsylvania Ave SE, Washington, DC 20003.

Three Zones of Transition

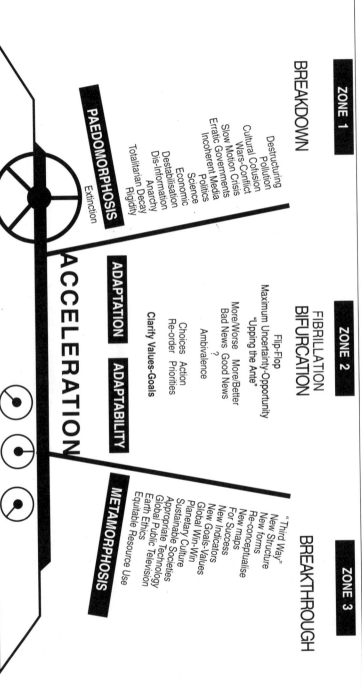

ZONE 1	ZONE 2	ZONE 3

BREAKDOWN

FIBRILLATION
BIFURCATION

BREAKTHROUGH

PAEDOMORPHOSIS

Destructuring
Pollution
Cultural Collusion
Wars–Conflict
Slow Motion Crisis
Erratic Governments
Incoherent Media
Politics
Science
Economic
Destabilisation
Dis-Information
Anarchy
Totalitarian Decay
Rigidity
Extinction

Flip-Flop
Maximum Uncertainty–Opportunity
"Upping the Ante"
More/Worse   More/Better
Bad News   Good News
?
Ambivalence
Choices   Action
Re-order   Priorities
Clarify Values–Goals

ADAPTATION   ADAPTABILITY

ACCELERATION

METAMORPHOSIS

" Third Way"
New Structure
New forms
Re-conceptualise
New maps
For Success
New Indicators
New Goals–Values
Global Win-Win
Planetary Culture
Sustainable Culture
Appropriate Societies
Appropriate Technology
Global Public Television
Earth Ethics
Equitable Resource Use

PLATE 1-1

Riding the Tiger of Change

It is hardly news to anyone that industrial societies are undergoing massive structural changes and realigning themselves in a process of economic and technological globalization. Today, this planetization process is visibly accelerating and three distinct zones of this unprecedented transition can be mapped to help decision makers negotiate the unfamiliar terrain: 1) The Breakdown Zone, 2) The Fibrillation Zone, and 3) The Breakthrough Zone.

Since all of us live in one or more of these zones and few forecasting methods are broad enough to capture such overall dynamics we must shift our attention from modelling *content* (i.e., the daily quantification of events and data) to modelling the wider *context* of these events and the overall *processes* involved. Attempting this heroic modelling task makes amateurs of us all, and yet it is crucial in creating the new conceptual tools required if we are to learn to interpret these events and to ride the tiger of change.

Within this overall context of accelerating globalization, evident in areas from banking and finance, satellite telecommunications, computerization, air transportation, militarization and the speedup of technological innovation, we can also expect increasing turbulence and new instabilities. Further, we should expect that more of the changes we see are *irreversible*, while taking note that most of our conceptual tools for mapping them—such as economics and conventional scientific approaches—are still based on Newton's ideas of mechanics and reversible models of locomotion in a clockwork universe. Therefore, we can also expect accelerating future shock (to use Alvin Toffler's term), even in formerly stable areas of our personal and political lives and institutions.

Simple Diagrams of Two Major Types of Cybernetic Systems

STABLE, EQUILIBRIATING SYSTEM
(morphostatic) (Structurally stable)

e.g., thermostat-controlled mechanical system; early agrarian or small-scale production economies (as conceived in market equilibrium supply-demand theories); reversible components and decisions

SYSTEM

feedback loop

System internally dynamic, but stable structure maintained and governed by *negative* feedback loops.

UNSTABLE, DIS-EQUILIBRIUM SYSTEM
(morphogenetic) (Evolving new structure)

e.g., living, biological systems, human societies; large-scale socio-technical economic systems; rapid innovation and evolving structurally; many irreversible components and decisions

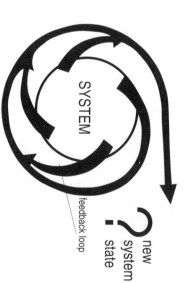

SYSTEM

feedback loop

new system state ?

System internally dynamic and structurally dynamic, governed by *positive* feedback loops, which can amplify small initial deviations into unpredictably large deviations, which sometimes break through thresholds and push the system to a new structural state.

PLATE 1-2

All this will occur in the context of swifter and larger shifts in environmental conditions, as new thresholds are overridden; as for example, where increased carbon dioxide in the atmosphere is now producing more climatic variability. Another effect to observe will be the *ambivalence* of these events, with more confusion and conflicting interpretation by scientists, governments and media, i.e., the is-it-good-news-or-is-it-bad-news syndrome. Our three-zone map may help give us a pegboard to sort things out for ourselves and pinpoint where we are in the picture. Since all three zones co-exist simultaneously, we might also remember that word maps, such as this book, are less effective than pictorial maps (see Plate 1-1) and that even then, flat surface maps are less representational than a three-dimensional globe—the real stage on which the three transitions are occurring.

Zone 1's paradigm paradoxes

Many countries still caught in the industrial paradigm seek to deal with its pathologies by trying to "reintegrate" marginalized groups and areas of society—precisely because the forces and underlying rationale of industrialization over the past two hundred years continually produce centralizing effects. These centralizing, and now globalizing forces continue to produce the very marginalization they seek to ameliorate. At the same time, the globalizing forces of technology and production; militarization; trade, finance and information; work, employment and migration; human effects on the biosphere; mass consumption and culture; as well as the interactions among them are now driving the geo-political realignments and internal restructuring of most countries and their domestic institutions. This general global restructuring reached a new threshold in the late 1980s and will accelerate in the 1990s, due to growing interlinkages and interactivity.

As the United States and the USSR slowly realized that the Cold War had begun to decimate their economies and that, in effect, *Japan* had won; a fundamental rethinking has begun regarding *what* "new world order" will emerge. Thus, the centralizing forces of industrialism at the global level are creating decentralizing forces at the national and local level—overturning old power centers and providing new opportunities for formerly marginalized people and regions to play a new role in a new world game, with new rules, and inevitably, new "scorecards" for evaluating "progress" and "success" in an era of global inter-dependence. This new global context will increasingly drive paradigm shifts in policy-research and tools of evaluation, in fact, an epistemological revolution which will restructure academic institutions and curricula. The single-

Differing Perceptions, Assumptions, Forecasting Styles Between Economists and Futurists

ECONOMISTS		FUTURISTS
Forecast from past data, extrapolating trends	⇨	Construct "What If?" scenarios; trends are not destiny
Now also use optimistic, pessimistic forecasts	⇨	Identify "Preferred Futures"— plot trends for cross impacts
Change seen as dis-equilibrium (i.e., equilibrium assumed)— all other things equal "normal" conditions will return	⇨	Fundamental change assumed (transformation assumed)— no such thing as "normal" conditions in complex systems
Reactive (invisible hand assumed to control)	⇨	Pro-active (focus on human choices and responsibilities)
Linear reasoning; reversible models	⇨	Non-linear reasoning; irreversible models, evolutionary
Inorganic system models	⇨	Living system, organic models
Focus on "hard" sciences and data	⇨	Focus on life sciences, social sciences, "soft," fuzzy data, indeterminacy
Deterministic, reductionist, analytical	⇨	Holistic, synthesis, seeks synergy
Short term focus (e.g. discount rates in cost/benefit analysis)	⇨	Long-term focus, inter-generational costs, benefits and trade offs
Data on non-economic, non-monetarized sectors seen as "externalities" (e.g., voluntary, community sectors, unpaid production, environmental resources)	⇨	Includes data on social, voluntary unpaid productivity, changing values, lifestyles, environmental conditions; maps, contexts, external variable (use post economic models: technology assessment, environmental impact, social impact studies)
Methods tend to amplify existing trends (e.g., Wall Street psychology)	⇨	Methods "contrarian" (e.g., look for anomalies, check biases in perceptions, cultural norms)
"Herd instinct" in investing, technologies, economic development	⇨	Identify potentialities that are latent
Entrepreneurial when "market" is identified	⇨	Socially entrepreneurial (Schwartz) (e.g., envision future needs, create markets)
Precise, quantitative forecasts (e.g., gross national product for next quarter of year; annual focus)	⇨	Qualitative focus (e.g., year 2000 studies, anticipatory democracy), data from multiple sources, plot interacting variables, trends in long-term global contexts

PLATE 1-3

RIDING THE TIGER OF CHANGE   27

discipline, fragmented approach to knowledge will need reintegrating, since most of today's problems lie at the interfaces between disciplines and require systemic, multi-disciplinary approaches. Similarly, the worldview inherited from René Descartes and Isaac Newton; that wholes can be understood from analyzing their parts in an essentially "clockwork" universe, with its focus on precision and exactitude, certainty and equilibrium is falling behind in understanding dynamic change and biological systems. Most policy research and evaluation tools are caught in this "time warp," mapping vanished systems with inappropriate tools, particularly those of macroeconomic management still based on equilibrium assumptions.

Ironically, the dangerous events in the Middle East are providing new opportunities for rapid social learning, as politicians realize that a more interdependent world can only be managed with more cooperation (despite the apparent "victory" of market economic theories rooted in competition). What is required is a new balance between strategies of competition and cooperation (both equally prevalent in all natural systems, despite Charles Darwin's focus on the former). New events are forcing pragmatic responses from which deeper lessons can be learned. For example, there is now a growing recognition of the festering global issue of maldistribution between the haves and have-nots; the marginalization of traditional cultures, such as that of Islam and its powerful reactions to Western "cultural imperialism" and technology; the byzantine global politics of natural resources, for example, oil, and the vulnerabilities of wasteful, fossil-fueled industrial economies, which Iraq was able to exploit. Many of these same issues surfaced in the GATT (General Agreement on Tariffs and Trade) Uruguay Round and other international arenas, as well as the newer issues of how to reduce environmental threats to the biosphere which will be thrashed out in the U.N. Environment Conference in Brazil in 1992. None of these issues can be solved unilaterally, and national leaders are beginning to understand the loss of sovereignty and the eroding power of nation-states; increasingly they cannot keep their promises to their voters to provide full employment, keep inflation and interest rates down, deal with deficits or manage their domestic economies in today's global financial casino.

This new Era of Global Interdependence has forced a greater reliance on the United Nations and all its agencies—the only supra-national entity available. This has created many new opportunities, even for the marginalized. For example, the United Nations (U.N.) has over the past forty years devoted much of its effort to humanitarian concern and activities on behalf of the world's poor and marginalized peoples. At last,

The Traditional GNP Economic Pie

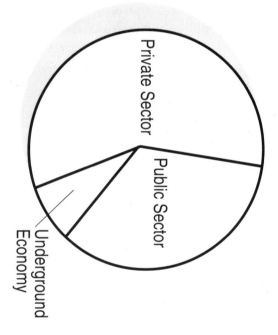

Private Sector

Public Sector

Underground Economy

PLATE 1-4

it is possible to engage high-level policy-makers in looking toward the root causes of world poverty that are inherent in the ideologies and epistemologies that undergirded the Industrial Revolution—from left to right and its prevailing worldview of "economism," a term coined by President Carlos Andres Perez of Venezuela, a co-chairman of the South Commission, whose final report is *Challenge To The South* (1990).[1] This latest, best voice for addressing the problems of the marginalized countries of the Southern Hemisphere goes well beyond the prescriptions of the Brundtland Commission's 1987 report, *Our Common Future.*[2]

What is emerging is an understanding that the left-right spectrum of economic ideologies that underlies macro-management approaches of capitalism, socialism, communism and all the "mixed" economies as well were, in retrospect quite superficial. Both Karl Marx and Adam Smith would have agreed on the underlying goals of industrialism: "modernization," technological efficiency and determinism, materialism, secularization, and generally expanding industrial production and rationalization of its methods around the Planet.[3] The surface argument about how to do this became very bitter and crystalized in the Cold War stand-off. These entrenched debates continue in spite of growing disbelief in the South that economies reach the magic "take-off" point immortalized by Walt W. Rostow in his *Stages of Economic Growth* (1960). Until quite recently, few decision-makers worried about *fundamental* issues such as whether the entire economic process of pursuing industrial growth (as measured by increases in per capita Gross National Product [GNP] and Gross Domestic Product [GDP], levels of savings and investment, inflation and interest rates, etc.) might be leading to *systematic* marginalization of the weak or whether Nature could continue tolerating increasing human numbers and industrial activities. Most focused on optimizing income distribution and industrial production while providing full employment in the formal, GNP-tracked sectors of their economies.

Historical and current evaluation tools used to measure industrial "success," deeply rooted in macroeconomic models, are now obsolete from perspectives of global equity and human development, as well as those of the global environment and resource management. Thus these evaluation tools also continue to re-enforce the marginalization of groups that do not conform to industrial values and areas which cannot compete with socio-technical regimes typical of industrialization. Whether such groups aspire to the well advertised goods of mass production, or whether they reject them and the ideologies of modernization on religious or cultural grounds or are simply overwhelmed by them, seems to make little difference. The result is often marginalization.

Total Productive System of an Industrial Society
(Layer Cake with Icing)

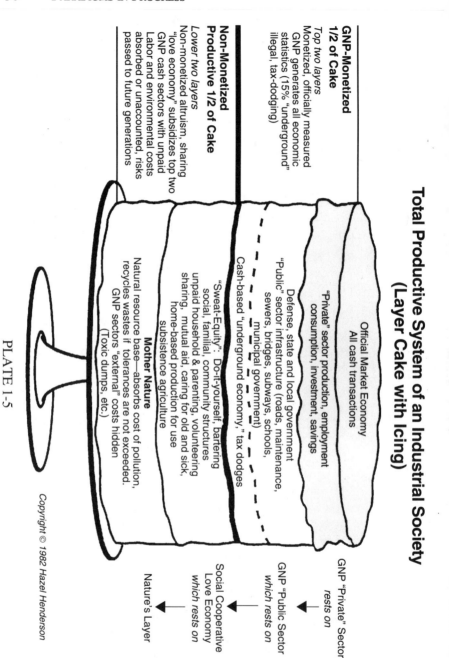

**GNP-Monetized
1/2 of Cake**

Top two layers
Monetized, officially measured
GNP generates all economic
statistics (15% "underground"
illegal, tax-dodging)

**Non-Monetized
Productive 1/2 of Cake**

Lower two layers
Non-monetized altruism, sharing
"love economy" subsidizes top two
GNP cash sectors with unpaid
Labor and environmental costs
absorbed or unaccounted, risks
passed to future generations

Official Market Economy
All cash transactions

"Private" sector production, employment
consumption, investment, savings

Defense, state and local government
"Public" sector infrastructure (roads, maintenance,
sewers, bridges, subways, schools,
municipal government)
Cash-based "underground economy," tax dodges

"Sweat-Equity": Do-It-Yourself, bartering
social, familial, community structures
unpaid household & parenting, volunteering
sharing, mutual aid, caring for old and sick,
home-based production for use
subsistence agriculture

Mother Nature
Natural resource base—absorbs cost of pollution,
recycles wastes if tolerances are not exceeded.
GNP sectors "external" costs hidden
(Toxic dumps, etc.)

GNP "Private" Sector
rests on

GNP "Public Sector
which rests on

Social Cooperative
Love Economy
which rests on

Nature's Layer

PLATE 1-5

Take the case of the generally sacrosanct goal of "full employment" which, mentioned in the introduction, has now been revealed as one of the major hoaxes of industrialism.[4] What economists and policy-makers actually meant by this term was the full employment of "heads of households" (i.e., only half of the adult population and generally male). Traditional subsistence societies in this worldview were to be "modernized" and brought into the industrial production system (generally more urbanized to take advantage of narrowly-calculated "efficiencies of scale" that ignored social and environmental costs). Similarly, women and children were assumed not to be "economically-employed" however many hours they worked to grow food, carry water, tend herds, take care of the young and the aged or infirm, etc., Women who further worked to educate children, pass on the culture, serve as community volunteers, were only considered by the "full employment" statistics if they were paid money for this work.[5] All this represented a colossal subsidy to the GNP measured sectors.

This hidden subsidy eroded as women moved into the paid work force due to wartime mobilizations and the lure of cash. The stresses on the GNP sectors that this imposed became clear after World War II and the statistical "response" to the flood of new labor force entrants was to redefine "full employment" from its definition of 2 percent unemployment in the 1950s and 1960s toward the some 7 percent figure of today. In this way, statistics and national accounts methodology was clearly *derivative* from the cultural assumptions of macroeconomic, industrial mindsets, while also playing a powerful role in enforcing the status quo and prevailing assumptions. Few dared to question whether an industrial economy could actually employ and pay *all* of its able-bodied adults, or whether this might "break the bank" or simply inflate the currency, denude the rural areas, and erode family and community life while leaving children and the elderly or sick unattended. By the late 1970s, as the exodus continued from rural areas and the labor forces swelled with more women and minority entrants, the statistics could no longer redefine the situation and the OECD began in the late 1970s to refer to the 1980s as a "decade of jobless economic growth."

Such examples foretold the widespread signs today of the collapse of the industrial/economism paradigm, evident in widening poverty gaps and increasingly visible ecological destruction, deforestation and desertification. More recent examples include the crisis of macroeconomic management in the United States where "laissez-faire," competitive, individualistic ideologies are preventing Congressional resolution of budget deficits, and the deregulation ideologies that led to the debacle in the savings and loan industry and the over-indebtedness and speculative binges on Wall Street and in the banking and insurance sectors. GNP growth driven models still confuse policies in many Third World countries, as well as such industrial countries as, for example, New Zealand, where the two major parties, from the left and the right are unable to offer the voters any alternatives to "Rogernomics" (the local version of Reaganomics and Thatchernomics) i.e., hyping GNP growth and headlong deregulation and privatization to make the numbers look good. Alternative home-grown, locally-autonomous models of economic development relying less on investment from distant capital markets and more on local credit unions, microenterprises and the informal, unpaid and barter sectors are not considered "serious." Consequently 35-40 percent of the electorate was "undecided" or planned to stay home.[6]

Therefore, one cannot expect that redesigning better statistics or approaches to evaluation can by themselves address or repulse these entrenched and powerful trends or the strategies and paradigms that drive them. However, many of the absurdities of these old industrial/economic growth models are now clearly visible, indeed, many are reaching crisis proportions, particularly in the Southern Hemisphere countries, as are the urgent problems of urban ghettos and rural decay in many industrial countries. Today, as politicians redouble their efforts to apply ever larger doses of fiscal and monetary medicine, even economic journals are noticing the anomalies. *Business Week* in the United States declared editorially, "Clearly, the major economic problems don't lend themselves to macroeconomic solutions."[7] In fact, as the U.N. Fourth Development Decade of the 1990s began, it became clear to more and more countries in the Southern Hemisphere that the entire GNP-measured economic growth model had not only derailed in rising debt, starvation and ecological devastation, but had gone into reverse.

Many now are convinced that this traditional economic development model involved a one-time historical process—unrepeatable, in any case. Now, ironically, industrial countries of the Northern Hemisphere are demanding that Southern countries, whom they proselytized for so long, should forego copying this industrial development model as too polluting. Needless to say, the new rallying cry of "sustainable development," as well as "green technologies" and "environmentally-friendly" products are still falling on deaf ears in the South.

The Breakdown Zone

In Zone 1, many of us feel that our lives and jobs are stultified, or that we are stuck in an unresponsive bureaucratic institution or corporation.

This is natural in a time of change since individuals always learn faster than institutions, in fact, institutions often rigidify, resisting change until they become brittle and shatter, while others simply stagnate or decay. Thus, this Breakdown Zone is where society and its obsolescent institutions are de-structuring. We need not panic, since de-structuring is a natural process like composting, creating rich new soil for regeneration. In fact, Nature shows us how some species actually regress to an earlier, larval stage in their development when their adult form has become too rigid and ill-adapted. This process, called paedomorphosis, allows the younger, less-structured (and therefore more adaptable) form to carry on the species. So it may help us to see Zone 1 as containing these "seeds," and remember that paedomorphosis leads to the many metamorphoses we will find in Zone 3, the Breakthrough Zone.

In Zone 1 it is not only institutional forms, cities, suburbs and rural areas that are de-structuring, but also cultural and political forms and value systems underlying them. For example, our culture and those of most other industrial societies are in a state of confusion as they shift to the not-yet-defined "post-industrial" phase. The Soviets and other socialist societies experiment with marketplaces to overcome lack of incentive and enforced cooperation, while in the U.S. people yearn for less individualistic, dog-eat-dog competition and retreat into their churches, new religions and cults in search of community and kindness. Both capitalism and communism are revealed as superficial ideologies concerned merely with methods of production and distribution, rather than as deeply-sustaining philosophies of life. Similarly, imposing one or the other of these two outdated European styles of industrialism on the rest of the world is failing, from Africa and Asia to South and Central America. China in spite of the setback of Tiananmen , still seems to be finding a "third way" as its coastal cities and provinces open further to the world economy. Enforcing industrialism as a single model for development is now inappropriate for the world's rich variety of diverse societies, each with its own unique expression to offer the global melting pot.

Thus Zone 1 is also a war zone, as conflicting cultures, ideologies and religions clash in the new global village—adding to the enduring competition between nations over territory and resources. The latest tragic example of such 1990s warfare is, of course, the still inconclusive Middle East conflict. Even if accidental nuclear exchanges are avoided, we can expect the proliferation of proxy wars, such as those in Central America, Africa and other Third World countries. Such overt and covert violence, together with continuing inequities and injustice will continue to fuel revolts, insurrections and terrorism while guerilla strategies and suitcase bombs will continue to be the natural response to military might and Starwars.

Zone 1 is also the "accident zone" and the zone of "slow motion" crises such as pollution. Accidents from Chernobyl and Three Mile Island, Times Beach, Love Canal and Bophal to the Challenger explosion are all effects to be expected as we humans attempt to manage and coordinate ever larger and more complex organizations and powerful technologies. Slow motion crises to watch included rising extinction rates of species, increasing loss of forests due to acid rain and spreading deserts in the Sahel and near the over-irrigated valleys in California.

The political arena of Zone 1 is best summed up as "the politics of the last hurrah," i.e., maladaption to change where governments of all ideological stripes rigidify and try to defend their borders against the waves of globalization now swamping their cherished national "sovereignty." This is most evident in the economic sphere, as somewhere around $500 billion (no one is sure) of footloose money sloshes around the Planet every 24 hours and electronically transferred funds are deployed by the new breed of 24-hour asset managers playing such new games as program trading in today's "global casino" so well described in the pages of *Business Week*. Information has become money and money has become information. As the global "fast lane" speeds up, money loses its meaning and ceases to function as a viable means of keeping track or score of the game.

It is in this light that Peter Drucker argued in *Foreign Affairs* (Spring 1986) that the commodity economy had "uncoupled" from the industrial economy; the industrial economy had uncoupled from the employment economy and that world trade had uncoupled from world financial flows. In his otherwise insightful article, Drucker does not go far enough by singling out these areas. In staying within the traditional paradigm of economic and money-based analysis, Drucker misses the non-money denominated sectors of total productivity and fails to see the extent to which this new global funny money game (or "symbol system," as Drucker terms it) now has very little to do with the realities of any sector of real-world production, consumption, investment or trade, not of any real geographic region or ecosystem on the Planet. Indeed, the 1990s will see the end of today's global money monopoly, as all those outside the money system learn myriad new ways to barter and "counter-trade" their commodities locally, regionally and globally via computer networks.

Meanwhile, politicians wrestle with domestic unemployment, trade, retraining and industrial policies (a hopelessly outdated concept), all of which deal with real geography and real people, and implementing such policies must take *years* of preparation and building. Yet all such domestic plans, however well laid and executed, are de-stabilized *daily*, as the currency exchange markets open each morning in London, New York and Tokyo. Treaties and economic theories alike, addressed to *international* competition and trade policies, or to domestic unemployment, inflation, deficits or interest rates are all swept along by this rising tide of financial flows, as well as Third World Debt, bouncing currencies and oil prices—all indicators of the need for global economic cooperation and a new Bretton Woods to write the necessary "win-win" rules for operating the new global economic "commons," i.e., a global "common ground" of all the players.

Some governments respond to Zone 1 conditions by reconceptualizing this new global commons, while others either rigidify, try to turn the clock back, attempt diversionary military adventures, fudge the figures or even indulge in dis-information, often confusing their own citizens by obfuscating the issues. The least adaptive political behaviors of course are totalitarianism or anarchy. Therefore if you find yourself in Zone 1 too much of the time, you may recognize that it is time to assess your options, recycle your skills and scan for opportunities to redeploy yourself and prepare for a well-informed leap into Zone 3, the Breakthrough Zone. However, to accomplish this you will need to explore and negotiate Zone 2.

The Fibrillation Zone

Zone 2 is characterized by the term "fibrillation" as when the human heart muscle temporarily vacillates under stress, either leading to a heart attack and possible death, or shifting to another regular rhythm. Thus in Zone 2, which is expanding rapidly as globalization accelerates, the atmosphere is one of "upping the ante" and a pervasive increase in risk and uncertainty. Zone 2 is a "critical mass" zone of *bifurcation* (a term used by mathematicians, chaos theorists and those in the physical and life sciences) meaning the many modes in which a system can or is about to change in its entirety or state. These dynamic, organic models of changing systems[8] include the modes of "catastrophe" of French mathematician, René Thom, who described seven different bifurcation modes of transformation; the "order through fluctuation" models of Nobel chemist Ilya Prigogine of Belgium and the "change through attraction" models of U.S. mathematician, Ralph Abraham, whose computer simulations of system change processes exhibit three organic "attractors" (point attractors, periodic attractors and chaotic attractors) which "pull" systems into new states as do magnets. They appear very unpredictable because the minute changes they cause can give rise to very different or large results. These advances in mathematical modelling are best summed up in James Gleick's bestseller *Chaos* (1987). From these models, it is possible to see how the de-structuring processes of Zone 1 give rise to the uncertainties and the maximum number of opportunities to shift gears, reconceptualize, redesign, and restructure, i.e., to ride the tiger of change into the third, Breakthrough Zone.

Zone 2 is also characterized by "flip-flop" processes, as whole systems enter this bifurcation zone of transformation, when they are poised on the "cusp" of these shifts in state. For example, a corporation in a state of rapid growth is suddenly confronted with a key choice, which when made, will either propel it into bankruptcy or to new markets in a restructured form. High-risk strategies are often most effective, while doing nothing can be the most dangerous "action." In Zone 2 more individuals, institutions and nations must make choices because they are nearing thresholds and pushing against their margins and boundary conditions. For example, today's nation-states boundaries and nationalistic belief systems have become dysfunctional. Giving up some "national sovereignty," e.g., over their domestic economics, is risky, but less risky than going it alone. Thus, in Zone 2, choices and actions are required— but unless the situation is also reconceptualized and remapped, the action may be maladaptive and relegate the system or person back to Zone 1. Thus, Zone 2 demands the most clear-eyed and rigorous re-examination of assumptions, priorities, goals and the very values that underlie them, since values are the basic driving force in all technical, economic and political systems. This re-examination is in itself a high-risk task, because old verities and old institutions must be challenged, which initially contributes to the destructuring process of Zone 1. Yet the price of *not* challenging the old forms is loss of leadership, those "attractors" which "pull" the system (in political terms, those with more attractive visions of the future) into its new state.

Another key aspect of Zone 2 is that we should expect more and better good news and more and worse bad news. This effect is evident in fluctuating oil prices and is simply another indicator of systems reaching margins and thresholds of maximum stress conditions. It helps explain why incremental changes are often ineffective. Only policies addressing *basic* causes which underlie problems can hope to succeed, while policies addressed only to ameliorating or suppressing symptoms can lead to worse results. For example, trying to deal with unstable domestic economies using narrowly focused and superficial remedies of traditional "flat earth" macroeconomic policies: inflating or deflating, regulating or deregulating, privatizing or nationalizing, raising or lowering interest rates, as if the society was a hydraulic system, can leave the patient worse, possibly irreversibly so. As mentioned, since globalization has changed the game, only global agreements can work, as well as fundamental re-evaluation of all economic sectors, re-analysis of data and developing of new indicators of performance beyond the simplistic model of the Gross National Product. National politicians must now spend at least 50 percent of their time on global interdependence issues in their attempts to "level the global playing field," as discussed later in this book.

Thus, Zone 2's proliferating good news and bad news becomes also evermore ambivalent, and it becomes increasingly unrealistic to view any news in such categorical, either/or terms. Media analysts can no longer help by merely reporting the events, since *interpretation is everything* and examining the underlying causes and assumptions of the actors and the audience becomes the key to deciphering the unfolding plot. For example, many futurists have focused on the so called Information Age's good news, and there is plenty of it: trends to greater participation, more informed citizens, decentralization, as well as the "high touch" which John Naisbitt, author of *Megatrends*, sees as balancing the less pleasant side of the high tech revolution, as well as the now widely touted labor "shortage." (i.e., More unskilled illiterates are unemployable and have joined the permanent "underclass." In 1991, unemployment rates for black males 20-24, was still 25 percent.) However, the full dimensions of the Information Age lead to more ambivalence: more efficient computerization of the military may trigger an accidental nuclear exchange; the rapid disruption of the world due to automation; health and privacy effects of the computer revolution; and, a growing glut of raw unevaluated data. As always, the limits of the Information Age hinge on the span of attention and time constraints of decision-makers, affecting their ability to *use* the torrents of daily information-overload.

So, if one finds oneself living in Zone 2, the best course is to dig deeper for the answers, to turn the issue or event (whether reported as "good" or "bad" news) around and look at all its facets, while surveying the widest range of interpretations offered by politicians, business leaders, unionists, academic forecasters or futurists. Zone 2 is the arena of trade-offs between *adaptation* and *adaptability*. If we or our institutions have become too well-adapted to now vanishing conditions, we will have less in our storehouses of adaptability to meet the new conditions—the "nothing fails like success" syndrome. Anthropologists call this The Law of the Retarding Lead. We see it operating today, where countries which are less industrialized, such as China, India and Sri Lanka, may be able to forge ahead by taking the best from all the earlier experimenters in Europe, North America and Japan, and leapfrog to a Third Way, thus entering Zone 3.

The Breakthrough Zone

This zone of breakthroughs was almost invisible during the 1960s and 1970s because it could not emerge until sufficient destructuring had occurred. As the Breakthrough Zone widened and led to the expanding Fibrillation Zone, so too, the breakthroughs grew and became more visible: new compacts among nations, such as those bordering the Mediterranean Sea to clean up their common pollution; the treaties to guard against the militarization of outer space and to protect the South Pole from exploitation; as well as the many United Nations sponsored conferences on Law of the Sea, and the global issues crosscutting national boundaries: food, population, health, education, habitat, renewable energy sources and science and technology for development. These brave beginnings to create new global social management technologies were coupled with new human capabilities in unlocking the basic code of life: the DNA molecule and such advances as the eradication of smallpox. A growing awareness of our human powers and responsibilities for more appropriate uses of our scientists and technologies to extend human lifespans and potentialities, end hunger and disease, led to the new dialogues between rich and poor nations of the Northern and Southern Hemispheres over a more just global economy.

New sensitivities emerged to appreciate the diversity and richness of ethnic cultures and, at last, a concrete vision of planetary identity flashed from space to a whole generation of the human family.

Zone 3 is where old "problems" and "crises" are revealed as new opportunities, and the good news in the bad news becomes apparent. Even the nuclear bomb had, indeed, kept the peace for forty years, and so the new round of proliferation forced millions of citizens to demand arms reduction treaties and a shift of resources away from the dangerously growing militarization, toward finally dealing with poverty, disease, hunger and war—the four horsemen of the *real* apocalypse. All through the 1970s and 1980s, citizen movements grew in all countries for peace, human rights, ecological sanity and government and corporate accountability. Socially responsible investments and successful mutual funds, such as the Calvert Social Investment Fund of Washington, DC, proliferated with these movements. Tyrannical regimes fell in Iran, Haiti and the Philippines, while others tottered, including South Africa, now reeling from citizen-spurred disinvestment and the courage of its own black citizens. Haiti's struggle for democracy and leadership crises may be viewed as a classic manifestation of fibrillation, the struggle to come to terms with and move beyond Zone 2. At the same time, the rising backlash to Western industrialism in Islamic cultures fueled conflicts in the Mideast and throughout the USSR. Similarly, the recognition of the outdated regimentation of old style industrialism, based on an inadequate understanding of human needs and potentials and with its limited awareness of Nature's crucial role in production, is now leading to more humane, participatory organizations, cooperatives, worker-owned and managed businesses and the burgeoning of smaller businesses and entrepreneurship, as well as production methods, inclusive of recycling and recovery systems that work with Nature and within ecological tolerances. As more workers and managers lost their jobs to "downsizing," they swelled the ranks of the self-employed, 8.7 million in 1991 or 7.7 percent of the workforce.[9]

Today, we are already moving beyond the Information Age, based on electronic technologies, to the Age of Light and its lightwave technologies: from lasers, fiber optics, optical scanners and computing, to photovoltaics and many other thermal and chemical energy-conservation processes based on a deeper understanding of Nature and modelling her processes—from solar collectors based on the chloroplasts in every green leaf to biotechnologies based on the genetic code, still in their moral infancy as they explore these new Faustian powers. As U.N. Assistant Secretary General Robert Muller reminds us in his *New Genesis* (1984), we are a very young species, in terms of our planet's development, and we have in our very brief history, learned a great deal, and as long as we refuse to panic or despair, we may yet learn the lessons of globalization now upon us. Our Planet is a perfectly designed, programmed learning environment, akin to one of psychologist B.F. Skinner's famous boxes— providing us with all the lessons and both positive and negative feedbacks needed to nudge us along the path.

We see the learning now occurring through the "crises" of our costly, mechanized, chemical and energy-dependent agriculture and its massive production of monocultured crops now glutting world markets. The future lies in lower-cost, lower-input forms of agriculture, in small-scale and boutique farms, in new crops, from jojoba and guayule to ethnic fruits and vegetables, specialty and organically-grown foods, fish farms and genetically engineered varieties tolerant of poor soils, excessive salt and lack of water.

Here too, we see that this planetary storehouse of genetic diversity is a "commons," just as are the oceans and the air we breathe. Therefore, we

Expanded Framework for Human Policy

PLATE 1-6

must also conclude global compacts as rapidly as possible to move toward "win-win" rules to manage these precious resources cooperatively, for the benefit of all the human family, rather than in the obsolete, self-destructive, competitive mode of today's corporations and biotechnology sector, whose research base has been underwritten by public funding and taxes. Such technologies are too precious and potentially hazardous to be left to the mercies of a few unscrupulous or careless companies, which can put others in jeopardy and foreclose the options of future generations. Similarly, doctrinaire, laissez-faire assumptions have hampered the wider development of the computer sector, where competitive, zero sum rules create a tower of babel of incompatibilities, preventing wider use of computers in the global, networking modes to which they are naturally suited, based on the random access model of telephone systems. Even in the United States in 1991, Senator Albert Gore of Tennessee was still struggling to pass legislation creating telecommunications highways and infrastructure to undergird a 21st Century society.

The threat of global economic chaos is forcing governments and economic advisors to throw out old ideologies and address the new agenda of stabilizing currencies and financial flows, and seeking more realistic *niches* of true comparative advantage and symbiosis. We see that head-on competition to produce a narrow range of goods in already saturating markets is now a destructive exercise in putting lower wages and further ecological destruction on the marketplace's auction block, and accelerating market economic activities into a global, zero-sum behavioral sink.

Thus, Zone 3 involves not only breakthroughs, restructuring, new forms and adaptations, but also a broad "politics of reconceptualization" of all the basic assumptions and conditions underlying the problems and crises of Zone 2. Knowledge is restructured from old, single disciplines, such as economics, into new trans-disciplinary policy tools, for example: from macroeconomics to "post-economic" policy studies including technology assessment, environmental impact statements, future studies, scenario building, cross-impact analyses, risk assessments, social impact studies and systems research—all with global, rather than national frameworks.

As these new maps clarify the new terrain, new criteria for success and new indicators and measures of performance and development are emerging; for example, the GNP is giving way slowly in many government agencies and academic textbooks to broader indicators such as Japan's Net National Welfare (NNW) and the Overseas Development Council's Physical Quality of Life Index (PQLI) and the Basic Human Needs

(BHN) indicator, developed by the U.N. Environment Programme as well as more recent indicators discussed in Chapter Seven. Using such indicators, a very different picture emerges and such countries as Sri Lanka and China are highlighted for achieving progress in health, education, shelter and environment, as well as growth of living standards (rather than per capita-averaged money income which often masks severe inequities in distribution). As these new indicators take hold, it becomes clear that countries such as China, are achieving their successes partly due to reprioritizing; for example, China's military expenditures have been reduced in the past 20 years. Similarly, Japan's success is due in part, to her concentration on serving civilian markets, rather than joining the deadly, costly competition of the arms race.

In Zone 3, we also see that the old "either/or" debate gives way to a "yin/yang view of complementarity. The debate moves beyond the *either* competition *or* cooperation argument, to the understanding that both these equally important principles are operating simultaneously, and at every level in all human societies and in Nature.

Already Zone 3 is replete with new concepts: such ideas as the ubiquitous images of emerging planetary paradigms and cultural identity; the concepts of sustainable forms of production, renewable resources, appropriate technologies and the new economics (or "ecologics" as some term it) of the carrying capacities of various ecosystems, not to mention the exciting new views of human nature and potentials growing out of brain and mind research, summed up in Jean Houston's *The Possible Human*. Zone 3 is replete with models and examples of "win-win," breakthrough strategies. However, they appear as "insignificant" to Newtonian-trained scientists with single disciplines or clockwork models, rather than as the "attractors" of the new organic, systems models such as those mentioned earlier. Similarly, most statistical "cameras" are still focused for vanishing phenomena of a more discrete, static, orderly world of the past. For example, social policy in the United States is still largely based on faulty, obsolete data. Similarly, economic statistics ignore the flows of services in world trade, now enormous, while economic models cannot embrace the newest and most pervasive of commodities: information. As information is not scarce, it conforms to "win-win" rules, rather than zero-sum competition.

Today, it is well for our mental health to remember that the supercharged atmosphere we are experiencing as we move further into flip-flop modes of Zone 2, is still the focus of most academics, statisticians and mass media. Thus the breakthroughs are continually overlooked or drowned out by the saturation reporting of the daily shocks, threats, confrontations and senseless violence of Zone 1, while the opportunities and choices of Zone 2 are under-reported or misinterpreted. For example, the widely covered insurance "crisis" partly caused by dud real estate, junk bond portfolios and "yuppie" insurance companies, lawyers and the jury system, is a golden opportunity to examine the limits of inherently risky technologies to address tasks that can be accomplished in other less risky ways; the Newtonian "clockwork" assumptions underlying most of our models for assessing risks and probabilities, *and* the overall social values implicit in the current insurance system.

The quiet building and restructuring taking place in Zone 3 is "slow motion good news" and cannot be summed up in 30 second pictures between commercial breaks on half-hour shows, and yet, it is vastly more important to our future than most of today's "photo opportunity journalism." For example, we hear of all the giant corporations that fail or close plants, while most of the 700,000 small new companies formed each year go unnoticed because the Census Bureau does not count companies with fewer than 20 employees. As the acceleration of change increases, "news" and "facts" will fall further behind the changing scene.

Here, once again, we find that many crises and problems are opportunities, for example, we find that the world population "problem" may actually be stabilized by saving lives. By preventing millions of needless early infant deaths from fatal diarrhoea in many countries, the World Health Organization (WHO) tackled both tasks by the simple, swift, inexpensive remedy of administering a drinking solution of water, glucose and salt. In so doing, this oral rehydration therapy (ORT) had reduced birthrates, rather than increasing them, as Newtonian-oriented studies expected. The really good news is that so many solutions are turning out to be simple and inexpensive, rather than requiring massive, costly new technologies. When crises and problems are fundamentally re-examined, solutions often arise in the rethinking process, as in the "lateral thinking" and creativity exercises used by many organizational development and transformation theorists. For example, massive, costly high-tech medical systems to "cure" disease are now giving way to less costly remedies: healthier lifestyles, less and better nutrition, more physical activity, education and prevention, as well as new understanding of the beneficial effects of less stress and more positive outlooks on life.

As our mass media begin to understand their role as a nervous system of the new body-politic of the human family, they may also search out and interpret the events and opportunities of Zones 2 and 3, thus reducing general stress levels and panic reactions, while amplifying our knowledge of all the healthy choices open to us. Clearly, the human species is at a new evolutionary juncture, and is undergoing the timeless drama of all species: the play between adaptation and adaptability, between maladaption, paedomorphosis, learning, transformation and metamorphosis. As we deal with the heightened stakes of the Fibrillation Zone with all its unavoidable choices, we can all do our part in taking the millions of necessary small steps and wise decisions, most of which we know intuitively, which together will amplify the "attractors" leading us toward further expansion of the territory of the Breakthrough Zone. The vision of successful globalization will govern the "win-win" politics of building an equitable, culturally diverse, ecologically-harmonious and therefore peaceful Planet. In this all-embracing context, all our individual self-interests become identical with the self-interest of our now truly interdependent human family.

Chapter One Footnotes

Portions of this chapter have been taken from an article by the same name which first appeared in *Inquiry Magazine*.

1 *Challenge to the South*, Oxford University Press, New York and London, 1990.

2. *Our Common Future*, World Commission on Environment and Development, Oxford University Press, New York and London, 1987.

3. Hazel Henderson, *The Politics of the Solar Age: Alternatives to Economics*, current edition from Knowledge Systems, Inc., Indianapolis, 1988.

4. Ibid., pp. 245-282.

5. Marilyn Waring, *If Women Counted*, Harper & Row, San Francisco, 1988.

6. As of July 1990 during a lecture tour by the author in New Zealand.

7. *Business Week*, September 25, 1989, p. 166.

8. Hazel Henderson "From Economism to Systems Theory." *Technological Forecasting & Social Change*, May 1990, Elsevier, New York.

9. *Business Week*, July 22, 1991, p. 14.

Note: Also highly recommended

Frank Feather, *G-Forces: Reinventing the World*, Summerhill Press,Toronto, 1989.

Lester Milbrath, *Envisioning a Sustainable Society: Learning Our Way Out*, State University of New York Press, Buffalo, New York, 1989.

Satellites, Boosters and Debris

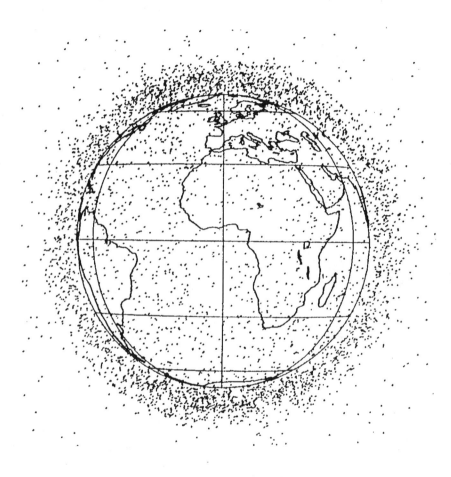

SATELLITES, BOOSTERS AND DEBRIS with a diameter of 10 centimeters or more swarm around the earth in this computerized printout by Lockheed engineers. Their printout is based on data from the U.S. North American Aerospace Defense Command.

PLATE 2-7

Living Earth's Lessons Co-Creatively

A Parable:
Locking Mother Earth into an Orbiting Space Prison?

We have all played the childhood game of "connecting the dots" to create a hidden picture. Space scientists today are dealing with a sinister new version: "How long do we have before the millions of dots of space junk currently orbiting our Planet and multiplying with every new space activity, become dense enough to form virtual prison bars, foreclosing humanity's future as an interplanetary species?"

Most space experts still down play the accumulation of space debris, noting that there have been, as yet, no serious accidents and that the likelihood of collisions with spacecraft is still low. However, many do acknowledge that this likelihood is increasing and NASA's Johnson Space Center in Houston already has a group designing armoring for spacecraft to allow absorption of direct hits from such space shrapnel. Thus the time may well be ripe for reassessing these risks, as well as our current policy assumptions which still tend to perpetuate such "rearview-mirror" thinking.

Space junk has been accumulating for decades, ever since Sputnik in the 1950s. The United States and the USSR are responsible for most of the some 7000 objects (spent rocket boosters and the like) of the size of a baseball and larger that are tracked by the U.S. North American Aerospace Defense Command (NORAD) and the 40,000 additional objects smaller than a baseball and larger than a pea, which were orbiting as of 1986 (Plate 2-7). At orbital speeds, even a pea-sized or smaller object can cause significant damage, such as the paint flake which damaged the space shuttle *Challenger's* windshield in 1984. The *Scientific American* drew attention to this growing problem in 1986 and reported that, even then, Strategic Defense Initiative (SDI) officials were studying this newest garbage crisis. This latest evidence of our throwaway mentality—now overwhelming our landfills, polluting the atmosphere and oceans here on Earth—may prove most devastating in space, as the ultimate testament to human ambitions and hubris.

SDI space debris crisis

It is becoming fashionable among U.S. defense related companies now that military contracting is the latest sunset industry, to switch their attention to more intensive lobbying for Star Wars (SDI) budget increases. Indeed as the Cold War winds down, Star Wars is seen as the last best hope for high-tech suppliers to diversify and replace lost terrestrial weapons contracts. Yet Star Wars is predicated on a strategy that would literally explode not only incoming warheads or satellites in space or lower orbits, but also explode the planet's existing space garbage problem—sooner or later—into a full-blown crisis. Like similar planetary issues such as the build-up of greenhouse gases and ozone depletion, human societies are still ill equipped to respond to such "slowmotion crises" affecting all constituencies of our global commons. Such common security issues require international diplomacy and treaties, as well as redefinition of the nature of threats and risks to human life.

The general weakness of many earlier arguments for Star Wars, as well as for anti-satellite weapons and the militarization of space, are well documented. They were authoritatively summed up in a report by the U.S. Congress Office of Technology Assessment released in May 1988 after being withheld by the Pentagon for seven months. The report was steered by an Advisory Panel representing a cross-section of elite U.S. scientists from major national laboratories including Sandia, Lawrence-Livermore and Los Alamos, universities including Caltech and MIT as well as major contractors including Hughes Aircraft, Honeywell, McDonnell Douglas, International Business Machines (IBM) and Digital Equipment Corporation.

This report concluded that the SDI program's timetable (based on such optimistic assumptions as "extraordinarily fast rates of research, development and production") was "an act of faith," and that it was likely to "suffer a catastrophic failure" on initial deployment, and that it might only be possible in the 1995-2000 period. It was also concluded that Soviet countermeasures could match U.S. deployment schedules, and that SDI could only be expected to destroy "a few to a modest fraction" of the weapons that could be deployed and that even the computer software programs required exceeded software engineering developments projected for the foreseeable future.

Generally, Star Wars much-vaunted "impenetrable shield" against space weapons depicted in so many idealized NASA and DOD mockups and videographed scenarios that saturated U.S. television screens in the 1980s turned out to be just scenarios, while thousands of scientists foreswore lucrative contracts and went public in newspaper ads to expose these flawed Star Wars rationales.

Changing global security context

Today, Star Wars has metamorphosed from Ronald Reagan's 1983 rationale as a defensive way out of the Cold War of Mutually Assured Destruction. The Bush administration's FY1991 budget called for a 22 percent increase to SDI's $4.6 billion on the grounds that it "makes more sense than ever"—refocused as both a limited deterrence-enhancing defensive system, as well as an offensive anti-satellite weapons system (ASAT). Yet doubts proliferate. Not only has the concept of the X-ray laser proved technically formidable, but, as many have noted, the ending of the Cold War has now rendered the whole SDI program irrelevant. Even more fundamental arguments for discontinuing Star Wars are compelling.

The debate about global security is now more often viewed in economic and environmental terms, rather than based on only military factors. Similarly, we are realizing the importance of diplomatic and negotiating skills in our interdependent world, that is, the "software" of conflict resolution and skillful diplomacy, rather than military hardware now so catastrophic that it is rendering war itself obsolete. In addition, the new strategic importance of satellites of whatever nationality in the emerging global security system of arms treaty verification and general "Earth-keeping" chores monitoring environmental conditions, *precludes* militarization of space. ASATs would inevitably knock out many such civilian and verification satellites, as well as routine telecommunications "birds', leading to dangerous disruptions and regional "blind spots" in treaty monitoring.

But worse, *any* testing let alone deployment of Star Wars technologies, including the new Brilliant Pebbles now being pushed by Livermore Laboratories and supported in the Bush budget proposal, would trigger the space garbage crisis scenario: connecting the dots swirling around our Planet and even further narrowing humanity's "launch windows"— jeopardizing, perhaps irrevocably, our ability to understand the solar system, our galaxy, as well as our hope for colonizing space.

Space clean-up

So far, the space debris dilemma has spawned some contracts to research methods of cleaning up the existing backlog of space junk, and companies such as JPL of California have stakes in this latest environmental clean-up market. Developing technologies to retrieve lost satellites are advancing and the United States has some demonstrated capabilities in these tasks in the space shuttle program. Ironically, it is the U.S.'s own space program and satellites that need protection from Star Wars.

Furthermore, on the diplomatic "software" front, it now seems that even verification tasks may become more routine and "lower-tech" depending more on surveillance by airplanes, as in recent agreements. Space is a common heritage of all humanity and its militarization not only betrays our children's future, but is now clearly unnecessary and unwise. In October 1990, the U.S. Office of Technology Assessment confirmed the extent of the space junk problem in its report: *Orbital Debris: A Space Environmental Problem*, noting that if space-faring nations do not work together to reduce the amount of orbital debris they produce each year, future space activities are likely to suffer loss of capability, loss of income and even loss of life as a result of collisions between spacecraft and debris. Yet NASA priorities remained fixed on Mars, rather than cleaning up the existing mess, while President Bush tried to revive the SDI budget in 1991, even though the USSR was less a threat. It would be ironic, indeed, if the SDI's siren promise of an ultimate defence "shield" created instead the "prison bars" that trapped humans into an Earth which became a vast orbiting penal colony, from which we could never escape—a fitting fate for a foolish species.

Thus the 1990s will see a great human drama unfold: Will we learn that our self-absorbed efforts to exploit the Earth are futile and change our perceptions and value systems to reflect the truth of Chief Seattle's words "the Earth does not belong to man—we belong to the Earth"? ◆◆◆

When we use the Earth, the living goddess Gaia, as our frame of reference, our epistemology, our study guide and curriculum, and when we learn to interpret her feedback signals responding to our actions, we can maintain that holistic, open awareness necessary for true learning. When our space programs and systems scientists fully embrace this awareness that *only the system can model the system*, i.e., the relevant system is Earth *itself* and its relationship with the Mother Star, the Sun, they will have a comprehensive enough context for modelling sub-systems, from ecosystems to human organizations and cultures. When our human family at last, see ourselves a responsible, conscious part of the living body of the Earth, co-creating the future in symbiosis, we will restructure our knowledge, our universities and schools and our relationships.

Let us now turn to examining how the Earth has always been our model and guide for optimal design of our tools, habitats and technologies. When we fully appreciate how much all of our human technologies imitate Nature, we may use the Earth more consciously to show us the best way forward into a new, ecologically-compatible, humanly sensitive model of "development." It is now better to drop the prefix "economic" altogether, for the sake of clarity, as I and Fritz Schumacher (author of *Small is Beautiful*, 1973) urged, since we both agreed that economics had become a form of "brain damage." Instead, I have urged that we use many of the more inclusive policy tools already available to us, described in *The Politics of the Solar Age*[1] and in my "Post-Economic Policies for Post-Industrial Societies."[2] As more humans assume full planetary identities and begin to empathize with the Earth and connect more viscerally once again with natural rhythms and processes, as well as with

A Post-Cartesian Scientific Worldview

(based on global view, biological and systemic life sciences, rather than inorganic, static, equilibrium or mechanistic models)

PRINCIPLES

INTERCONNECTEDNESS	at every system level
REDISTRIBUTION	recycling of all elements and structures
HETERARCHY	networks and webs, intercommunication rather than hierarchies; many interactive systems variables; self-organization, autopoesis, mutual causality
COMPLIMENTARITY	replaces either/or, dichotomous logics and re-frames with meta-logics of "yin-yang" and "win-win" rather than zero-sum games
UNCERTAINTY	from static, equilibrium, and mechanistic models to probabilistic, morphogenetic, oscillating and cyclic models. Biological view of self-organizing, self-replicating, self-referential living systems
CHANGE	focus on irreversible phenomena as well as traditional reversible models, evolutionary view, macro-scopic time/space, change as fundamental, certainty as limited

PLATE 2-8

each other, the many states of denial and barriers to consciousness created by our old boundaries, nationalistic, academic and ideological, begin to fall away. We see ourselves and our Planet more clearly, and our Earth's relationship to our life-supporting Mother Star: the Sun. This stage of human awareness and the many reconceptualizations growing out of it were the subject of *The Politics of the Solar Age*, where we would remember, as all earlier cultures before industrialism knew, that our Earth is nourished by that daily flow of life-giving photons from the Sun. Thus, the Solar Age of awareness is also offering the opportunity for us to go beyond both the Industrial Age and the Information Age, and mature into the dawning Age of Light, both with the arrival of lightwave technologies, and the flowering of our consciousness in a *new* Age of Enlightenment.

Since the 1960s, many fruitful metaphors of transition have emerged which have helped map the ongoing restructuring of industrial societies. Daniel Bell's *The Coming of Post Industrial Society* (1973) found instant resonance, even as a "rear-view mirror" image of the maturing and decline of the Industrial Revolution. Barbara Ward's unforgettable image of *Spaceship Earth* in 1966 pointed to today's reality of the globalized economy. World attention began to expand beyond old rivalries between the two major styles of industrialism: capitalism and socialism, which had crystallized in the East-West cold war, gradually embracing a larger North-South dialog between the industrial countries and the rest of the world. In *Creating Alternative Futures* (1978), I summed up this emerging global view as The End of Economics, since economics (from left to right) was primarily concerned with industrialism as a method of producing material goods efficiently and with greater technological virtuosity. (See Plate 1-3: Differing Perceptions, Assumptions, Forecasting Styles between Economists and Futurists.)

New images of post-industrial society proliferated in the 1970s as the restructuring of industrial societies accelerated. Further globalization increased the general turbulence, forcing new awareness of the infeasibility of nuclear war and competitive nationalism. Alvin Toffler's *Future Shock* (1970) set the stage for his breathtaking view of the human journey through the "first wave" (agriculture) and the "second wave" (industrialism) to the emerging *Third Wave* (1980), a globalizing human culture based on information, more appropriate use of technology, demassifying of regimented industrial uniformity with more productive, pro-active individuals outgrowing consumerism. This view of a more globalized, decentralized culture with human-scaled technologies and the growth of human potential was amplified and echoed by many futurists, including John Naisbitt in *Megatrends* (1982). Schumacher had asserted this view most clearly in his *Small is Beautiful* and had emphasized with me, the ecological dimensions and moral implication of these changes.

Robert Theobald also outlined in several books, including *Alternative Futures for America* (1970), what he called "the Communication Era," and a shift toward community empowerment, automation, greater dissemination of information, and redefining work and leisure as the fruits of automation to be shared widely. He proposed a guaranteed income for all, an idea he shared with conservative economist, Milton Friedman, who urged a similar "negative income tax." Both perspectives transcended the view of scarcity in traditional economic theory. The idea of overcoming scarcity by automation was also part of Herman Kahn's image of *The Next 200 Years* (1967), a continuous hyper-industrial boom which would eventually reach all of the people on the Planet. Schumacher and I, on the other hand, saw "scarcity" transcended: firstly, by restructuring societies to recognize that it is through self-chosen tasks and personal challenges that we express ourselves and grow; and secondly, by rethinking "satisfaction" of "needs" in traditional economic theory from beyond its materialistic bias which viewed "needs" as "insatiable" and had set industrial societies onto their slippery, unsustainable path of continual GNP-measured "economic growth" which destroyed Earth's life-support systems. My own view of citizen action in both *Creating Alternative Futures* and *The Politics of the Solar Age* was that information disseminated more broadly could enable the rise of networks of citizens which could crosscut old power structures, facilitate learning, and initiate a widespread politics of reconceptualization, transforming our fragmented worldview into a new paradigm based on planetary awareness as well as a new view of human nature. (See Plate 2-8: Post-Cartesian Worldviews)

Furthermore, the dawning of the Solar Age meant much more: a shift to renewable resource management and sustainable forms of production long advocated by ecologists and promoted by colleagues at the Worldwatch Institute, the Cousteau Society, the Council on Economic Priorities and the Calvert Social Investment Fund. The Solar Age was also premised on a new view of science that revered the Earth and worked cooperatively with Nature, rather than in the old manipulative, exploitive modes of industrialism. To me, the Solar Age would go beyond the Information Age, which had become an ubiquitous image, glibly confirming old ideas of "economic progress" and coinciding with the rise of the "services sector" as Daniel Bell had predicted (and which I named "the bureaucracy sector"), as well as the astonishing growth of information technologies, computerization and automation.

However, the Information Age is no longer an adequate image, even for the present, let alone as a guide to the future. It still focuses on hardware technologies, mass production, narrow economic models of efficiency and competition, and is more an extension of industrial ideas and methods than a new stage in human development. Information is an abundant resource, difficult to contain, hoard and sell. It does not conform to scarcity economics, but is best shared and free-flowing, rather than a material commodity. This demands new rules: from the old competitive zero-sum, "I win–you lose" rules, to the new win-win rules of cooperation—from local to global, flattening hierarchies and empowering citizens in our global village. But focusing on only the information aspects of these changes can blind us to all of the *dis*-information or propaganda in this media-dominated environment. Mere information has simply led to overload of ever-less meaningful billions of bits of fragmented raw data—rather than the search for meaningful new patterns of knowledge. (See Plate 2-9: Information Quality Scale.)

My view of the dawning Solar Age involves this kind of repatterning of the exploding Information Age, nothing less than a paradigm shift, where we take off the old spectacles of all the narrow separate disciplines: economics, sociology, physics, engineering, psychology and the rest, and compost all these fragments into a holistic view of the entire human family, now inextricably linked by our globe-girdling technologies into one emerging planetary culture. This view is shared by many with whom I have been privileged to work: William Irwin Thompson in *Pacific Shift* (1985); Fritjof Capra in *The Turning Point* (1981); Barbara Marx Hubbard in *The Evolutionary Journey* (1982); Erich Jantsch in *The Self-Organizing Universe* (1980); Peter Russell in *The Global Brain* (1982) and Jean Houston in *The Possible Human* (1982).

The Age of Light, which is explored further in Chapter Nine, transcends the inorganic view of industrial science and technology: that the Earth is inert matter to be exploited and manipulated. Since the Earth is reconceived as Gaia (after the Greek Earth goddess), a living planet, the most appropriate view is organic: the sciences of living systems, which are dynamic and self-organizing. Biological sciences become more useful spectacles for mapping a living planet and the teeming richness of its ecosystems, and it is no accident that biotechnologies are proving to be our most Faustian new tools. The Solar Age is an image that reminds us that the light from the sun is what powers our extraordinary blue Planet and it is the sun's stream of photons which drives all of Earth's processes: the cycles of carbon, nitrogen, hydrogen, the water cycles and climate "machine." It is these light-driven processes, which

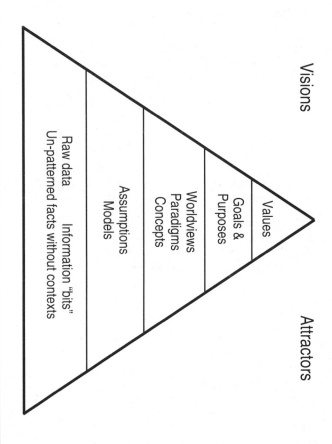

Information Quality Scale

i.e., meaning of information as relevant to human purposes

Visions

Attractors

Values

Goals & Purposes

Worldviews Paradigms Concepts

Assumptions Models

Raw data   Information "bits"
Un-patterned facts without contexts

PLATE 2-9

are then mediated by the photosynthesis of plants, that maintain conditions for we humans to continue our evolution beyond the Information Age. Plate 9-50 shows how technologies, however new, still mimic Nature.

The logic of the emerging post-Cartesian science will at last transcend "objectivity" and dualism. It will be based on self-referential, autopoetic logic, where the observer must account for his or her logical position in the system they seek to describe. This will produce a more honest science where the role and impact of the observer is clearly acknowledged as affecting the phenomena or experiment. It will also provide "full disclosure" of the personal reasons and motivations of the scientist for studying one phenomenon rather than another, since the first normative decision of any scientist is to decide what to pay attention to, among the infinite numbers of data sets "out there." Post-Cartesian science will be a science with reverence, gently descriptive and exploratory without the compulsion to intervene. It will produce a revolution in technology from "hardware" to "software," where we will think more carefully before intervening, and a production problem will not always conjure up visions of factories and machines. Instead, we will scan ecosystems for signs of redundant potential or situations where natural ecosystem production can be augmented, as described in more detail in my other books.

With such new sensibilities, one can envision the further direction of the human enterprise, as we learn to co-create our future with our Earth. As Walter Truett Anderson notes in his book, *To Govern Evolution*,[3] we must accept the responsibilities of our many and continuous interventions in reshaping eco-systems, rather than deny this role we have played historically. The new page of the human agenda open before us involves much learning: in fact, how to restore some of the damage we have created, to re-forest and re-green the Earth. This must be the fundamental task of any new "development" and will test our skills, ingenuity and understanding as never before, since so many of our ecosystems are simultaneously under stress and exceeding thresholds, such as the space debris now threatening our satellite communications and the widening hole in the ozone layer. The hour is late and the stakes higher than ever, but we have no other course than to learn how to intervene more responsibly to heal the Earth. As we redefine "development"[4] and proceed beyond the Cold War to the emerging scenario of "Mutually Assured Development," we can envision what an emerging planetary trade system might look like, after a new, more equitable global monetary system and successive sets of trading bartering and currency agreements emerge.

One can imagine such a future world trading system based mostly on "software" rather than "hardware" (i.e., goods and materials). Every

Emerging Era of Global Interdependence Geo-Political Realignments

1945-1988
"Cold War Era"
Super-powers
Bi-polar world

GAME:
"Mutually Assured Destruction"
Military confrontation
Ideological struggle for "3rd World"

1988-?
Multi-polar World
Super-powers decline
Japan won Cold War
MEGA Trade Blocs

GAME:
"Mutually Assured Sustainable Development"
New national strategies
Multiple ideological struggles over approaches to "development"
"Progress" rethinking economics beyond left and right convergence
Green movements

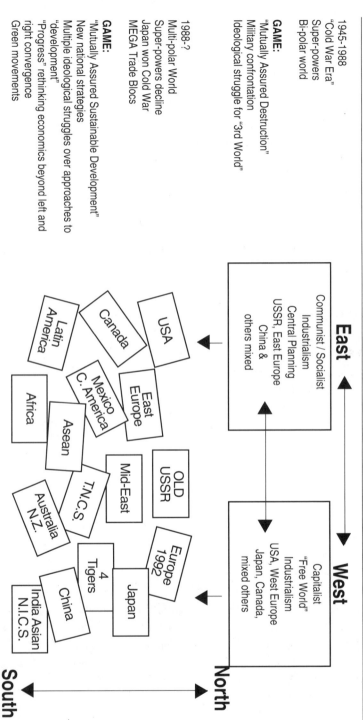

East

West

Communist / Socialist
Industrialism
Central Planning
USSR, East Europe
China &
others mixed

Capitalist
"Free World"
Industrialism
USA, West Europe
Japan, Canada,
mixed others

USA
Canada
Latin
America
Mexico
C. America
East
Europe
Africa
Asean
Mid-East
T.N.C.S.
OLD
USSR
Australia
N.Z.
4
Tigers
Europe
1992
Japan
China
India Asian
N.I.C.S.

North

South

PLATE 2-10

region will have the basic skills to produce the basic "stuff" of daily living: food, shelter, transportation, basic goods manufacturing, and the process of mimicking new products and innovations from industrial countries, such as the instant "cloning" of new computers and electronics, will become indigenized as the norm. Technological innovation and the funds spent on research and development will be ever less-recapturable, by companies, states or nations, since this innovation is knowledge-based and is becoming the newest "commons," despite efforts to patent and impound it as "private property." This is seen as a "dilemma" for corporations and nations, as they still try to compete for technological advantage, and set up new trade blocs in Europe, North America and Asia.

However, from a planetary perspective, we may view such nations and companies as "ripe seedpods," reaching the maturation of their potential and inevitably scattering their knowledge into the global commons. The effort to impound innovation must become ever more costly and doomed to failure, and as all societies learn to produce the basics for their own, global trade will shift toward "software" and the exchange of the best expressions of different cultures combined with the uniqueness of their local eco-systems. This true "niche" strategy, is not competitive, but cooperative, since these quintessential learning expressions of each culture, whether as computer software, literature, innovations in governance (such as the earlier inventions of parliaments and juridical systems), or as new blueprints for problem solving, will tend to be ever more unique. This kind of ephemeralized world trade system is already visible; for example, the Dutch can export their hard-learned technologies for dyking out the seas with little competition since no other society can match their experience. Likewise, one of the most successful British exports since World War II has been eccentricity, i.e., the Beatles, punk fashions and Boy George—perfect exports for a natural resource limited island society. One can imagine an entire economy built on music, rather as Austria was during the heyday of Mozart and its great musical period. As we turn our attention to identifying such "cultural DNA," we will value the great spiritual traditions, art, and poetry which all societies have borrowed from each other, just as highly as the consumer electronics and automobiles which predominate in world trade today. As the industrial countries of the Northern Hemisphere age, their maturing and shrinking populations will need and value ever more highly the young people in their own and other societies of the Third World. Already, there is a growing awareness that the basic investment today must be in people, to draw out young minds and keep learning as a lifelong activity.[5]

Differing Models of Markets and Commons

	Economists	Futurists / Systems
	Markets	**Open Systems**
	Private Sector... • Individual decisions • Competition • Invisible hand • Anti-trust	• Divisible resources • Win-lose rules • (Adam Smith's rules)
	Commons	**Closed Systems**
	Public Sector... • Property of all • Monopoly under regulation • Consortia	• Indivisible resources • Win-win rules • Cooperation • Agreements

Note: One must remember that all such schematizations are, at best, approximations and often culturally arbitrary.

PLATE 2-11

Development will be reconceptualized as investments in people and in the restoration and maintenance of ecosystems. Already the new demographic realities of aging industrial societies are forcing new thinking. A cover story in *Business Week* of August 10, 1987, trumpeted the new "worker scarcity that may last to the Year 2000." Today in most industrial societies, jobs go unfilled either because they are too ill-paying to offer a living, or because young people are growing up poor, untrained and illiterate, even in the United States, where between one in three and one in five adults are functionally illiterate. Similarly, a report issued by the New York based business-oriented Committee for Economic Development, released in September 1987, called for increased public investment in the health and education needs of young children, and cited studies showing that $1 invested in quality preschool education would return five times that much in lower costs of public assistance and crime.[6] Thus, even economists are slowly learning about social and environmental costs, and that prevention is always better and cheaper than repair or cure. Perhaps Americans will find that their very best "export" is their Constitution and Bill of Rights, which may continue serving as a magnet for bright, adventurous people from all over the world, who will continue to give their best to their new homeland.

The internal restructuring processes all countries are undergoing range from the "hollowing" shift from manufacturing to services in the United States and from glasnost and economic reforms in the old USSR to the shifts toward democracy in Eastern Europe and Latin America. These restructurings are accompanied by inevitable trade and security realignments between countries as they seek to learn new ways of playing in the new "global ballpark" and riding the roller-coaster of world trade. Much of the new agenda lies beyond old left-right debates about how to stay "competitive" (either militarily or economically) in the "global ballgame." The new agenda (implicit in the new talk of "level playing fields") is nothing less than creating some new rules and taking a necessary measure of responsibility for managing and maintaining the new "ballpark" itself: the global economy (now indivisible), the spread of technology, arms control and disarmament, and maintaining the global commons of our rivers, oceans, ecosystems, atmosphere and space.

This new agenda of "Planet management" is graphically laid out in such studies as *Gaia: An Atlas of Planet Management*, edited by Norman Myers and a team of scientists, and Worldwatch Institute's *State of the World* reports. The new agenda is thrust upon us—ready or not—and can provide the greatest learning experience and cooperative development opportunity for the human family to take the next step in our journey on this Planet. All of the industrial capacity of every country and region is needed for this new Planet management task: to restore and re-green desert regions, re-forest eroding areas, develop more vigorous and diverse food crops and distribute them more rationally; to protect the Earth's storehouse of genetic resources; to achieve the goal of the World Health Organization of health for all by the year 2000, to build needed infrastructure in many countries (particularly those of the Southern Hemisphere) and thereby, to create viable markets for the civilian products of a redesigned trading system. As if all these challenges were not attractive enough for those nations and military-industrial complexes still engaged in the old games of competition and mutually assured destruction, there is also the exciting new game of cooperative development in space and further exploration of the solar system, now clearly beyond the resources of any one nation.

Since this new agenda is almost self-evident, a common-sense approach to our global future espoused by countless scholars, scientists and millions of citizens, what is holding things up? And why is the world not yet embarked on this **new** game: Mutually Assured Development? The answer is that the new game, in fact, has already **begun**! However, old perceptions and now dysfunctional belief systems are still preventing most people, including so-called leaders in government, business and mass media, from **seeing** this new game unfolding before our very eyes.

The new game is unfamiliar (by definition) and it is very different from the old, competitive, zero-sum (I win-you lose) games that most of us were taught (evident, for example, as the underlying *premise* of our adversary legal system). The new game is cooperative, where no one wins unless everyone wins and individuals make out *better* if they consider the needs of others, and *worse* if they act selfishly. For example, if some people insist on standing up to see better in a crowded football stadium, everyone else is eventually forced to stand up, and while *no one* sees any better, *everyone* is more uncomfortable. Win-win games are always the rule when a system of resources is "common property," or a "commons" and can only be used indivisibly by all, such as the air we breathe. Those resource systems which can be used individually without inflicting harm on others are more familiar to us as "markets," where competitive rules, such as those of Adam Smith's famous invisible hand seem to work best. We see now that as all the niches get filled up in any market, it turns into a commons. Part of the new scenario and evidence that the new game is emerging can be seen in the fact that both the Soviets and the Chinese are rethinking their approaches to resource management by reinstating market games. At the same time, the globalization process is also creating new "commons" out of what all countries used to consider "free" goods, such as water and air, the electromagnetic spectrum, genetic biodiversity and space.

However, the key to understanding both of the fundamental games is *feedback*, the information on the effects of these strategies on each other and the whole, so that continual course-correction is possible. Thus the old left-right debate sees the virtues only in one or the other strategies, competition *or* cooperation. Today we have learned from feedback that all social systems (like all other living systems) require balance between cooperation and competition—both are vital strategies for survival and success, and even more important, both must learn and correct their courses from *feedback*, to remain healthy. Just as the human body remains healthy by using constant *feedback* (information on air temperature, stressful situations, sounds, vision and all the senses), so a society is successful inasmuch as it structures itself to take advantage of *feedback*: from its own citizens (democracy), from the environment, from other countries and from new conditions of change, such as the increase of human numbers to an unprecedented five billion. Thus it is no longer a matter of left or right, competitiveness or cooperation, but the extent to which a society can structure itself to *utilize feedback* and where appropriate, to change the game and write new rules.

Today, the accelerating globalization process is precisely that of re-cognizing whole systems, which in earlier and less crowded times seemed like "free" markets for all: the air, the oceans. Now, as "commons," they will require win-win rules. The word "commons" derives from fourteenth-century England, where each village had a "common" greenspace, where all could graze their sheep. The now famous "Tragedy of the Commons" relates to the behavioral error of villagers who tried to maximize their own gain by grazing more of their sheep on the "common"—until overgrazing destroyed it for all.

In today's globalization, we now see how we have created the newest "commons": the new, indivisible global economy itself. Each nation and multinational corporation tries to maximize its own position in an all-out competitive game that can only destroy the global economic commons and bring on a worldwide collapse or depression. Each player, unlike in 1929, is now privy to vastly more information and *feedback*, so as to be able to *simulate* the results of a contemplated individual action ahead of time. Thus, each player is also seeing that they must give up or pool some cherished individual "sovereignty."

Thus, the world's economic actors, in spite of themselves and their former ideologies, are moving toward some kind of new framework of agreements: on currencies, trade debt and management, analogous to a new "Bretton Woods," which now must include all players. This shift towards building a Win-Win-World is almost imperceptible but signs *are* visible: from the treaties already signed to eliminate ozone destroying chlorofluorocarbons (CFCs) to the U.N.'s Earth Summit in 1992. We see the same shift to cooperative strategies in manufacturing and marketing as production of automobile and consumer electronic items becomes ever more internationalized. The national base of a multinational company is becoming less relevant, along with bilateral trade statistics, as well as national economic indicators and strategies, now that financial markets have moved to 24-hour asset management in the global arena. Feedback too, is becoming more instantaneous as televised news and opinion outflank government officials and diplomatic channels, producing rapid course-corrections, such as in the debates over global warming.

The old win-lose games are now beginning to damage their players— most notably in the aftermath of military competition between the United States and the USSR Mr. Gorbachev still tries to revive his sinking economy, while the United States struggles to understand its own relative decline in the world and its nosedive into being the deepest debtor nation. Meanwhile, the Japanese are spearheading the new game, by creating the world's most successful economy based on civilian goods and becoming the world leading bankers with 25 percent of the planet's capital reserves. Old cold warriors still complain that the Japanese achieved this consumer goods driven economy by U.S. decree and "under the U.S. nuclear umbrella." True enough—but this was our old win-lose game and we can hardly fault the Japanese for creating a new game by *adhering* to U.S. rules.

Today, many farsighted proposals are emerging from the most globally-minded, visionary thinkers in Japan: seeking to recycle their yen surpluses in more creative ways than the petrodollar recycling of the past decade. New "Marshall Plans" are being proposed, where Japan hopes to be joined by other countries which participated in the Marshall Plan which rebuilt Europe and world trade some forty years ago. Dr. Masaki Nakajima, former Director of Mitsubishi Research Institute has been promoting his vision of a Global Infrastructure Fund for ten years. All these proposals are now gathering international support from leading public and private sector citizens.

Several recent conferences have explored these new "Marshall Plan" proposals to assist developing countries of the South, which range from dam building and other large infrastructure projects of questionable ecological design to desert-greening and reforestation. The Tarrytown

Conference, which I convened in New York with entrepreneur Robert L. Schwartz in May 1987, focused on agreement on a new model of development, beyond economics and focused on ecological sustainability and "trickle-up" rather than "trickle-down" development.[7]

The U.N. Conference on the Relationship between Disarmament and Development, held in New York in September 1987, moved to break the logjam in the old win-lose thinking. The Reagan Administration caught with its "paradigms" down, foolishly boycotted the Conference. The Soviet Union decided to join, and offered a proposal of its own to create an international channel for funds saved from future disarmament agreements to Third World economic development. Of course, there is much rhetoric to be expected from nations still playing old military games, because so many are still major arms merchants to the world (a business worth almost one trillion dollars per year). Until old definitions of progress move beyond GNP growth and "security" is redefined beyond the military view, future tragedies, like the Gulf War, are inevitable as well. However, the one hundred and forty-five countries and five hundred non-governmental organizations attending the Conference attested to the growing power of the new "mutually assured development" game.

Thus, the new game of building a Win-Win-World is already underway, since it is the only game possible for human survival. Many countries are reinterpreting "development" in their own cultural contexts. If Northern Hemisphere industrial countries and their government officials decide to get behind the new development proposals of some of their own visionary citizens, such as that presented in the U.N. Commission on Environment and Development's 1987 report, *Our Common Future*, then a critical mass for the much more attractive game of "mutually assured development" will be unstoppable. We need to take off our nationalistic blinders and identify and support "planetary citizens" of all countries, who have transcended their old "patriotic" identities and now identify fully with the entire human family and with Mother Earth herself. The Earth indeed, is a perfectly programmed learning environment, more wondrous and efficient that one of B.F. Skinner's boxes, giving her children all the positive and negative feedback loops to nudge us in the direction we can go to develop to our fullest.[9]

All of the natural systems of Planet Earth exhibit both strategies of competition and cooperation equally and in balance: the competition between species, groups, organizations and individuals, as well as ideas, keeps unhealthy overgrowth at bay. The cooperative strategies between all these same players are equally important—creating the "glue" which keeps the groups and individuals orchestrated and creating the rules of

Social Implications of Six Emerging (Post-Cartesian) Principles

- **INTERCONNECTEDNESS** — planetary cooperation of human societies, living systems policy models

- **REDISTRIBUTION** — justice, equality, balance, reciprocity, sharing

- **CHANGE** — redesign of institutions, perfecting means of production, changing paradigms and values

- **COMPLEMENTARITY** — unity *and* diversity, from "either/or" to "both/and" logics

- **HETERARCHY** — distributed networks and intelligence, no rigid organizations or hierarchies

- **INDETERMINACY** — many models, viewpoints, compromise, humility, openness, evolution, "learning societies"

PLATE 2-12

interaction. As I testified before the U.S. Congress Joint Economic Committee in 1975, economists must now change their models and assumptions to conform to the new reality: "inputs" to production are energy, resources and knowledge and the "output" must be more fully-human beings.

Thus in general terms, we are quite aware of the basic principles on which a New World Order must be built. Fundamentally, these principles are becoming enumerated in some of the earlier indices of development that go beyond the growth of GNP, for example PQLI (Physical Quality of Life) and BHN (Basic Human Needs) developed in the 1970s. They are (as I stated them in *Politics of the Solar Age*):

- the value of all human beings;
- the right to satisfaction of basic human needs (physical, psychological and meta-physical) of all human beings;
- equality of opportunity for self-development for all human beings;
- recognition that these principles and goals must be achieved within ecological tolerances of lands, seas, air, forests and the total carrying capacity of the biosphere;
- recognition that all these principles apply with equal emphasis to future generations of humans and their biospheric life-support systems, and thus include respect for all other life forms, and the Earth itself.

Historically, human development can be viewed as many local experiments at creating social orders of many varieties, but usually based on partial concepts, that is, these social orders worked for *some* people, at the expense of *other* people, and were based on the exploitation of Nature. Furthermore, they worked in the *short*-term, but appear to have failed in the *long*-term. Today, all these experiments of local and partial human development, when seen in a planetary perspective, have been failures in one way or another, based on some form of short-term exploitation (destabilization).

Today, we know that such societies are impossible to maintain and that the destabilization on which they have built themselves is now affecting their internal governmental stability and the global stability of the Planet. Interestingly, these instabilities can all be stated in scientific terms:

1) in classical equilibrium thermodynamics, in terms of the First and Second Laws: the Law of Conservation and the Entropy Law, that all human societies (and all living systems) take negentropy (available forms of energy and concentrated materials) and transform them into entropic waste at various rates, and that we

can measure and observe these ordering activities and the disorder they create elsewhere (for example, the structuring of European countries in their colonial periods at the price of much concomitant disordering of their colonies, culturally and in terms of indigenous resources);

2) in terms of biology and the evolutionary principle, "Nothing fails like success," that is, the trade-offs between short-term and long-term stability and structure, adaptation versus adaptability;

3) in terms of general systems theory, the phenomenon of suboptimization, i.e., optimizing subsystems at the expense of their enfolding systems;

4) in terms of ecology, as violations of the general principle of interconnectedness of ecosystems and the total biosphere, that is, the continual cycling of all resources, elements, materials, energy and structures. This interconnectedness of all subsystems on Planet Earth is much more fundamental than the interdependence of people, nations, cultures, technologies, and so forth.

Thus, the aspirations for a new world order are not only based on ethical and moral principles, important as these emerging planetary values will be for our species' survival. The need for a new World Order can now be *scientifically* demonstrated. We see the *principle of interconnectedness* emerging out of reductionist science itself as a basis, and the concomitant ecological reality that redistribution is also a basic principle of Nature. Since all ecosystems periodically redistribute energy, material and structures through bio-chemical and geophysical processes and cycles, all human species' social systems must also conform to *principles of redistribution* of these same resources that they use and transform, whether primary energy and materials or derived "wealth," (capital, money, structures, means of production) and "power" as well as continually changing institutions.

We can see six principles emerging in Westernized science itself, implying human behavioral adaptation of the kind now emerging. These post-Cartesian principles, as noted in the Introduction and elaborated in Plate 2-12 are: Interconnectedness, Redistribution, Change, Complementarity, Heterarchy and Indeterminacy.

Will it be breakdown or breakthrough? Stress is evolution's tool and today we are being stressed to change and evolve as never before. In this sense, the new resource limits and challenges we face are good news. They are stressing us to grow up—to become all that we can be—to discover "the possible humans" that we are.

Chapter Two Footnotes

1. Hazel Henderson, *The Politics of the Solar Age: Alternatives to Economics,* current edition from Knowledge Systems, Inc., Indianapolis, 1988.

2 Hazel Henderson, "Post-Economic Policies for Post-Industrial Societies." *ReVision,* Winter 1984.

3. Walter Truett Anderson, *To Govern Evolution,* Harcourt Brace Jovanovich, New York, 1987.

4. Collected papers (including the author's) from The Other Economic Summit in London, 1984-1985, in *The Living Economy,* Ed. Paul Ekins, Routledge and Kegan Paul, London.

5. See for example, *Florida Sunrise,* Report of the Speakers Advisory Committee on the Future (on which the author serves), which reached the conclusion that education was the prime factor in "economic development," and urged that the State "invest in people," Florida House of Representatives, The Capitol, Tallahassee, Florida.

6. *The New York Times,* September 7, 1987.

7. *INQUIRY,* "Saving the World—Japanese Style" Ziauddin Sardar, Vol. 4 No. 7, London, July 1987.

8. *The New York Times,* August 23, 1987, p. 1.

9. For a review of some of the possibilities, see:

> Jerome Clayton Glenn, *Future Mind: Artificial Intelligence, Merging the Mystical and the Technological in the 21st Century,* Acropolis Books, Washington, DC, 1989.

> Fritjof Capra, *The Turning Point,* Simon & Schuster, 1982.

> Robert Ornstein and Paul Ehrlich, *New World, New Mind,* Doubleday, New York, 1989.

> Anna F. Lemkow, *The Wholeness Principle,* Quest Books, 1990.

> David Loye, *The Sphinx and the Rainbow,* Shambala, New Science Library, Boulder, 1983.

> Mary E. Clark, *Ariadne's Thread,* St. Martin's Press, 1990.

> William Irwin Thompson, *Gaia: A Way of Knowing,* Ed. Lindisfarne Press, New York, 1987.

> Erich Jantsch, *The Self-Organizing Universe,* Pergamon Press, London, 1980.

> E.F. Schumchaer, *Small is Beautiful,* current edition from HarperCollins, New York, 1989.

> John Button, Ed., *The Green Fuse,* Quartet Books, London, 1990.

> The Schumacher Lectures, 1983-1988.

> *Rethinking the Curriculum: Toward an Integrated Interdisciplinary College Education,* Ed. Mary E. Clark and Sandra A. Wawrytko, Greenwood Press, Westport, CT, 1990.

> Helena Norberg Hodge, *Ancient Futures,* Sierra Books, San Francisco, 1992.

Old Unsustainable Economic Development Treadmill

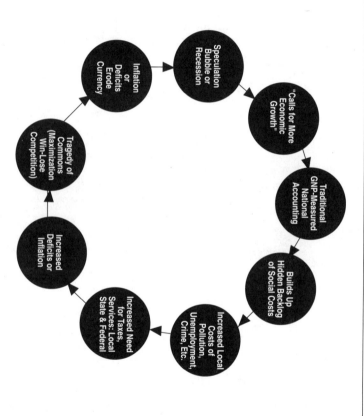

PLATE 3-13

CHAPTER 3

From Economism to Earth Ethics and Systems Theory

Environmentalism heretofore has been generally known as a "safe," middle-class issue. Who could be against clean air and water, tidying up the neighborhood, recycling and preserving species and wilderness? This was the kind of platform on which George Bush felt comfortable and which was even espoused by Britain's Margaret Thatcher.[1] However, the further one is drawn into environmental issues, the more the truth—long-recognized by environmentalists—emerges. Environmentalism implies nothing less than a major emergent philosophy, global in scope, which challenges virtually every prior Western philosophical system. Just as new voices, such as that of the U.S. State Department's Francis Fukuyama, announce anew the end of history and human ideological evolution,[2] the entry onto the world scene of environmentalism portends the newest major contender. This emerging eco-philosophy, in whatever culture it has arisen (and there are Green Parties now in more than a dozen countries) shifts our focus from anthropocentrism to biocentrism, i.e., from attention on human and cultural affairs to the affairs of Planet Earth as a living system of interdependent species. This Gaia hypothesis of two bioscientists, James Lovelock and Lynn Margulis, first proposed two decades ago, has penetrated Western culture and is helping drive the new eco-philosophy.[3]

Suddenly, with this new ecological perspective, most of the proud saga of human history is telescoped into a brief account of a recently arrived, two-legged species currently experiencing a classical, unremarkable "breeding storm," as biologists would say, exhibiting similar behavior patterns to other species, such as deer, rodents, and marsupials. When a species overruns its ecological niche, behavior of phenotypes (i.e., individual members of the species) changes. They may become aggressive or apathetic, beginning to ignore their young, or show signs of cannibalism, etc., until their diminishing habitat causes starvation and disease, and the changing ecology reduces their numbers to fit the limited carrying capacity. Ethical conclusions drawn from such biological views of humanity range from callous calls for "triage"[4] to propositions that we are instinctively altruistic.[5]

Most of the edifice of knowledge and culture in industrial societies is shockingly belittled by such new worldviews growing out of our rising awareness of our dependence on the planetary biosphere. Particularly violated is our Western cultural heritage—the Enlightenment as "progress," scientific rationality, and the march of positivism—not to mention our Judeo-Christian traditions, which see humans (or at least men) at the apex of the pecking order of creation, with dominion over all other species and the Earth.[6] Yet, even here eco-philosophy has created a ferment, and many of these religious orders have held soul-searching conferences over the past decade and have retooled the notion of "dominance" to the more species-ecumenical (but no less arrogant) idea of "stewardship. "[7] Humanism too has been accused of vulgar anthropocentrism—a charge it has found unavoidable.[8]

It is not surprising that the new generation of environmentalists began, during the 1960s, to roam the world in search of other cultural and religious traditions which held the Earth and other life-forms in higher regard.[9] Thus, elements of Buddhism, Taoism, Hinduism, and Islamic traditions were combined with ecological wisdom from many ancient indigenous cultures, from Australia's Aboriginals to Native Americans. These were, in turn, interwoven with insights glimpsed from the prehistory of neolithic matrilineal worshippers of the Great Mother Earth, in all her iconic forms, by Erich Neumann,[10] Marija Gimbutas,[11] Joseph Campbell,[12] and Riane Eisler.[13]

The overarching search was for value-systems with radically expanded spatial and time horizons. Environmentalists believed that only by thus reconceptualizing the brief history of the human species and its place on this ancient, living Planet could deeper ethical principles be found.[14] These longer time frames might engender greater concern for future generations and promote human survival as our numbers continue to explode. It also seemed necessary to many environmentalists, including me, that the Planet Earth itself would need to be "re-sacralized," as in earlier times, as embodying the spirit and wonder of the creation.[15] We hoped that this might become an antidote to the array of anthropocentric philosophies of human superiority and domination of Nature which had helped fuel the spectacular, if ambivalent, successes of the Industrial Revolution.

All of this seeding of new perceptions, values and paradigms continued throughout the 1970s and into the 1980s, when environmentalism was thought to be in decline. It was indeed eclipsed in the United States by Reaganism and in Britain by Thatcherism and by the peak of the dominant paradigms of industrialism, materialism, technological optimism, and general obliviousness to the natural resources on which it was based —which some now refer to as "economism."[16] However, environmentalism continued to flourish in other countries, particularly in Germany with the rise of the first Green Party.[17] In the United States, after eight years of Ronald Reagan's "politics of denial," there is in the 1990s a resurgence of interest in real-world problems that were left festering during this last great materialist spree: poverty, homelessness, illiteracy, a gamut of global restructuring issues, and the worsening state of the Planet itself. Indeed, in the late 1980s, the Planet took over as the great teacher of humanity. As Nature's feedback turned negative—acid rain, ozone depletion, dying lakes, and growing deserts, all plainly visible from satellite photographs—human attention at last began to focus on what disastrous, often irreversible, effects we had wrought on our life-support system.

Today, as politicians and corporate executives rush to jump on the environmental bandwagon, they too are unraveling the deeper message: our entire industrial value system, which the technologically "advanced" nations of the Northern Hemisphere have been busy prescribing and promoting to the nations of the Southern Hemisphere in the name of "economic development" and progress, has come unstuck. Indeed, as many desperate, indebted, ecologically ravaged, and starving countries have pointed out, after three decades of development, the process has gone in reverse, and it is clear to many of them that the European model of industrialization is not repeatable.[18]

The irony is that the challenge of eco-philosophy and the challenge from the so-called Third World are equally aimed at *both* major methods of macroeconomic managing industrialism, i.e., centrally planned, socialist societies *and* free-market, mixed models of capitalistic industrialism.[19] Indeed, both share the same underlying goals of *industrialism*, and most of the economist followers of both Adam Smith and Karl Marx, from left to right, share their enthusiasm for industrialism as the best answer to human aspirations; from Walt W. Rostow's *Stages of Economic Growth* treatise in the 1960s to Fukuyama's much-quoted "The End of History" in 1989, to Deng Xiaoping in China and many in the restructuring

Emerging Era of Global Interdependence

(New playing field of globalization processes, realignment and restructurings)

Driving Forces: six great globalizations:

1. Globalization of industrialism/technology
2. Globalization of finance/communication/information (round-the-clock trading roller coaster)
3. Globalization of employment, work, migration
4. Globalization of human effects on biosphere-pollution, etc.
5. Globalization of militarization (trillion $ arms sales, nuclear, chemical weapons)
6. Globalization of consumption, culture, media-driven world citizenship movements

And 7th Globalization (feedbacks):   Interactions
                                          Responses
                                          Re-alignments
                                          Re-structurings

PLATE 3-14

Communist world, the goal of industrial economic development is still dominant. The notion has barely dawned among them that global environmentalism and its underlying eco-philosophy constitute a major overarching paradigm that will from now on compete with economism and industrialism in both East and West, as well as North and South, in the 21st century.

Increasingly, political parties, corporate ethics statements, major magazines, and new journals are espousing environmentalism[20]—only to learn that its inescapable conclusions challenge almost everything they have been taught to believe in: economic growth, technological progress, the Protestant ethic, materialism, individualistic market competition, even scientific theories based in the mechanistic worldviews of Isaac Newton and René Descartes.[21] A case in point is a recent survey of the environment, "Costing the Earth," published by the London-based *The Economist*.[22] The intellectual contortions of the editors were evident in the title, as well as in an editorial, "Growth Can Be Green," which made heroic efforts to salvage the now dysfunctional discipline of economics, whose narrow, short-sighted accounting systems have proved clearly culpable in causing many environmental problems. Economic growth could be reformed and "green growth will indeed be somewhat slower than a dash for the dirty variety,"[23] *The Economist* admitted, adding that:

> at present, most economic activity takes little account of the costs it imposes on its surroundings. Factories pollute rivers as if the rinsing waters flowed past them for free, power stations burn coal without charging customers for the effects of carbon dioxide belched into the atmosphere, loggers destroy forests without a care for the impact on wildlife or climate. These bills are left for others to pick up—neighbors, citizens of other countries and future generations.

It is worth quoting *The Economist's* change of heart further:

> conventional statistics of economic growth are . . . particularly blind to the environment, National income accounts (Gross National Product) take no notice of the value of natural resources: a country that cut down all it trees, sold them as wood chips and gambled away the money . . . would appear from its national accounts to have got richer in terms of GNP per person. Equally, they show measures to tackle pollution as bonuses, not burdens. . . . It would be easier for politicians to talk rationally about effects of sensible environmental policies on growth if governments agreed to remove some of these oddities from the way they keep their economic books.

This rapid rethinking and exposing of errors in economic theory and practice which they have not noticed for 50 years is to *The Economist's*

Emerging Era of Global Interdependence

```
┌─────────────────────┐
│  6 Globalizations   │
│  New Differentials  │
└─────────────────────┘
```

+

```
┌──────────────────────────┐
│        Feedbacks         │
│ Interactions - Responses │
└──────────────────────────┘
```

← Requiring a paradigm shift in knowledge/research methods

- Loss of National Sovereignty
- Acceleration and
- Irreversibility of Changes

From focus on exactitude, static equilibrium, classical reductionism

Toward focus on research methods/policy tools based on systems view:
Dynamic, non-linear, probabilistic, feedback driven models of dis-equilibrium (e.g., chaos theories)

PLATE 3-15

credit. At least environmentalists can be grateful that their unheeded and identical critiques of the past 20 years are, at last, being heard. Yet, kissing such a massive turnaround off as a new verity, which economic theory has already embraced, is little more than barefaced intellectual sleight of hand, to which many others in the profession are also resorting. Rather, summed up in these short paragraphs is nothing less than a social, economic, and philosophical revolution that has hardly begun. Implementation of these new environmental insights and goals will require a greater restructuring of today's industrial societies than even the extraordinary restructurings we witnessed in the late 1980s.

Meanwhile, this kind of intellectual glibness of our overcrowded, competitive economics profession seeks to gloss over their centuries of erroneous theorizing. Economists are now embracing environmental values without even pausing their pontificating long enough to reflect on the implicit ethics of eco-philosophy. When they do, they will find values far too long term and intergenerational to ever fit into any purely economic formula.[24] It is for this reason that I have spent the past 15 years lecturing and writing about the *end* of economics as a generalized theoretical approach to public policy. Instead, I have pointed to the many *post*economic policy tools and interdisciplinary models readily available for mapping longer-range issues and the dynamic behavior of rapidly restructuring complex societies.[25]

Today, at last even the business press is replete with jokes about economists and their forecasting failures, and, as noted, *Business Week* pronounced recently, "Clearly, the major economic problems don't lend themselves to macroeconomic solutions."[26] Many honest economists who have transcended their discipline are beginning to admit publicly that they too are shifting to newer, sharper policy tools. For example, Herbert Simon, when accepting his Nobel Prize in Economics, stated that he had not used economic methods for a decade, and had switched to game theory and other decision sciences.[27] Plate 1-3 (Differing Perceptions, Assumptions and Forecasting Styles between Economists and Futurists) summarizes the different approaches used by economists, futurists, and systems theorists, showing clearly the new focus on longer time horizons and broader social factors. In Plate 3-16 (Emerging Change Models), the major new change models now being used to map dynamic systems are outlined.

Today social change and the general restructuring of nations and their institutions are being driven by at least six massive globalization processes, which I have explored elsewhere:[28] the globalization of (1) technology and production, (2) work, employment, and migration,

Emerging Change Models

Earth System Science

Interdisciplinary: plate tectonics, biogeochemical and solar-driven processes, strato and meso-sphere (N.A.S.A. Program on Global Change International Division, Washington, DC, 20546)

Catastrophe Mathematics

Models at least seven modes in which systems change their states, i.e., bifurcations (Rene Thom, *Structural Stability and Morphogenesis*, Paris 1972)

Cybernetic Models

Homeostasis and metamorphosis governed by feedbacks, negative and positive (Magoroh Maruyama, "Paradigmatology" in H. Henderson, *Politics of the Solar Age*, 1981)

Order through Fluctuation Models

(Ilya Prigogine, *From Being to Becoming*, San Francisco, 1980)

Chaos Theory Based on Attractors

Point, periodic and chaotic Attractors can "magnetize" systems into new states (Ralph Abraham, *Dynamics: The Geometry of Behavior*, Santa Cruz, 1984)

PLATE 3-16

(3) finance, information, and debt, and the new factor that money and information have now become interchangeable, (4) the global scope of military weapons and the arms race, (5) the human impacts on the planetary biosphere, and (6) the emergence of a global culture and consumption patterns. The seventh great globalization process involves reaction to the prior six, i.e., these new interdependencies are driving the current restructurings and realignments between nations. The most striking effect of all this interactivity is the loss of sovereignty for every nation, with national leaders no longer able to deliver on their customary promises to protect their citizens in time of war, to shield them from pollution and environmental hazards, to maintain full employment, or to "manage" their domestic economies. The variables needed to control these conditions have now migrated beyond domestic reach, into the global arena. Furthermore, all this interactivity accelerates change and is clearly irreversible, and this requires a shift in our knowledge-structures, curriculum, and research methods, which, as mentioned, is now under way. In recognition of this disarray, diverse grassroots movements are expanding their successes of the past 25 years in challenging obsolete policies and now are actually toppling governments, as in Eastern Europe and throughout the old Soviet Union.

The now widespread interest in new indicators of development and global sustainability criteria has produced much debate in academic circles. The International Institute for Applied Systems Analysis in Austria has produced some good work in this area, for example, R.E. Munn's review of non-linear, interdisciplinary models for global change which are adaptive and cross-cultural.[29] The Worldwatch Institute's *State of the World Report, 1988* assesses capital investments required as a "down payment" on sustainability, in six areas: (1) protecting topsoil and cropland; (2) reforesting the Earth; (3) slowing population growth; (4) raising energy efficiency; (5) developing renewable energy; and (6) retiring Third World debt. The Report then sets out two alternative global security budgets: (1) continuing the projected $900 billion spent annually on military security; and (2) global security defined in sustainable development terms, where the military budget component falls each year from $845 billion in 1990 to $751 billion in the year 2000, while the sustainability budget rises from $46 billion in 1990 to $149 billion in 2000.[30]

The major drivers towards these new "common security" definitions will continue to be the economic exhaustion of the United States and the breakup of the USSR, as well as the acceleration of the globalization forces already discussed. Tremendous political activity on the part of the

Values Bifurcating in Post Industrial Societies

Short View (Peaking of Old Values)	Long View (Emerging Values)
• Reductionist, "Micro-Rigorous"	• Integrative, "Macro-Rigorous"
• Quantitative	• Qualitative
• Hierarchical, dominator	• Participatory, partnership
• Greed, individualistic, competitive	• Concern for community, cooperation
• Speculation, paper asset shuffling	• Socially responsible investing
• Borrowing, leveraged buyouts, etc.	• "Valdez" principles, Sullivan and other investing criteria
• Budget and trade deficits, international debt	• Investing in people: the new "Wealth of Nations"
• Debt financing, credit cards	• Increase savings rates, balance budget
• Program trading "futures", options, etc.	• Reducing arms budgets
• Consumption values and addictions	• Frugality, search for "inner" satisfactions & personal growth
• Addictive society and organizations	• Globalizing education
• "Lifestyles of the rich and famous"	• Shopping guides for a better world
• Advertising geared to infantile desire	• "Eco-labeled" products
• Crisis model of problem solving, "Band-aid" remedies	• Pro-active, preventive, problem-identification
• Technological "fixes"	• Systemic reconceptualizing and redesign
• Gross national product and macro economics	• New indicators of development for major social trends geared to provide feedback to specific social goals
• Trading licenses to pollute the environment	• Rise of green parties and movements
• Low environmental concern	• Treaty of Montreal, etc.
• Non-ratification of Law of the Sea treaty	• Government priorities in negotiations, conflict resolution
• Government priorities in armaments, hardware	• "Green" levies and user fees
• Tax code subsidizes resource depletion	• Concern and debate over ethics, values
• "Business as usual," "Economism" has won	

PLATE 3-17

"global citizens" of every nation will be needed to force these priorities onto politicians and other leaders in business and academe, unions, and other social groups. The more we have better social and economic indicators to provide better feedback on our current course, the sooner political will can be mustered for the necessary shift in policies. Particularly, we need to know the social costs of our current course, from the some $30 billion the United States will have to spend to clean up toxic dumps, to the $60 billion per year that smoking costs in medical care and absenteeism in the United States. These data are available—although few governments pay to have them collated—for example, in the approach by Dr. Peter Draper in the United Kingdom, which made it possible to relate what kinds of consumption led to what kinds of disease, e.g., sugared cereals and tooth decay, so that such social costs could be charged to manufacturers.[31]

Another driver toward global cooperation is the increasing need in industrial countries to coordinate technological policies in high-tech sectors and use scarce research and development (R & D) funds more rationally. The global need for a massive technological transformation is now clear: from obsolete capital, energy and materials intensive technologies based on non-renewable sources to minimizing energy and materials content and recycling all components. (See Plate 3-19: Restructuring Industrial Societies.) Only by "greening" our human technologies, increasing their sophistication and basing them on biological foundations can humans hope to move their societies into alignment with the ecological realities. At the same time, massive funding must shift toward incentives to invest in these technologies, as well as ecosystem restoration and population control. Here, the U.S. government is still in the neo-classical economics paradigm, believing in "the magic of market forces," rather than conscious policy. For example, the Bush White House decries "industrial policy" (i.e., government subsidies to R & D and specific technologies) while at the same time refusing to acknowledge that the U.S. government's existing R & D budget priorities (i.e., 47 percent to defense during the 1980s, and increasing, so far in the 1990s to 61 percent defense-related) *is in itself an industrial policy*—rather than market-driven.

Competition in the marketplace, as we have seen, is not an appropriate strategy when the marketplace has become interlinked or over-crowded, and turned into a commons. In the case of U.S. research and development strategies, domestic-based U.S. chip makers recognized this shift in their environment, i.e., the chip *market* has gone global and the domestic market has turned into a "commons," requiring a shift from win-lose to win-win rules. Thus American manufacturers of computer chips have been lobbying the Bush Administration since it took office to (1) relax antitrust laws, so that they could cooperate and pool their R & D funds (since the cost of gearing up to produce the next generation of memory chips is now over $1 billion and unaffordable for any one company); and (2) frame a specific industrial policy toward such technological innovations to keep the United States from losing the lead in yet another area. So far, they have been frustrated in their drive to shift priorities away from defense and NASA's $40 billion space station toward critical technologies, such as super-conductivity, computing, and materials or changing the mission of U.S. National Laboratories from defense to industrial technologies with a view to making (global) competitiveness a top priority.[32] The chip-makers went to Congress and promoted The National Cooperative Production Act, which relaxes anti-trust laws to allow a joint R & D program, but in August 1991 it ran into another paradigm problem: Congress wanted it to exclude any co-production or R & D ventures with more than 30 percent "foreign" ownership—i.e., the Congress does not yet understand the globalization of investment, technology and production, where even by 1985, 40 percent of all U.S. "imports" were intra-company, from U.S. companies owning overseas operations. Predictably, the White House announced it would veto the legislation.[33]

In the last analysis, a fundamental understanding of the role of money itself must be propagated. *Money* is information used to track transactions and to keep score between firms and individuals—it is not a commodity in itself. The global financial system today, which has reduced money to a series of blips on thousands of computer trading screens, has now made it possible to see that money and information are equivalent and interchangeable. These new insights are producing many demands for reform, when such money symbol systems are used to dominate human affairs, such as in the case of Third World debts. Similarly, overusing the price system to accomplish social policy has become a bad habit in the United States, whose "free market" economy is actually a crazy quilt of administered prices, tax credits, subsidies and incentives, all managed by the narrow policy tools of fiscal and monetary string-pulling, while international economic relationships are giving way to crude, bouncing dollar policies and interest rates, feeding global instabilities. Reform of monetary policies and the role of central banks in issuing money and credit are growing in the West.

In the emerging age of interdependence, the new global systemic view is allowing new questioning of all our traditional disciplines, including economics, and the proper role of money itself, in relation to tangible wealth and human labor, skills and knowledge. Here again, grassroots groups with little investment in the dominant paradigm are leading the way, such as the now proliferating Local Exchange Trading Systems (LETS) pioneered in Canada by Michael Linton, as well as community land trusts, co-housing projects, New York's Community Capital Bank, micro-lending clubs, and community development groups, such as the First Nations Financial Project, spearheaded by Native American Rebecca Adamson, which creates enterprises and offers management and marketing skills to the first inhabitants of North America. Even in the United States, new cooperatives are burgeoning. The Institute for Community Economics, Springfield, Massachusetts; *Bank Notes* from the National Cooperative Bank in Washington, DC; and *Economic Alternatives* from Co-op America, Washington, DC, are all ongoing sources of news on such developments.

Today, a dozen of America's 500 largest corporations are co-operatives, mostly in food production. In addition, 21 U.S. co-ops now boast sales over $1 billion annually, some in retailing such as Ace Hardware Stores. Worker-ownership is also growing. The National Center for Employee Ownership (NCEO) of Oakland, California, points to growth of Employee Stock Ownership Plans (ESOPs): 9,870 plans now cover 11.3 million workers, or 13 percent of the civilian workforce. In spite of the use of ESOPs as a defense against hostile takeovers, employees also benefited by a tripling of their stock assets since 1980 to $120 billion. I have urged more ESOPs since the 1970s.

As all development paths are now interlinked and interactive via mass communications, and as mentioned in Chapter Two, this will move the world trade system to one of less "hardware" and more "software" as knowledge diffuses even more rapidly. Multinational companies will have fewer opportunities to "recapture" R & D investments, as when IBM introduces a new computer line, "clones" produced by others appear swiftly in the world market. This trend represents what I have termed the "bursting seed-pod" model of world trade, where mature industrial companies and countries release their knowledge and "scatter" it, in spite of patents. This is fiercely resisted by corporations and trade negotiations and helped scuttle the Uruguay Round of GATT in 1991. Yet, since information "flows" and is not "scarce" in the same way as are goods, it can be shared in a win-win game. Enormous efficiencies can thus be gained and environmentally sound technologies shared, with huge savings in energy, transportation and distribution. As countries are forced to think harder about their true niche, they will seek *creative* advantage, and

Relative Decline of the United States in the World

Some Overlooked Fundamentals

- Investment lag in "human capital" resources

- Energy sector still relatively inefficient

- Health sector

- "Waste" management

- Environmental costs and resource depletion rates

- Aging, decaying inefficient infrastructure

- Inefficient tax code

- Consumer oriented culture

- Short term view

- Productivity in the services sector lags

PLATE 3-18

become more unique in their exports and less subject to competition. Each country's unique gifts can be offered to each other, and all can savor the growing diversity of the human family, just as today, we savor each other's food, art, music and culture.

As industrial societies move further into this "services" and "amenities" view, beyond production *per se*, emphasis also shifts from obsolescence/innovation cycles to durability and overall optimization. An underlying problem with all national income accounting is the focus on *flows*, rather than *stocks*, emphasized in what is still, the fundamental Western book on overhauling economic models, *The Entropy Law and the Economic Process*, by Romanian scientist Nicholas Georgescu-Roegen. China already portrays this wider, more systemic view, which augurs well for overall performance and efficiency. The China 2000 studies are a model for other countries, including the United States, where similar studies such as the *Global 2000 Report* to President Carter in 1979 have been ignored. Today, the new "Solvency School" led by Paul Kennedy, author of *The Rise and Fall of the Great Powers*, and including James Chace, Mancur Olsen, David Calleo, George Kennan and others, has gained widespread credibility. The U.S. citizenry is waking up at last to the reality of the *relative* decline of the United States in a new multipolar world of vigorous new trading partners. The importance of the battle over indicators can be seen as essentially political; and the more suspect and meaningless conventional economic indicators of "progress" become, the more politicians must resort to polls of public opinion which are shallow for the most part. New evidence of the "declining productivity flap," which I examined in *Politics of the Solar Age*, confirmed my "mindless computerization" and rising social costs hypothesis. *The Economist* explored the problem in its article "Too Many Computers Spoil the Broth," and found that the rise of computer purchases from 11 percent of all durable equipment in 1970 to 51 percent by 1989 had produced almost negligible, if any, increase in labor productivity— producing too much useless information, often creating "information-overload" on managers. (August 24, 1991, p. 30) Poor energy efficiency, as noted, is another cause.

Even though this decline is real (see Plate 3-18: Relative Decline of the United States in the World), a key political task in the United States is to cast its relative decline in *positive* terms—not in the shallow claims of some commentators that the United States has "won" the Cold War and that capitalism has been vindicated, but rather, to outline the positive vision of a safer, multipolar world which is now poised to build a new age of interdependence and global cooperation toward Mutual Sustainable

Development, with all our rising industrial partners and the developing countries of the South. As debates continue at many levels the newer definitions of "security" in economic, social and environmental terms, the U.S. debate can adjust to the new global realities—particularly if new social indicators of progress are set up. Today, two-thirds of Americans agree with the Solvency School that the United States has become weaker compared to other countries, while 45-50 percent believe that America is "slipping dangerously" according to a 1988 poll by Stanley B. Greenberg.[34]

The Solvency School, while correctly pointing out the mutual economic exhaustion of the superpowers, overlooks the more fundamental set of stresses that their rivalry places on human communities and on natural systems that I have outlined, since, of course, few indicators of these dimensions are publicized. Only when such indicators provide scientific, timely feedback on a full range of variables and within broader and global parameters, can nations steer their ships of state with instrument panels of sufficient accuracy and sensitivity to continually course-correct on their paths to sustainable development. Clearly, most data are already available—on education, health, literacy, life expectancy, infant mortality, shelter, water and air quality, to complement per capita income averages. Other categories needing work are human rights and political participation, and much data on these are available from Amnesty International and other human rights organizations. More inaccessible, but also available are "shadow price" equivalents for unpaid services and production, including barter and counter-trade—as well as for much of the productive work of natural systems. For example, renewable energy resources are actually far more abundant than fossil fuels, and when the "energy supply-siders" take off their old-paradigm economic spectacles, they will see that over the next 30 years, industrial countries could reduce their energy use per capita by a half, without harming their economies.

A December 1990, Worldwatch Paper 100 outlines all of the efficiency increases and cost reductions, making the shift to solar thermal and photovoltaics, wind power, biomass, hydrogen and the still enormous potential for efficiency gains in building design, lighting, insulation, etc. For example, over the past two decades, solar electricity has fallen from $30 per kilowatt hour to 30¢. And, if electric cars were used for 25 percent of all U.S. auto travel, total electricity use would only rise 7 percent. Solar based hydrogen can be used to generate this electricity and hydrogen fuel cells for such electric cars are already 70 percent efficient (compared with less than 25 percent efficiency for gasoline engines).

Capital availability is the crux and symptom of both the globalization process and the largely unanticipated restructuring of the U.S. economy.

The capital markets have been deregulated in the United States, and capital has become highly centralized as a result of this and the global search for advantageous interest rate and currency differentials in the now tightly interlinked world financial markets. This leaves most localities short of the liquidity they need as their locally generated money is "vacuumed out" of their communities by branches of the major money-center banks. This chronic deficit of liquidity for local circulation and trading as well as investment and other factors, is the basic cause of their vulnerability. Not surprisingly, new forms of computer-assisted barter, skills exchanges and other limited purpose local "currencies" are in use in thousands of U.S. and Canadian localities.[35] Meanwhile, capital is only available to those large-scale, successful enterprises which localities are forced to try to lure in head-on competition with other cities and states, as well as all other countries.

At the same time, on Wall Street billions of dollars of hot, hungry money competes fiercely for fewer and fewer opportunities in higher and higher technology start-ups, in the hopes of at least one big winner. No enterprise that does not offer at least annual 30 percent returns on investment is even considered, while millions of modest, useful, small-scale enterprises meeting local and regional market needs are too short of capital to expand and many are forced into bankruptcy when they experience a temporary cashflow crunch. Thus many local needs for locally produced goods and services which would build a stable local economy remain unmet, and many people must drive long distances to shop for vital goods and services at regional outlets of large, multinational companies. In this way, local initiative is choked off in much the same way as in a centrally planned economy. This kind of absurdity occurs when market power is allowed to dominate rather than serve a balanced role in resource allocation. Of course, traditional economics recognizes this in monopoly theories, and the U.S. government is supposed to regulate such monopolies. However, political power, campaign contributions, lobbyists, advertising, and the commissioning of "research" allows many of these monopolistic corporations to control mass media, large areas of production and weapons manufacture, and to capture enormous government contracts and influence policies.

Many U.S. localities are waking up to the impossibility of playing the old "plantation model" of economic development, since it leaves them wide open to the new world trade rollercoaster, vulnerable to sudden investment shifts, currency swings, bouncing interest rates and lower wage competition, while their well laid local plans are disordered as financial markets open in cities around the world. In Florida, a 1987 report, *Florida Sunrise*, shifts emphasis from the plantation model to one in which education and investment in its citizens are seen as a new path to development.

Thus, the old "growth" view of economic development has hit these kinds of new snags, and most states in the United States are now developing "growth management" plans and "development impact fees" which assess construction and development companies with part of the infrastructure costs their projects will incur. Many large companies which lose out in these new struggles with local governments, or refuse to pay "impact fees," simply move over the Mexican border and set up the now familiar maquiladoro plants in politically weak Mexican border towns. These towns, too, are becoming overburdened with the influx of migrants looking for jobs, and their tax bases are insufficient to provide infrastructure and basic services. All these issues emerged in the U.S.-Mexico Free Trade Agreement. Not surprisingly, many state and city officials and politicians are now learning that development in today's world requires a dual approach: first, to learn to play a much smarter role in the global fast lane and find export strategies not easily copied by others, i.e., genuine niches of true *comparative* (not competitive) advantage, *partly* based on Adam Smith's concepts; second, to develop a home-grown economy, to provide basic security and meet local needs with local resources in smaller-scale enterprises. One can see common elements in this approach in the United States and that of China's contract agriculture system, now spreading to the old USSR.

Intellectual "lags" are evident not only in the social and policy sciences, but also in academia, with its narrow focus on fragmented disciplines and tenure reward-systems. Similar lags in our institutions, including government, business, labor, and religious denominations, create frustrations, since individuals learn much faster than institutions. Thus we see, as these great global changes roll onward, the three zones of this great transition already described in Chapter Two: 1) the breakdown zone, where old institutions and forms are destructuring; 2) the bifurcation zone, of greatest uncertainty, as people move to reposition themselves as old ground becomes shaky; and 3) the breakthrough zone, where we see new forms emerging and new structures, knowledge, values and goals. We also see in the most mature industrial societies, such as the United States and Britain, a classic bifurcation of industrial values occurring (see Plate 3-17: Values Bifurcating in Post-Industrial Societies), with the peaking of the short-term, expansionist values that were so successful in the past: competition, greed, material consumption, and individualism, leading to massive debt, the twin deficits, addiction, and other social problems we are now facing. On the other hand, we see the emerging of new values more suited to the postindustrial stage, in a globally interdependent 21st century: greater emphasis on cooperation, savings, longer-term investment and management strategies, environmental conservation and sustainable forms of development (defined as meeting the needs of current populations without foreclosing options for meeting those same needs of future generations).

The new era, as we move into the 21st century, is that of global interdependence and mutually assured development, since no nation still thinks it can achieve world hegemony. Most see that our entire Planet is becoming a single global commons, since we all must share its atmosphere, oceans, and electromagnetic spectrum. Even the global financial system, which grew out of conditions of a competitive world marketplace, has emerged as a seamless commons of currency traders and 24-hour asset managers, stock markets, and debtor and creditor nations—all in the same boat. As discussed, when former marketplace's niches are all used up and it becomes massively interlinked, its condition changes to that of a commons (any shared resource) and win-win (cooperative) rules apply. If win-lose rules are still applied, as if it were a market, then the result is lose-lose, as detailed in Chapter Two. Economic theory is now trying hard to catch up with research on how to manage these common resources, since these are the issues of the future. However, in most economics textbooks, theories of these commons are usually relegated to a mention, or footnoted under the more familiar term "market failures." Systems theorists reframe these issues as those of open systems (markets) and closed systems (commons), and view their allocation issues more in terms of game theory. (See Plate 2-11: Differing Models of Markets and Commons) Two useful texts in this field are *The Evolution of Cooperation* by Robert Axelrod (Basic Books, 1984) and *No Contest* by Alfie Kohn (Houghton-Mifflin, 1986).

Today's restructuring debates, whether of perestroika in the old Soviet Union or economic reforms, deregulation, etc., elsewhere, are all debates about two key issues: (1) *What* is valuable under new conditions? and (2) *Who, what, when, why, where* and *how* to regulate or deregulate? This is because all economies are, in essence, sets of rules derived from various cultural value systems, which determine, in diverse ways, what goals are important and what activities and jobs are valuable in attaining these goals. The failure of economic models of development concerns their inability to embrace these diverse goals and values, which differentiate cultures, and attempt instead to impose formulas regarding "correct" policies, capital/labor ratios, and models of "efficiency" and "productivity" that are not only alien to many cultures, but which we now know also ignored the productive role of natural systems.

The new debate about what constitutes "sustainable development" is about all these issues and going beyond neat formulas to decode the various "cultural DNA" of each specific society to find out what their people consider important and what "menu" of goods, services, and amenities they consider optimal. Breaking through economist rhetoric, it is now clear that *the role of government is primary*, whether intervening to foster market *or* "command and control" methods of governance, in both industrial and "developing" countries.[36] Similarly, in companies, the role of management is key, where rethinking top-down styles and devolution of authority, as well as new social awareness and concern are paramount, as described in *The Knowledge-Value Revolution* by Taichi Sakaiya (Kodansha International, 1991).

From economism to systems theory

Many see that it is less a matter of whether a country is centrally planned, mixed (as most are), or capitalistic, since the effects of the underlying industrial model are similar, but more a matter of whether societies are *cybernetically designed* to incorporate *feedback* at every level of decision making, from the family and community to the provincial and national levels, from those people *affected* by the decisions. Thus, the instinct of leaders in centrally planned societies (and over-sized corporations!) is to decentralize decision making and incorporate more of this feedback, whether by using prices (hopefully corrected for social costs) or votes, i.e., democracy. But, as discussed in Chapter Two, prices and votes are not the only forms of feedback that complex societies need to course-correct their decision making. Other vital feedbacks include genuinely free, even muck-raking mass media (especially television), civic and other consumer and worker organizations, free associations of all kinds, including business groups—as long as none can drown out the others or obtain unfair access to the political and economic processes— and of course all the newly perceived feedbacks from Nature. All of these new issues are much better suited to the expanded, interdisciplinary frameworks of systems theory, futures studies, and posteconomic policy tools such as technology assessment, environmental impact statements, social indicators, and the like, than the cul-de-sac of economic theory. A macroeconomic management focus, in addition, can simply precipitate debates back into the old left or right axis of the Cold War struggle between communist and capitalist ideologies.[37] The restructuring societies of Eastern Europe and those of the former Soviet empire could use fewer ideologies of the old "magic market forces" think tanks, and more of the newer wave of management innovation promoting worker-ownership, cooperative styles of leadership and the emergence of new values. Recent books that would help are Willis Harman and John Hormann's *Creative Work* (Knowledge Systems, 1990); Jeffrey Hallett's *Worklife Visions* (American Society for Personnel Administration, 1987); *Equitable Capitalism*, Ed. Stuart Speiser (Apex Press, 1991); Pauline Graham's *Integrative Management* (Basil Blackwell, 1991) and *Second to None* by Charles Garfield (Business One-Irwin, 1992); as well as Fred Emery and Eric Trist's classic, *Toward a Social Ecology* (Plenum Press, 1973).

Today, we can take off these old ideological spectacles of "economism" and also see that the history of the 20th century has largely been about experiments at governing human societies at current, unprecedented population levels. As a biological species, we have no repertoire of experience or behavior beyond that learned in small communities and tribes in decentralized, rural, agricultural settings.[38] In this century, most of the experiments at urbanization, nationhood, and agglomerated governance of larger, diverse regions and ethnic populations have been less than satisfactory, for we are a young species. Efforts at synthesizing ideologies capable of organizing larger loyalties and productive efforts, whether around kings, generals, or religious leaders, or massive public undertakings, crusades, and even the ubiquitous fomenting of xenophobia, have all proved unstable. They have culminated in such ghastly organizing efforts as Hitler's Third Reich, two world wars, Stalin's gulags, and Mao's China. Now the game has changed irrevocably, and we humans must learn to overcome our disabling belief-systems: all those "isms," from nationalism and tribalism to religious intolerances and communism, capitalism, and even industrialism. It remains to be seen whether environmentalism can avoid crystallization into yet another set of dogmas.

As we approach the 21st century, we humans are truly at a turning point. It will now avail us little to continue to argue about who is to blame for the past colossal mistakes. Neither is it helpful to perpetuate Cold War rivalries by rubbing salt in the wounds of the Soviets, the Eastern Europeans, or the Chinese about the demise of communism. It is time to give a decent burial to both Karl Marx and Adam Smith and reframe the old debates in much broader contexts and interdisciplinary terms. In any case, we can remember that most of humanity's failing organizational endeavors were undertaken, at least, in the *name* of progress and improvement of the human condition. Today, we have all learned much from these experiments, however horrible, and leaders of both socialist

Restructuring Industrial Economies

Obsolescent Sectors (Unsustainable, entropic)

• Industries, companies based on heavy use of non-renewable energy and materials
• Bureaucratic, large, less flexible
• Non-recyclable products, packaging
• Military contracting
• Products involving toxic, non-biodegradables, polluting materials, throwaway items
• Planned obsolescence
• Chemical pesticides, inorganic fertilizers
• Heavy farm equipment
• Polluting, inefficient capital equipment, process machinery, processing systems
• Extractive industries with low value added
• Fossil fuels, nuclear power generation
• High tech hospital based medical care
• Highly processed foods
• Advertising encouraging waste and polluting practices
• Shopping center developers
• Speculative real estate development
• Large, fuel-inefficient vehicles
• Mono-culture farming
• Hardwood and tropical forest products

Emerging Sectors (Sustainable, low entropy)

• Industries, companies based on efficient use of energy and materials and human skills
• Entrepreneurial, small, flexible
• Recyclable products, re-manufacturing
• Conservation, innovation
• Fuel efficient motors, cars, mass transit
• Solar, renewable energy systems
• Communications, information, services
• Infrastructure, education, training
• Space communications satellites
• Peace keeping, surveillance of treaties
• Efficient capital equipment, processes
• Restorative industries, re-forestation, desert greening, water quality management
• Health promotion and disease prevention
• Organic agriculture, low till systems
• Integrated pest management
• Pollution control, clean up and prevention
• Natural foods
• Waste recycling and reuse
• Community design and planning
• "Caring" sector

PLATE 3-19

and capitalist countries can learn something from each other. State-enforced cooperation requires leavening with incentives for individuals, and state-enforced competition and individual profit-maximizing require ethical frameworks, such as those we seek today. Socialist leaders are exploring mixed, regulated market economies in the West and find little that conforms with our neoclassical economics textbooks. Instead they see the similarities of predominantly government-regulated and created markets, which they seek to learn more about. For example, Deng Xiaoping's economic reform dictum is "government regulates markets and markets guide enterprises." The Chinese are falling behind in democratic reforms, but are ahead of the Soviets in economic reforms.

Nowhere are the cries heralding the triumph of capitalism and the marketplace more hollow than in the new brand of economism, which labels itself "environmental, or resource economics," or even the more pretentious "ecological economics"—desperately trying to catch up with events and new policy issues. As I discussed in *Politics of the Solar Age*, one of the problems is the overcrowded state of the economics profession and the excessive numbers of new graduates rolling off academic production lines, leading to the "ambulance-chasing effect" we see in the legal field. Here again, we see the same kind of bifurcation of economists' values between short- and long-term concerns: between economists who have staked out the market niche of helping bale out the declining sectors of industrial societies (i.e., companies irretrievably committed to unsustainable or excessive resource- and energy-intensive processes, goods, and services, from nuclear energy and devastating weapons systems to non-recyclable packaging and private fossil-fueled automobiles) and those economists who have thrown their lot in with the emerging sectors based on ecological principles of long-term sustainability (e.g., companies in renewable energy, conservation, recycling, remanufacturing, renewable-power mass transit, health maintenance, disease prevention, organic farming).

Economics, when in the service of these two divergent sectors and their goals and values, naturally looks very different. For the *unsustainable sector*, it tends to be the economics of rearguard actions: playing for time, lobbying against regulation, promoting "market" solutions, such as trading pollution licenses and the like. For the emerging *renewable sector* (mostly start-ups and small companies) economic analyses are geared to fighting the old giants and their market power and prior dominance over the rule-setting, quantifying the social and environmental costs of prior subsidies and incentives, etc., Thus, at last, economics is unmasked, not as the "value-free" science it claims to be, but merely a profession (with little quality control at that), with all the biases and social value commitments

The Economic View

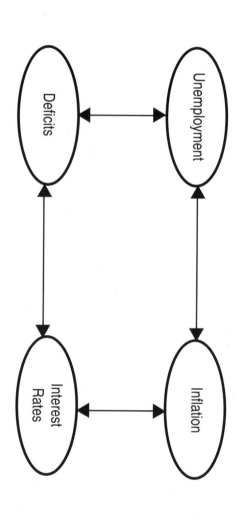

PLATE 3-20

of any other profession. From this standpoint, economics too is an ideology all the more suspect in its quantitative and technical pretensions. Economics has colonized our democratic processes by casting important clashes between old and new values as "resolvable" via cost/benefit ratios and risk analysis, with all the discredited underlying baggage of welfare economics: Pareto Optimality still foisted on an unwary public, as discussed in detail in *Politics of the Solar Age*. For example, the value of a salt marsh (one of the most productive systems on the Planet) is compared with in-filling for a housing development in price-determined terms, by using the "willingness to pay" principle, which asks voters with no financial stake in the housing development how much they would be willing to pay so as to keep it a marsh! These absurdities, which are common to most applications of this kind of economics, need no further comment.

Values are the primary forces in all human societies (despite Marxian theory). Values drive all the different economic systems, which, as mentioned, are simply programs of rules (in computer terminology), as well as their outputs: various configurations of technological "furniture" and diverse infrastructures, education systems, norms, etc., Indicators, such as the GNP, perform the "comparator" function, to see that the program is running properly according to the rules. When there are changes in external conditions, such as all societies are experiencing as today's globalization processes accelerate, citizens must find many new forums beyond merely voting occasionally in elections, in order to clear the backlog of issues and values clarification that must be hammered out. This must be done in vernacular language, not further confused by economic algorithms concealing obsolete values and assumptions. We see these new forums at corporate annual meetings, on TV and radio talk shows, and in the massive increase in most industrial societies of citizens movements for consumer and environmental protection, corporate responsibility, human rights, animal rights, etc., and all their myriad newsletter and press releases.[39]

No wonder the old two-party politics is failing, dominated as it is by the interest groups of the unsustainable sector and their prior market and political power. Until the new values and ethical concerns are given their due in political parties and the mass media, voters will continue to defect from the process. For similar reasons, macroeconomic management is failing, using models that are still too short-term, static, and based on the assumptions of equilibrium, all at heroic levels of aggregation—levels of investment, interest rates, and unemployment—which do not allow for the necessary detail and questions, such as what *kind* of investment, and

A System View of the Global "Vicious Circle" Economy (Fast Feedback Loops)

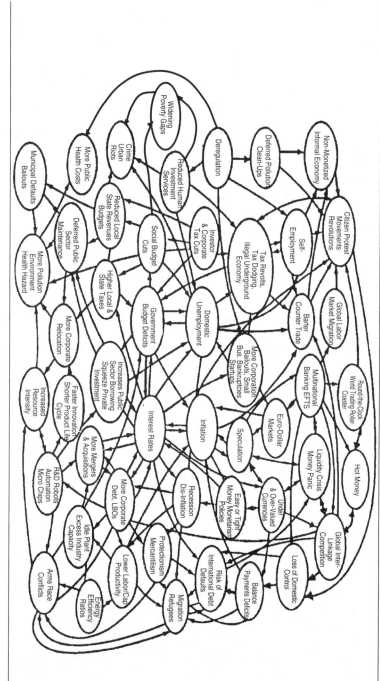

PLATE 3-21

Copyright © 1980/91 Hazel Henderson

productivity measured by what *criteria*? New consensuses cannot be located because all these macroeconomic indicators cannot deal with the new specific and structural issues in the real world (see Plate 3-20: The Economic View and Plate 3-21: A System View of the Global Economy). Thus, today we see many new initiatives to reformulate the GNP and augment these macroeconomic indicators with specific indicators of social performance—in health, education, environmental quality—in many countries, discussed in Chapter Six.

The debate now shaping up between economics versus long-term environmental ethics has been brewing for over a decade. Economists whose intellectual investments and clients are tied to the declining sector have been lobbying environmentalists and insisting that it is *we* who need to learn economics, rather than *they* that need to learn ecology and systems sciences. Economists still claim that economics provides the best overall theoretical framework for policy, while environmentalists insist that it is economics which must now find its place in broader, interdisciplinary models.[40] Obviously, economists prefer market "solutions" and their own narrow models of "efficiency" and "productivity," with which they are familiar, as well as the propensity to reduce everything possible to money coefficients or "shadow" prices. Ecologists and system theorists use many other coefficients—time, hectares of land, infant mortality, literacy levels, etc.—and this "politics of research methods and epistemologies" shows few signs of resolution.[41] The Bush Administration has endorsed, predictably, such "market solutions" as effluent taxes, incentives (i.e., subsidies), pollution licenses, etc. All these should have a place in the mix of options. However, the most controversial proposal is that these licenses to pollute should be able to be traded between companies in newly expanded markets, so that companies in compliance with air quality standards, for example, can sell their rights to spew out more pollution to companies who are still violators or to companies who want to come into the area and site a new polluting facility.[42] This perversion of market theory was used in some cases during the Reagan Administration, and I have made detailed arguments against it elsewhere (*Politics of the Solar Age,* pp. 245-282). Such policies grow, like noxious weeds, out of neoclassical market theory and economic textbooks that do not recognize the way markets are distorted by power and unequal access to information and income opportunities.

This kind of misapplication of market theory to political, social, and public health problems grew out of the famed Chicago School of Economics, and its leading proponent is Milton Friedman, coauthor of *Free to Choose,*[43] which highlights the main concern of his theorizing:

individual freedom in the market, rather than the new concerns of the global commons. These doctrines of the Chicago School have pervaded many of the nation's law schools and are taught as "Law and Economics." They assume that our democratic political system is simply analogous to yet another marketplace, where conflicts can be worked out between private parties and interest groups, using such welfare economic principles as compensation for damage caused to others by market activities, or their willingness to pay to avoid harm, etc., thus avoiding the need for much regulation. Some of these ideas do still work in small communities where the social fabric is still intact and moral and ethical sanctions still apply to control purely self-interested behavior. However, it is hopelessly outdated where *common* resources must be shared, i.e., air, water, or open space, in today's crowded urbanized societies, where win-win rules are needed for equitable access. Even Judge Bork, in his unsuccessful confirmation hearings for a Supreme Court seat, testified that he had abandoned his belief in much of this theorizing behind Law and Economics.

Although these misplaced market theories are perhaps most of all inappropriate for dealing with our environmental and global commons, they are espoused by many in the Environmental Protection Agency (EPA), the Congress, and even some environmental groups with persuasive staff economists. The marketing pollution license proposals are often thrown in with the whole range of other less-questionable uses of the tax code, subsidies, incentives, and other price signals, which can nudge change as well or better than some regulations (such as higher gasoline taxes, which are essential, in my view). On the whole, I favor taxing and user-fee approaches for producers over subsidies and incentives. Subsidies too often create a set of "client" companies or whole industries which then acquire market power to lobby for perpetuation of such subsidies—creating tilted playing fields for newer market entrants. For example, *"Project 88: Harnessing Market Forces to Protect Our Environment,"* a study sponsored by Senators Tim Wirth and John Heinz, contains many useful policy proposals to create new markets and price signals.[44] At least the truth that it is *humans* that create markets and not God, or magic forces is clearly stated, and the costs to taxpayers of these additional bribes is acknowledged, along with attempts at comparisons with new revenues from effluent taxes and comparisons with regulation and costs of legal and enforcement delays and of the endless lawsuits involved. The assumption is that all these intricacies and interacting variables can be modeled with economic tools, and that those environmentalists who participated were fully cognizant of the flaws in these models. However, economic theory is so perversely impenetrable that one has to be an expert in order to critique its deeply buried assumptions, and it is more likely that the noneconomists were overawed or did not wish to display their incomprehension. However, the report also includes recommendations that markets be created to trade pollution rights and licenses as well for controlling air pollution, acid rain, greenhouse gases, and surface and ground water pollution. These need much more critical examination and rebuttal on many grounds.[45]

These marketable licenses to pollute imply that a *right* to pollute exists, in spite of protestations to the contrary, and since there is currently no constitutional right to pollute, the whole approach sends the wrong signal. The spectacle of private companies trading together the rights of third parties to breathe clean air is sinister. Human rights cannot be abridged so easily, particularly when neither the potential victims nor their representatives are seated at the negotiating table. Thus, creation of these types of pollution markets invades the social and political arena in new ways that must be widely debated and not discussed merely within economic concepts of "efficiency." For example, the Project 88 report was directed by economists with funds provided by foundations. A citizen-based group, the Environmental Policy Institute, served only as "fiscal agent" for the project "as part of an effort to stimulate diverse points of view about environmental problems." Various environmental group representatives agreed to be listed as only "contributors, reviewers or staff," with further caveats that the report did not necessarily reflect the views of their groups or the "fiscal agent's other funding sources." As an old science and public policy hand, Project 88 looks to me like the brain child of a particular financial and economics constituency more committed to the rearview mirror issues of bailing out the declining unsustainable sector than focusing on creating markets and price signals to fertilize the growth of the emerging, sustainable sectors of the future.

The arguments used in favor of marketing pollution licenses include: (1) Regulation hasn't worked well and pollution is a fact of industrial life; (2) Since pollution can't be eliminated, why not just recognize this reality and tax or license it? (3) We need to use both the carrot of subsidies and the sticks of taxes and regulations; (4) Offering the right to trade their pollution permits enables companies that are cleaner to make more money by selling these permits to dirtier companies, and (5) These policies will give us more "efficiency" and "bang for the pollution-control buck."

These arguments are less than persuasive for the following additional reasons beyond the constitutional one already cited. (1) It is egregious to claim that regulation hasn't worked well, since much progress has been made, and only during the Reagan years did it begin to fail badly, since the policy of his Administration was to deregulate the entire economy, and the EPA was singled out for systematic budget cuts and generally decimated. (2) One of the real blocks to better enforcement has been that the burden of proof in pollution and toxic hazards in the environment was placed on the general public, the EPA and other enforcement agencies, rather than, as in the case of the Food and Drug Administration, on manufacturers, which bear the burden of proof that the substance has been tested until it meets the GRAS (generally regarded as safe) standard. This reversed burden of proof allowed endless, costly legal delays and required enforcement agencies to hire thousands of scientists and lawyers to testify during appeal processes that dragged out over years. This generally prevented the logical regulation of these hazards *at the source.* The California Toxics Law, Proposition 65, implemented in 1988, puts the burden of proof back into the marketplace, saving taxpayers millions of dollars and speeding up the regulatory process, applying toxic status to more chemicals in 1989 (only *12 months*) than the EPA managed under the Toxic Substances Control Act in the past *12 years.*[46]

Thus the fight over marketing pollution licenses has only just begun. As Jon Mills, former Speaker of Florida's House of Representatives said, "If these rights exist, what is to stop me and a group of my environmentalist friends from going into that same market and out-bidding all the polluting companies? We could take them off the market—but then, that's what we *pay our government enforcers* to do! Oh, you say that only *polluters* can enter these markets, *not* law-abiding citizens? What is fair about that?"[47] I might add, what will stop us then from setting up markets to trade licenses to commit *felonies*? And will there ever be enough money in the public treasury to bribe *everyone* to abide by the laws? Nevertheless, the trading of pollution licenses was allowed in the 1991 Clean Air Act. Previous experience in the 1970s makes this ominous. As Richard Ayres, chairman of the National Clean Air Coalition notes, the number of "pollution credits" owned by a company depends on how much it has reduced its emissions, which has to be certified by EPA. In the 1970s experiments there was a lot of real chicanery in calculating accounts, such as selling rights on a plant that closed years ago. And an analysis in *Business Week*, "The Right to Pollute Shouldn't be for Sale" concluded that they might end up giving us dirtier air and water, or at least creating pollution "hot spots" unless trades are monitored closely. We will pick up this subject again in Chapter Seven.

The good news about all this cultural confusion over our changing values and goals, ethics and regulations, is that these issues are reaching higher thresholds of public awareness and debate—in the Congress, on Wall Street, in the corporate sector, and in the community, in schools and in the family. The whole world has changed and we are now debating how we need to change the game, the rules, and the scoring system

Arguments for using "the magic of market forces" to achieve social and regulatory goals has been a constant and sensible refrain in American politics. Our confusion was that we were blinded by economic dogma to *also* hold the contradictory belief that we did *not* actually create these markets, but rather that they were derived from some original state of grace or "human nature." As noted elsewhere, invoking "human nature" to buttress one's political beliefs or policy is a very old strategy. Furthermore, while it is true that, as Adam Smith said, humans have a propensity to barter—indeed we have been doing it since we came out of the caves—the social innovation of creating a nationwide system of markets as the primary resource-allocation mechanism is a fairly recent and brilliant human invention (*Politics of the Solar Age*, pp. 155-241). It was only some 300 years ago in Britain that a package of social legislation to create this national system of markets was introduced and passed by Parliament. It rolled back ancient cultural customs of feudal obligations and right and the older resource-allocation methods still used by many societies (including ours and Britain's): reciprocity and redistribution.[48] In fact, one of the most critical errors of economic theory has been the omission of the informal, unpaid sectors from its models (parenting, do-it-yourself, mutual aid, volunteering, food-raising, bartering, etc.), what I refer to as the "love economy," which all societies bogging down in "economism" are now rediscovering (see Plate 1-5: Three Layer Cake) as the *unseen* half.

So, of course, we should create new markets to help eliminate pollution or keep it within Nature's regenerating tolerances. But let us *take credit* for our intelligence, rather than keeping up the pretense that these are "magic forces," or that the propensity of humans to barter was *invented* by Adam Smith, or that capitalism is the only context in which they are or can be used. And let us remember that all human societies depend on sets of explicit and implicit values, ethics, and morals—the more of which can be agreed to and inculcated as part of our *responsibilities* which go along with our rights, the less police and external enforcement will be needed.[49] Indeed, we can use markets much more than we do now to shift our wasteful, unsustainable sector into the future and create whole new industries based on cleaning up and recycling, as well as future sustainability and even environmental enhancement and restoration.

To move forward and achieve these goals, there already is a wide consensus among economists and environmentalists that we must, as

Exploring the Evolving Global Playing Field

New markets

- Telecom services
- Desert greening
- Pollution control
- Renewable energy
- Recycling, eco-resource management
- "Caring" sector (day care, counseling, re-hab, nursing)
- Infrastructure (extending transport, telecommunications, etc.)
- Eco-restoration, bio-remediation

New commons

- Space, Earth systems science
- Electromagnetic spectrum
- Oceans, water resources
- Atmosphere, ozone layer
- Security, peace-keeping
- Forests
- Health
- Global economy

PLATE 3-22

soon as possible and by a range of appropriate means, move to full-cost pricing, i.e., internalize as quickly as possible all the longer-term social and environmental costs of production back onto the company balance sheets, so that the products and services may be truly priced. Obviously, there are many long-term costs that we cannot hope to fully account for, such as depletion of ozone, public health risks, etc., which is why we can never rely on only prices. Other forms of feedback, mentioned earlier, must all be used where most apt for the problem at hand. These external costs can be internalized by regulations, mass media exposés, votes, public opinion, consumer action, boycotts of offending products and "*buy*cotts" of environmentally superior products,[50] larger bounties on recyclable cans and bottles, not to mention the sales efforts of pollution control companies, recycling and conservation companies, and of course, the continued educational campaigns of environmental groups and their lobbying efforts. Better consumer information and product labeling, such as the Green Seal in the United States and Germany's Blue Angel eco-label, are already creating marketing opportunities:[51] in pesticide-free, organic foods, natural cosmetics, environmentally sound lines of recycled paper products, household cleansers, solar and energy-saving light bulbs and fixtures, as well as the upstream industries helping old companies change their processes, conserve their energy, and recycle their "by-products" and former "pollution" and "waste" back into their production stream or find new uses for these unappreciated resources.

Of course, all these new markets are either values-driven or regulation-driven. For example, at a recent meeting of the World Business Council, one of my fellow speakers, Dean L. Buntrock, President of Waste Management, Inc., a multibillion-dollar corporation, began his talk by stating clearly that his company and its spectacular growth was "regulation-driven." Moving further upstream to the securities markets, we see the outstanding success at promoting better environmental practices of the socially responsible investing movement, whose investors now account for $650 billion worth of assets screened for their longer-term social and environmental concerns. Here again, changing values created this growing market niche, at first scoffed by Wall Streeters. The movement's Valdez Principles and Sullivan Principles (covering investment in South Africa) are now regularly covered by the financial press for their effects in corporate boardrooms.[52] The energy conservation market is still holding its own, from its creation by OPEC and energy-efficiency standards set in the 1970s and not completely rolled back in the Reagan era. This market is poised to resume growth in the United States as we rediscover our energy dependence on imports has *increased* and that our competitiveness internationally is still hampered by the fact that it takes the United States two and a half *times* as much energy to create an equivalent unit of GNP as it does Japan or our European trading partners. With new problems posed by global warming trends, the shift from fossil fuels to further conservation and alternative, renewable energy is inevitable. In fact, in my own environmental work, it is necessary to move even further upstream and survey all these social and values shifts as well as globalization and planetary ecosystem trends in order to see where new markets are emerging, as well as new commons, and where new win-win rules still need to be negotiated and new treaties written.

The new opportunities in both the new markets and the new commons include all manner of environmental restoration and enhancement, reforestation, and new uses for renewable, less-toxic plant-substitute inputs into hundreds of manufacturing processes. As I predicted in my earlier books and papers,[53] the paradigm shift from focusing on mechanical, inorganic sciences and production methods of early industrialism to the postindustrial focus on biological systems and information-rich methods has now occurred. I described this paradigm shift as one in which a problem of production would no longer instantly invoke visions of machines, factories, or hardware, but would engender more careful thought and scanning of eco-systems for their inherent capabilities and their untapped potentials which human knowledge can use and augment and shape to our needs more deftly. An example of this kind of rethinking of what "development" means on a living, crowded Planet is the budding industry of desert-greening, which promises to be a huge, global market well into the 21st century. Many different methods are practiced today, and some areas, such as my home state of Florida, have all the native plant species and agricultural biotechnologists to create a new export industry, along with our water-quality management technologies now being honed by environmental necessity. Venture capital companies are now beginning to see the new opportunities, and several new firms were launched in 1990.

New visions of world trade in the 21st century go far beyond the confines of economic theories of nations competing via comparative advantage or protectionism in a global marketplace. In the new era of global interdependence, countries will learn strategies beyond competing over today's narrow range of goods, such as automobiles and consumer electronics. They will practice the other two important trade strategies: *cooperation*, when commons require win-win rules, such as in space development, and most important, *creativity*, i.e., rethinking the game itself. Today, we are trying to impose industrial conformity on all trading partners by extending economic theories of protection to today's lengths of trying to homogenize everyone's social and cultural values, as in the "structural impediments" debate between the United States and Japan. Instead, nations can learn that each culture and its host ecosystem has produced truly unique gifts to offer in world trade, and the game will shift from "hardware" (shipping goods around) toward "software" (expertise, technique, social innovations). This "cultural niche" model is derived from *ecological* theory (where diversity is a basic principle) and mirrors the cooperation and symbiosis that is just as common in Nature as competition. Competition, cooperation, and creativity are all important strategies, appropriate in various circumstances, and no economic algorithm from either socialism or capitalism can be applied dogmatically.[53]

By far the largest global environmental ethics market is now emerging out of the winding down of Cold War arms expenditures and preventing a new arms race in the wake of the Gulf War. Citizens must demand that the Cold War's arms reduction yield a peace dividend—in spite of arms producers' lobbying. The rechanneling of some of these trillion dollar annual budgets is urgent so as to cope with the real horsemen of the apocalypse: poverty, hunger, disease, ignorance, and destruction of our planetary life-support system. Growing world trade in these basic goals of all humanity awaits only our fuller recognition that our tightly interwoven global economy is also a commons, requiring more win-win rules and agreements on debt, currency fluctuations, special drawing rights, and rethinking what a "level playing field" might look like, once we take off our economic spectacles. Debt must be dealt with beyond the currently fashionable swaps for Nature and equity (often band-aids based on murky ethical premises). The world's bankers and finance ministers need to face up to the fact that the de facto default has occurred already, and most of the recent remedies merely acknowledge some of this reality. Writing off Third World countries' debt is a necessary, but not sufficient starting point for further recycling of surplus nations' currencies—yen, Deutschmarks, etc.—into more organized secondary markets for discounted "country junk bonds," as I have termed them.[54]

As Third World debt is put behind us, the global playing field can be buttressed by placing an ethical floor under it, one composed of an extended girder work of agreements and protocols on toxic chemicals, worker and consumer protection, environmental standards, and eventually leveling some of the really serious differentials in wages (measured not in GNP terms, but in purchasing power parity equivalents [PPPs]).[55] These differentials in exploiting human labor, just like excessive differentials in consumer and worker safety and environmental protection, are what drives the excessive, unhealthy migrations of populations across borders looking for work and companies looking for short-term market advantage. These massive migrations further fuel the globalization processes and the 24-hour-day financial casino, where money is divorced from real wealth and becomes mere blips of information on thousands of trading screens, where time windows of opportunity to exploit differentials in currencies and interest rates are collapsing to mere nanoseconds.

Much of this ethical girder work of treaties, agreements, and protocols to raise the ethical floor to level the global playing field is already in place, through the United Nations special agencies and such treaties as that in Montreal in 1987 on chlorofluorocarbons and the Law of the Sea, which has been waiting for the United States to ratify it after a decade of delaying tactics. Only when this ethical girder work is in place, can ethically aware, responsible companies live up to their moral codes without fear of unfair competition by others willing to cut corners and exploit people and the environment for short-term gain.

Most of the great ethical and moral leaders in the short history of our human family have preached similar ethical imperatives, usually encoded in the classic systems theory statement of The Golden Rule, and reminded us that the "god" is within us as well as without. We have free will, reason, and compassion, and the intelligence to read the feedback signals from every level of our societies and environment. Beyond individual rights, too, lie our concomitant responsibilities. Exploring these issues is a new journal, *Rights and Responsibilities*, edited by Amitai Etzioni, author of *The Moral Dimension: Toward a New Economics* (1989). No subject is more important to our survival than exploring our values, ethics, and potential for altruism as well as broader self-interest. For when our individual self-interests are seen in the larger context of the human family on Planet Earth, we see that they are all identical, as Elise Boulding shows in her prophetic book, *Building a Global Civic Culture: Education for an Interdependent World* (Teachers College Press, Columbia University, 1988). It is in every one of our broadest self-interests to help create and undergird the ethical and environmental markets of the 21st century, since they provide our best assurance of survival and truly human development.

Chapter Three Footnotes

1. *The Economist*, September 2, 1989, citing the growth of "green" policies from 1973 and E.F. Schumacher's *Small is Beautiful* to Mrs. Thatcher's "conversion from Iron Lady to Green Goddess."
2. F. Fukuyama, "The End of History?," *The National Interest*, Summer 1989.
3. W.K. Stevens, "Evolving Theory Views Earth as a Living Organism" *New York Times*, August 29, 1989.
4. G. Hardin, *The Limits of Altruism*, Indiana University Press, Bloomington, 1977.
5. P. Sorokin, *The Ways and Powers of Love*, originally published by Beacon Press, Boston,1954.
6. Hazel Henderson, *Creating Alternative Futures: The End of Economics*, G.P. Putnam and Sons, New York, 1978.
7. M. Daly, *Pure Lust*, Beacon Press, Boston, 1984.
8. D. Ehrenfeld, *The Arrogance of Humanism*, Oxford University Press, Oxford, 1978.
9. Fritjof Capra, *The Tao of Physics*, Shambala Press, Berkeley, CA, 1983.
10. E. Neumann, *The Great Mother* (Manheim, R. trans.), Bollingen Series, Princeton University Press, Princeton, NJ, 1955.
11. M. Gimbutas, *The Goddesses and Gods of Old Europe*, University of California Press, Berkeley, 1982.
12. Joseph Campbell, *The Power of Myth*, Doubleday, New York, 1988.
13. Riane Eisler, *The Chalice and the Blade*, HarperCollins, San Francisco, 1987.
14. The Native American ethos of submitting all policies to the test of their effects on the "seventh generation" which typifies this longer-range ethic, is explored by Gary Paul Nabhan in *The Desert Smells Like Rain*, North Point Press, 1982.
15. Hazel Henderson, "The Politics and Ethics of the Solar Age," Horace Albright Lecture, University of California, Berkeley, 1982 (monograph).
16. The South Commission, *Toward a New Way to Measure Development*, Caracas, Venezuela, foreword by President Carlos Andres Perez of Venezuela, 1989.
17. Charlene Spretnak, and Fritjof Capra, *Green Politics*, E.P. Dutton, New York, 1984.
18. *The Economist*, September 23, 1989, carried a special article, "Survey: The Third World," which outlines the classic "economism" view, i.e., that these countries should not give up hope and that the 1980s were a "temporary setback."
19. *The Economist's* editors, in their survey cited above, do not include ecological criteria in comparing Third World countries, which they espouse so vigorously in their Survey of the Environment.
20. *New York Times*, "Environment Magazines Spring Up," September 28, 1989.

21. Hazel Henderson, *The Politics of the Solar Age: Alternatives to Economics,* current edition from Knowledge Systems, Inc., Indianapolis, 1988.

22. *The Economist*, "Costing the Earth," September 2, 1989.

23. *The Economist*, "Growth Can Be Green," August 26, 1989.

24. David Collard, in *Altruism and Economy*, Oxford University Press, 1978, makes a heroic effort to tease out from economic theory the few papers and studies on the subject of longer-term ethics.

25. Hazel Henderson, "Post-economic Policies for Post-industrial Societies," *Re-Vision*, Winter-Spring, 1984-85.

26. *Business Week*, September 25, 1989, p. 166.

27. H. Simon, "Rationality as a Process and Product of Thought" (Nobel Memorial Lecture), *American Economic Review*, 1978.

28. See the Introduction to the current edition of *Politics of the Solar Age*.

29. R.E. Munn, "Environmental prospects for the next century: implications for long-term policy and research strategies," *Technological Forecasting and Social Change*, p. 33, 1988.

30. Lester Brown, et al., *State of the World Report 1988*, WorldWatch Institute, Washington, 1988.

31. P. Draper, "Economic conventions: health vs. wealth," *Royal Society of Health Journal*, 1977.

32. *Business Week*, July 15, 1991, p. 128.

33. *Business Week*, July 29, 1991.

34. Stanley B. Greenberg, "The '88 Election," *World Policy Journal*, Summer, 1988.

35. For example, the Local Exchange Trading System (LETS) developed in Courtenay, BC, Canada by Michael Linton, Landsman, Inc.

36. *The Economist*, September 23, 1989, in its Third World Survey agreed that "in the 1950s and 1960s, economists set the third world on the wrong track" and that *government intervention* (whether expert or inept) was the key variable.

37. *The Economist*, September 23, 1989, in its Third World Survey, for example, frames its entire 58-page discussion of these "development issues" *within* economic theory, as if these macroeconomic management variables were *primary* (grade and export policies, currency differentials, fiscal and monetary approaches), rather than recasting these issues in line with their discovery that all these policies are simply policies of *government intervention*, which is primary. Social, cultural and environmental variables were largely ignored.

38. *Business and Society Review*, #70, Summer 1989. In "Do Good Ethics Ensure Good Profits?" social scientist Amitai Etzioni and anthropologist Lionel Tiger point to these deeper cultural and anthropological factors, and how our history of living in small groups allowed us to rely on "full disclosure" and social sanctions—mechanisms we need to reinvent to fit our crowded world of today.

39. Hazel Henderson, "Information and the New Movements for Citizen Participation," *Annals of the American Academy of Political and Social Science* 412, pp. 34-43, 1974.

40. Hazel Henderson, "Ecologists Versus Economists," *Harvard Business Review*, July-August 1973.

41. Hazel Henderson, "Toward an Economics of Ecology," *Columbia Journal of World Business* VIII(3), 1972.

42. *New York Times*, "Searching for Incentives to Entice Polluters," October 8, 1989.

43. M. and R. Friedman, *Free to Choose: A Personal Statement*, Harcourt, Brace, Jovanovich, New York, 1980.

44. "Project 88: Harnessing Market Forces to Protect Our Environment, Initiatives for the New President," Public Policy Study sponsored by Sen. Tim Wirth, Colorado, and Sen. John Heinz, Pennsylvania, 1988.

45. *New York Times*, October 8, 1989. "Searching for Incentives to Entice Polluters" contains additional objections raised by David G. Hawkins, senior attorney of the National Resources Defense Council to the Bush Administration plan to apply such trading rights to automobile pollution, where reduction of pollution is not fungible, as it may be in the case of specific pollution or toxic substances.

46. C. Russell, "California Gets Tough on Toxics," *Business and Society Review* 70, pp. 47-54, 1989.

47. Jon Mills, Director of the Center for Government Responsibility, Holland Law Center, University of Florida, Gainesville, in personal communication with the author (24 August 1989) and taped for the PBS television special "Profit the Earth," first aired on April 16, 1990.

48. K. Polanyi, *The Great Transformation*, Beacon Press, Boston, 1944.

49. See, for example, Draft Declaration of Human Responsibilities for Peace and Sustainable Development, presented to the U.N. General Assembly by the Government of Costa Rica and President Oscar Arias Sanchez (1989 Fall Session).

50. See, for example, *Shopping for a Better World*, published by the Council on Economic Priorities, 30 Irving Place, New York, NY, yearly editions, also *Seventh Generation, Coop America* and *Real Goods* catalogs.

51. These new labeling systems include Germany's Blue Angel Seal and Canada's Eco-Seal, both offered to companies that can comply with environmental standards regulated by the government.

52. *New York Times*, "Who Will Subscribe to the Valdez Principles?" September 10, 1989.

53. Hazel Henderson, "The Imperative Alternative," *Inquiry*, London, June 1986.

54. *Redefining Wealth and Progress: New Ways to Measure Economic, Social and Environmental Change. The Caracas Report on Alternative Development Indicators,* Knowledge Systems, Indianapolis, 1989, pp. 29-37.

55. *The Economist*, "Feeling Poor in Japan," June 11, 1988.

Action Plan For The State of The World's Children

The year 2000: what can be achieved?

The following is the full list of goals, to be attained by the year 2000, which were adopted by the World Summit for Children on September 30th 1990. After widespread consultation among governments and the agencies of the United Nations, these targets were considered to be feasible and financially affordable over the course of the decade ahead.

Overall goals 1990-2000

• A one-third reduction in under-five death rates (or a reduction to below 70 per 1,000 live births-whichever is less).
• A halving of maternal mortality rates.
• A halving of severe and moderate malnutrition among the world's under-fives.
• Safe water and sanitation for all families.
• Basic education for all children and completion of primary education by at least 80%.
• A halving of the adult illiteracy rate and the achievement of equal educational opportunity for males and females.
• Protection for the many millions of children in especially difficult circumstances and the acceptance and observance, in all countries, of the recently adopted *Convention on the Rights of the Child.* In particular, the 1990s should see rapidly growing acceptance of the idea of special protection for children in time of war.

Protection for girls and women

• Family planning education and services to be made available to all couples to empower them to prevent unwanted pregnancies and births which are 'too many and too close' and to women who are 'too young or too old'.
• All women to have access to pre-natal care, a trained attendant during childbirth and referral for high-risk pregnancies and obstetric emergencies.
• Universal recognition of the special health and nutritional needs of females during early childhood, adolescence pregnancy and lactation.

Nutrition

• A reduction in the incidence of low birth weight (2.5 kg. or less) to less than 10%.
• A one-third reduction in iron deficiency anaemia among women.
• Virtual elimination of vitamin A deficiency and iodine deficiency disorders.
• All families to know the importance of supporting women in the task of exclusive breast-feeding for the first four to six months of a child's life and of meeting the special feeding needs of a young child through the vulnerable years.
• Growth monitoring and promotion to be institutionalized in all countries.
• Dissemination of knowledge to enable all families to ensure household food security.

Child health

• The eradication of polio.
• The elimination of neonatal tetanus (by 1995).
• A 90% reduction in measles cases and a 95% reduction in measles deaths, compared to pre-immunization levels.
• Achievement and maintenance of at least 85% immunization coverage of one-year-old children and universal tetanus immunization for women in the child-bearing years.
• A halving of child deaths caused by diarrhoea and a 25% reduction in the incidence of diarrhoeal diseases.
• A one-third reduction in child deaths caused by acute respiratory infections.
• The elimination of guinea worm disease.

Education

• In addition to the expansion of primary school education and its equivalents, today's essential knowledge and life skills could be put at the disposal of all families by mobilizing today's vastly increased communications capacity.

PLATE 4-23

Source: UNICEF, New York

Beyond GNP
Re-membering Wholeness

The emerging Earth Ethics blur old boundaries and show the ways GNP measured "progress" ignored other realities. For example, the fate of the world's children, the fate of the Earth and the future of the human family are, of course, inextricably linked. Yet the prevalent mindset in today's world systematically denies many such linkages and the seamless web of relationships by which humans live with each other and Nature. Some other examples of such denials of reality include the recent contentions of the United States Government that "no linkage" exists between disarmament and development, as the reason that the United States did not participate in the 1988 U.N. Conference on Disarmament and Development. Denial of such obvious linkages is not merely a strategic stance governments use, but is part of a much deeper mindset that predominates governments, business, the media, academia and most modern institutions, which allows and even encourages fragmented perspectives that prevent us from remembering that the world we inhabit is whole. The effect of this mindset in journalism and media is the compulsive reporting of events, however trivial, at the expense of examining the deeper processes and trends that underlie them. For example, the reportage of the recent tragic conflict in the Mideast soon lost sight of the deeper causes and focused on the daily military briefings where the minutia of every sortie and engagement were amplified ad nauseam and the countries involved became the "theater." This sanitizing of the War and celebrations of the victory masked the ghastly realities of at least 150,000 Iraqi deaths, the huge civilian casualties, the ecological devastation of Kuwait, the plight of the Kurds, the failure to dislodge Saddam Hussein and the persistence of the repressive Kuwait monarchy—leaving many Americans in a state of moral schizophrenia.

This kind of compartmentalizing of reality and its analytical, reductionist worldview took hold of the human imagination in Europe during the seventeenth century and became the hidden mainspring of the industrial and scientific revolution—what we now call the Era of Enlightenment.[1] After centuries of domination by the church in medieval times, this radical paradigm shift away from faith was heralded by the new breed of secular thinkers, including Galileo, Kepler, Descartes, and Newton. What we know today as the Cartesian worldview spread its core ideas: that the material and secular world could be studied and manipulated for human purposes; that dreams of paradise could be pursued here on Earth, rather than only in Heaven; and, that the powerful method of enquiry we now call "reductionism" (understanding wholes by examining their parts) could, to paraphrase Francis Bacon "force Nature to give up her secrets to man." This was the formula, the "cultural DNA-code" which gave rise to the unprecedented flowering of human capabilities we call the Industrial Revolution. It was potentiated further by earlier Judeo-Christian beliefs that God, the Father, had charged humans (or specifically, men) with dominion over the Earth.

Without doubt, this Enlightenment period produced a cornucopia of scientific inventions, new technologies and improved the lot of millions of people. It was probably inevitable as a developmental path for a species like humans, blessed or cursed with an opposing thumb and hind-legged stance which left their hands free for invention. The worldview of Descartes and Newton reduced the universe and the mysteries of our living Planet, Gaia, to that of a giant clockwork, which could be understood by our rational, left-brain mode of cognition. This, in turn, spawned increasing numbers of specialists and progressive fragmenting of academic disciplines. This shattered the wholeness of creation until even atoms were split to yield up their awesome power to human use.

Today, the powerful and often—unintended consequences of this narrow view of reality which the English poet William Blake called "Newton's sleep" are unavoidable: polluted skies, toxic dumps, oil spills, advancing deserts, shrinking forests, broken families and communities, and millions of neglected children, 40,000 of whom die every day from starvation, millions of others malnourished or roaming the streets of our cities, homeless and abandoned. Today, some three hundred years after this Scientific Enlightenment began, its cultural power still lives—dominating the policies of most of the world's leaders. The latter-day arguments and segmenting of reality continue, for example in this century's debates between communism and capitalism which led to the Cold War. In retrospect this debate was quite superficial. Both Karl Marx and Adam

Smith and their followers agreed about the basic *goal* of industrialism itself—differing only over the best ways to go about the task *efficiently*. This pursuit of narrowly-defined production efficiency gave rise to economics and its rationalistic formulas for employing the Earth's resources and people, which became the pre-eminent, powerful discipline offering the policy tools of macroeconomic management to governments. (See Plate 1-3: Differing Perceptions, Assumptions and Forecasting Styles Between Economists and Futurists.) Children and women, still viewed as chattel, became the lowliest workers in the early factories. Factories themselves were based on the Cartesian idea of removing production from its cultural roots in the home and community and splitting and rationalizing the process into hundreds of mindless tasks. Today, as industrialization spreads around the world, urban areas grow cancerously; rural communities are left, together with traditional cultures and peoples, in the backwash of "economic growth" and "progress." Groups such as Appropriate Technology International are trying to reverse this damage.[2]

In the 1990's, all these "side-effects" of pursuing an ever-rising Gross National Product (GNP) are too visible to be denied and their causal connections too obvious to the naked senses for clever rationalizations. People everywhere are awakening from this "technological trance," as theologian Thomas Berry calls the Cartesian worldview. News media have helped enormously in this awakening—albeit, long after all the environmental destruction and social costs had given birth to the environmental movement in the 1960s. Twenty-year-old environmental horror-stories, well-documented in thousands of environmental groups' newsletters suddenly became "news" about 1989, and began appearing in the news magazines and on television. The Earth Day 1990 crescendo of coverage began leading to articles about the rise and fall of the environmental "fad." "Green marketing" became the newest weapon in the advertisers' arsenal to increase consumption.

Linkages and interconnections between all these separately reported stories and events and the overall impact on the Earth of our mass-consumption-driven economies, became unavoidably obvious. The losers in the industrial race also became more visible: the "less-developed countries" could only develop like the Northern industrial countries if the North became more frugal and shared the Earth's remaining resources more fairly. The "marginalization" of rural and ethnic peoples, women, children and the weak began to be seen as an integral part of the process of blindly pursuing GNP-growth and the Cartesian definitions of efficiency and progress.

Concerning the children: Keeping our promises

In September 1990, another leap in awareness was achieved when 71 presidents and Prime Ministers were maneuvered into the first World Summit for Children, signalling an emerging paradigm of acceptance of the inter-connections of life by taking public responsibility for the condition of the world's children. Children had, through history, been viewed as small adults and willing workers, then made "serfs" in the early industrial factories, and sometimes, wards of the state, as traditional, extended, and then even nuclear families were shattered by the advance of industrial progress. Children fell between all the stools in the fragmented, Cartesian world: whether as pawns in family custody battles or neglected by both the family and the state. At the World Summit for Children, a new commitment was made: to try to end child deaths and child malnutrition on today's scale by the year 2000 and to provide basic protection for the normal physical and mental development of all the world's children. The Summit exposed the "quiet catastrophe": not only the 40,000 child deaths each day, but the 150 million children who live on with ill health and poor growth,[3] the 100 million 6-11 year-olds who are not in school. At last, these shocking statistics were publicly *linked* at the highest levels to the fact that the means of ending this quiet catastrophe are now both available and affordable. This linkage also signalled that the rationalistic, narrow, "left-brain" approach was expanding to include once again, the more "right-brain" moral and intuitive grasp of whole systems needed to address the world's intractable "problematique": environmental destruction, poverty and social neglect amid rising populations and shrinking resources, with soaring debt accompanying growth of GNPs in more and more countries. (See again Plate 3-13: Old Unsustainable Economic Development Treadmill.)

The World Summit for Children, however, took the giant step of linking many of the formerly disparate parts of the story, thus laying the groundwork for their historic promise and their Plan of Action by the Year 2000. (See Plate 4-23: Action Plan for the State of the World's Children 1991.) Another vital linkage was highlighted between population growth and infant mortality which reversed the Malthusian view that mortality rates must balance with birth rates. Rather, the reverse is true regarding child mortality: when children survive with such cheap, simple remedies as oral rehydration therapy (ORT) for diarrhea, birthrates can be reduced. *The State of the World's Children, 1991* notes that the total cost of such inexpensive prevention and treatment programs is $2.5 billion annually (what Soviet citizens spend each month on vodka, or the annual U.S. advertising expenditure on cigarettes). The payoff is saving the lives of nine million children. Such grotesque figures and anomalous comparisons show clearly the difference between money and wealth, and point to the absurdities of defining "progress" by GNP-growth. In the United States, the "richest" country, one in five American children live in poverty; more than ten million children have no health insurance; half a million drop out of school each year and the United States is 22nd among nations in child mortality rates and 29th in low birth-weight babies.

This is all part of the real decline in the United States during the 1980s, masked by the rising GNP and stock market. Meanwhile, the "downward mobility" of American workers, whose real incomes have not increased for a decade, accelerated. As reality broke through in the 1990s, a permanent underclass was "discovered," and even *Business Week* commented on the widening gap between rich and poor,[4] and in August 1991, ran a cover story "What Happened to the American Dream?" exploring the plight of the "Under-30s," who are finding home ownership out of reach, where even two-job families cannot make ends meet and where few expect to earn as much as their parents.[5]

All of these painful linkages of previously separate sets of data is another step toward "re-wholing" our understanding of the world—just as the pictures of the Earth from space show us this truth again. It is not surprising that the grassroots movements to heal the Earth and to care for the world's children are more effective in pressing these agendas on politicians than those of specialists and academics. The powerful, reintegrating, passionate concern showed by grassroots groups, whether the Chipko movement in Asia and the Greenbelt movement in Africa to protect and restore forests, or the world-wide efforts to prod media to write stories about the plight of children, have helped elevate children, as well as the environment in global priority-setting. Yet another linkage is the picture of the world's problems is that complex set of issues surrounding the role of women which is forcing another rethinking of the "development" debate. Two important new studies of these issues are *If Women Counted*, by former member of the New Zealand Parliament, Marilyn Waring (HarperCollins, 1989) and *Women and the World Economic Crisis* by Jeanne Vickers (Zed Books, 1991). Another useful study at last tackles the appalling sexism at the United Nations itself, *Making Women Matter: The Role of the United Nations* by Hilkka Pietila and Jeanne Vickers (Zed Books, 1990).

Many developing countries almost gave up on the North-South dialogue of the past decade, as their proposals for a New International Economic Order were ignored. The South Commission, co-chaired by Julius Nyerere, former President of Tanzania and President Carlos Andres

Perez of Venezuela, charted a new course at its meeting in Kuala Lumpur in 1987. The Commission resolved to redefine "sustainable, equitable, people-centered development" without the help of traditional, Eurocentric industrial development theorists. The term, "sustainable development" has gained wide acceptance since it was advocated in *Our Common Future* by the World Commission on Environment and Development, chaired by Dr. Gro Harlem Brundtland of Norway. Much imaginative work to operationalize these new concepts of development is under way, such as that in Venezuela. In fact, China's 10 years of improving living standards are not reflected in its GNP, and prove that per capita-averaged income and current national accounts conventions are by no means the best indicator of overall welfare or progress. However, China has lagged behind the USSR in democratic reforms. Both countries follow in the spirit of Karl Marx's original invention of the word "socialism," i.e., a more inclusive, systemic view, beyond economics, despite operational failures.

Broader views of development are essential because from this context comes the criterion of sustainability, i.e., providing equitably for the needs of the present generation without jeopardizing the needs of future generations. Thus, today's task of redefining development is much more than just avoiding the boom-bust cycles of market dominated, capitalistic economies, or the rigidities of Soviet, Stalinist-style central planning, but also to correct the excessive pollution and depletion of the Earth's resources that both these development models cause—now precluding the opportunities for the South. In the United States and other mature industrial societies the excesses of mass consumption have brought moral crises: from eroding ethical standards, drug abuse, crime, illiteracy, widespread homelessness and hunger to an increasing gap between rich and poor, as well as splintered families and communities.

The basic problem is that industrialism's ideology, crystallized in economic theory, is an unscientific basis for sustainable, equitable development and an expanded theoretical framework is needed, based on broader, interdisciplinary concepts as discussed in Chapter Three. Some economists are currently exploring chaos models and those developed from the life sciences in the hope of overhauling their discipline. The need for a "positive" normative goal-oriented approach to managing an economy was stressed by few economists—notable exceptions being Robert Heilbroner and Adolph Lowe.[6]

Once we transcend the box of economism and its false universalism, we can see how many intractable debates between economists, such as those about planning vs. markets and competition vs. cooperation, etc., can be overcome. The key issues are less whether countries are market systems or centrally planned, as many economists still believe, but rather, the extent to which they function *cybernetically*, i.e., incorporate at every decision level the necessary feedback loops from those people and resource systems affected by the original decisions as discussed in Chapter Three. (See again Plate 1-2: Simple Diagrams of Two Major Cybernetic Systems.)

Seeing the economy whole

Unfortunately, as technology becomes more complex, and social and technological interlinkages increase, managerial scale and scope must also increase to attempt control of this complexity. Each order of magnitude of technological and managerial scale in the market sector calls forth an equivalent order of magnitude of government regulation (particularly in democracies where citizens demand it politically).

From a general systems theory perspective, all economic systems are sets of *rules*, devised to fit the specific culture, values and goals of each society. Thus, even so-called free market or *laissez-faire* economies are designed by humans and *legislated* into existence, while prices and wages reflect the values of each society and its state of knowledge of its real situation in the physical world. In fact, the notion of "objectively set," "free market" prices is revealed as a myth (albeit a politically useful one) since all markets are, in one way or another, created by *human*, rather than any "invisible" hand. Resource allocation methods, whether planning, prices, regulation, rationing, barter or reciprocity, are only as good as the state of human knowledge.[7]

This decision theory view of economic systems as "games" with human rules, i.e., as management systems employing many feedbacks and strategies, allows an overview of planning, market and other tools of policy. As mentioned, both competition and cooperation are equally useful strategies which must be continually balanced in all societies. Systems scientist Stafford Beer has been designing such models for many years and is currently applying them under a United Nations grant in Uruguay.

Ecological and natural resource decisions and prices are only as good as human scientific knowledge and must be based on sound science in systematic, dynamic models. Many systems theorists, including Fritjof Capra, Leonard Duhl, and the World Health Organization itself, have proposed substituting "health" as a basic criterion for development, i.e., healthy land and water, healthy cities, healthy public policy—all for healthy people as the goal.[8] The Chinese government in a joint project with the World Resources Institute is focusing on a key cause of environmental destruction, the waste of resources, and how they can be conserved by correcting prices to include social costs incurred. Full-cost pricing will provide a more accurate market allocation method, albeit that additional accounting for environmental and social costs will produce an inflation effect, since most countries have been overstating productivity for decades. For example, the National Academy of Sciences 1991 Report, *Policy Implications of Greenhouse Warming* calls for "full-cost pricing" to more accurately assess fossil fuel use and mitigation of greenhouse gas emissions. In response the Oil, Chemical, and Atomic Workers Union (OCAW) pointed out that the report did not go far enough in calculating full-cost prices, because, the report omitted the costs of retraining and unemployment benefits for the laid-off workers in such polluting industries.[9]

The GNP-growth models of economic development, derived from macro-statistics and "business climate" models, (such as those of the U.S.-based accounting firm of Grant Thornton, prepared for its clients in their corporate location decisions) now clearly marginalize local areas, businesses and workers in the informal as well as the formal economy, not to mention further exploiting local environments and natural resources. At prevailing international interest rates, banks linked to the global economy with branches in local communities simply "vacuum" out local deposits and throw them onto the global electronic funds transfer systems. As discussed, this aggravates local deficits of currency to complete local trades and investing and reinforces the marginalizing effect of the "business climate" approach to GNP-measured economic growth.[10] I have termed this a latter-day "plantation model," i.e., a local area must compete with other local areas to "lure" a large enterprise to locate a plant to employ local people. To do this, the community must put itself on the auction block by offering tax holidays, cheap land, cheap labor, low tax rates, few environmental regulations (or regulations of any kind) and be unfriendly to labor unions. This disempowering and foolish strategy is best underscored by the fact that in the United States, for example, at least 25,000 local municipal and state governments and business development groups put out glossy brochures extolling this type of "business climate"— all chasing some 500 location decisions annually. Today's global economy makes it worse.

Grassroots approach

As humans re-whole their fragmented perception, they begin to see that the "luring outside investors" approach to development become self-defeating and ever more risky. Today for a whole generation of technology the innovation to obsolescence lifecycle can be three years or less. Thus, focusing on the "home-grown economy" is a safer approach. This basic strategy offers a minimal "safety net" until the world trade roller coaster is tamed by new global agreements, such as those to which the G-7 countries are already moving (in spite of their "free market" preferences).

The commonality in the new approaches in the United States, one of the world's most mature industrial societies with one of the highest per capita averaged income and GNP levels, is the now widely shared insight that sustainable development must begin locally from the grassroots and basic agriculture, rather than the failed trickle-down model of industrialism. A good example of the grassroots approach is the Sarvodya Shramadana movement in Sri Lanka, which fosters development in the Buddhist tradition as "awakening of all" in over 8000 villages, which themselves are incorporated as "enterprises." (Further information from Sarvodya-U.S., One Madison Avenue, New York, NY 10100.) The industrial model saw rural communities and farmers as backward people to be mobilized into industrial production. But, as has been discovered in most countries, there are few such easy short cuts to sustainable development, which involves steady efforts and prevention of harmful, unanticipated consequences which are often expensive to remedy, or even irreversible.

The U.S. Office of Technology Assessment (OTA), on whose Advisory Council I served during its start-up years from 1974 until 1980, released a study in June 1988 on *Grassroots Development* in Africa, which surveys efforts to enable the poor to participate in the process of development. OTA assessed 19 countries in which such projects had been funded by a new agency set up by the U.S. Congress, the African Development Foundation (ADF). Between 1984 and 1987, the ADF awarded grants to 114 projects ranging from $700 to $250,000, two-thirds of which were for agricultural activities and for potable water, raising vegetable crops for local consumption, improving animal health, renting tractors, helping set up cooperatives and the like. OTA's study confirmed the validity of ADF's assumptions concerning participation as the key to healthier forms of social and sustainable development. The World Bank is examining other grassroots development models such as Bangladesh's Grameen Bank, and the New York and Amsterdam headquartered network of Women's World Banking, with local affiliates in 55 countries. Another cooperative model is that of Seikatsu in Japan— a highly successful multi-million dollar buying club organized by women.[11]

A now widely perceived key to sustainable development seems to involve what the World Bank refers as to as "capillary lending," where channels are sought to pass through large sums of money to many village organizations—bypassing government and political influences in capital cities. Thus, it is questionable whether the World Bank can yet recycle recent Japanese surpluses effectively.

Seeing the informal sectors

All these new grassroots lending policies, both in mature industrial societies such as the United States, Canada, and many European countries, as well as in developing countries, again prove that old left or right ideologies associated with economic models are obsolete. For example, the World Bank is pressured from both left and right to stop its massive, inappropriate projects geared to host-country governments and infrastructures, which have led to some $30 billion of overinvestment in centralized energy projects on a world basis. Conservatives demand the grassroots, private sector approach in the name of the free market, while liberals want less environmental damage and maldistribution of income. Still the blindest spot is hardly addressed, i.e., the informal economy of unpaid productivity, work still uncounted in any national accounting models. These informal sectors still provide the basic safety nets in all societies, even those in the United States, Canada and Western Europe. Sociologists (rather than economists) collect these data, using methods of counting productive hours worked, whether paid or unpaid. Most of these studies, in France, Sweden, Canada and the United Kingdom, show that roughly 50 percent of all productive work is unpaid,[12] while other studies show that fully 80 percent of all the world's capital formation and investment is not monetarized,[13] a fact that millions of subsistence farmers, rural entrepreneurs and most of the world's women know only too well.

Accounting for unpaid production is a way to address price inflation and pinpoint specific ways to keep prices in line with true value. A good example of the problem of per capita averaged income statistics based on only monetarized production is evident in Japan. The U.K. journal, *The Economist*, noted the problem in its 11 June 1988 issue under the headline "Feeling Poor in Japan." The article pointed out that the Japanese GNP-averaged per capita income is the equivalent of $19,200 year (ahead of the U.S.'s $18,200). But when the Organization for Economic Cooperation and Development (OECD) worked out what the money actually buys in each country, i.e., its *purchasing power parity*, Japan looked rather poorer. Each Japanese had only $13,100 compared with the $18,200 for each American. The difference, of course, involves the various quality-of-life indicators.

However, while purchasing power parities are an important new social indicator, they still do not get at the full range of social costs and benefits in each country. In Japan, *The Economist* pointed out, extra consumer goods are consumed in ever more unpleasant surroundings and even New Yorkers have 10 times as much green space per capita, and while Japanese life expectancy is in the 80s, homes are prohibitively expensive due to exorbitant land prices and standard commuter trips to work in cities are over an hour each way. In the U.K. "real" purchasing power has remained flat for over a decade, while nominal wages have increased. One of the key tasks is to examine the unpaid, informal sectors, and where necessary, create barter systems locally, so that real welfare may be increased without increasing wages and inflation. A recent example of such community problem-solving includes the 25 cent vouchers that merchants sell in Berkeley, California, so that people can give them to panhandlers and the homeless sure in the knowledge that they will be exchanged for food, not liquor or cigarettes. Another is from the tightly-knit community of Great Barrington, Massachusetts, where a typical small business encountering the 1991 credit crunch decided to expand his delicatessen by selling "Deli-Dollars" for $9.00 each, which could be redeemed for meals at $10.00 in six months. Such low-cost ways of financing small businesses are legion. Further information can be obtained from the Self-Help Association for a Regional Economy (SHARE) in Great Barrington, Massachusetts. The interchangeability of money and information is a key to building local "information societies" based on barter and skills exchanging networks, in the same way that barter systems are employed when countries wishing to trade with each other do not have foreign exchange for this purpose, as for example, the barter trade between China and the USSR and the 25 percent of all world trade now conducted in such barter, or counter-trade systems. Similarly, the countries in the South could set up highly sophisticated computerized counter-trading networks to create multiple South-South trade systems, bypassing the current financial and trade channels.

The blindness of national accounting

The pressing need to overhaul national accounting as currently defined by the U.N. System of National Accounts (UNSNA) is underlined by Chilean "barefoot economist" Manfred Max-Neef, winner of the Alternative Nobel Prize, who notes that "nearly half of the world's population and over half the inhabitants of the Third World are statistically invisible in economic terms." Hernando de Soto documents the extent of Peru's informal sector, which accounts for 38.9 percent of that country's GDP, in *The Other Path*, while Marilyn Waring dissects the UNSNA statistics to show how they reinforce the domination of women in most countries in *If Women Counted*. President Perez of Venezuela offers a new paradigm for development indexes based on his concept of "integral development" and deals fundamentally with quality of life rather than quantities of goods and services produced. Perez' formula includes: (1) satisfaction of basic needs and to treat humans as indivisible beings; (2) self reliance where possible; and (3) sustainability defined as equitable distribution within in-built environmental standards.

A comprehensive review of existing economic indicators and their reformulation is under way in the United Kingdom, under the auspices of the New Economics Foundation, directed by Victor Anderson. Research in the Netherlands is proceeding along similar lines, based on the work of Roefie Hueting, Wil Albeda and others, including accounting for natural resource stocks and the non-monetarized work in the informal sector. Many researchers in Europe, including the U.K.'s Gershuny and Robertson, Sweden's Ingelstam and Ackerman, Italy's Giarini, Canada's Dyson and Nicholls, and Germany's Huber have studied the non-monetarized informal sectors of production, but as yet these are not included in national accounting in any integral way. Italy's Orio Giarini, author of *Dialogue on Wealth and Welfare* and *The Emerging Service Economy*, believes that it will be necessary to incorporate the non-monetarized sectors in order to understand the post-industrial, services economies now emerging in Europe and North America. James Robertson's *Future Work*, reaches the same conclusion and he has coined the term "ownwork" for the increasing numbers of part-time or self-employed, autonomous workers in the United Kingdom and North America. Indeed, as noted earlier, self-employment is on the rise in the United States, the United Kingdom and other mature industrial countries—sometimes as a result of risk-taking and often due to corporate "downsizing."[14] Both Robertson and Giarini agree that this type of work must be accorded much higher status and part-time work also must gain more prestige, and the encouragement of these new services sectors and their expansion will complement the formal, monetarized sectors. These views accord with my own work in *The Politics of the Solar Age* and that of Scott Burns in *The Household Economy*, as well as, the new U.K. study *Wonted Work*, by Graeme Shankland, Bootstrap Press, NY, 1988.

Re-wholing the population debate:
hawks and doves find common ground

Nowhere has there been more evidence of fragmented thinking as self-defeating than in the field of population policy. But even here, new paradigms are slowly emerging. Population debates in the 1990s will center around issues of North-South equity, ecologically sustainable technologies and, at last, issues concerning the world's women are being addressed.

The population control policy "hawks" of the 1960s tended to focus strictly on gross population increases, particularly in developing countries of the South. The hawks' views were widely perceived as having racist and sexist overtones; the poor, women and even the babies themselves were often portrayed as "the problem." Anxieties about food, resources, scarcity and allocation dominated. Technology was often seen as the answer; condoms, the pill and sterilization programs were the major weapons in this Malthusian struggle. Not surprisingly, head-on clashes ensued between North and South at U.N. conferences on the environment and population in the early 1970s. Developing countries articulated their own theories. From their perspective, the population problem was one of overconsumption and wasted resources in the industrial North.

The "doves" in both North and South argued that, in order to more accurately represent resource consumption patterns, gross population figures should be interpreted differently. For instance, the "Indian Equivalents" formula should be widely encouraged (an American baby's impact on world resources is at least 50 times that of an Indian child). By these calculations, the U.S. population must be figured in the tens of billions, and viewed as the biggest contributor to the global population problem.

The debates between the hawks and doves with their polar-opposite views dominated the 1970s and 1980s, forcing more systemic discussions of the role of technology and the impact of industrialization as interpreted by economists' GNP-measured formulas of growth and progress. Women, the life-givers, and children, the victims, both were still widely ignored in these raging debates.

As worldwide women's movements took off after the U.N. Mexico City Women's Conference in 1975, the population issue deepened to examine more closely the demographic transitions which were assumed to automatically accompany industrialization and GNP growth. Women claimed that not only did this type of development squander the earth's resources, but that the drop in fertility which occurred was more a function of the economic, social and political liberation of women than of industrialization per se. Mature industrial societies in West Europe began to fall toward zero population growth in the late 1980s as women claimed their human rights and opted to have fewer children. At the same time, the cost of raising a child skyrocketed and divorce created legions of struggling single parents—often women. By the late 1980s, policies were

World Population Trend and North-South Distribution

North

South

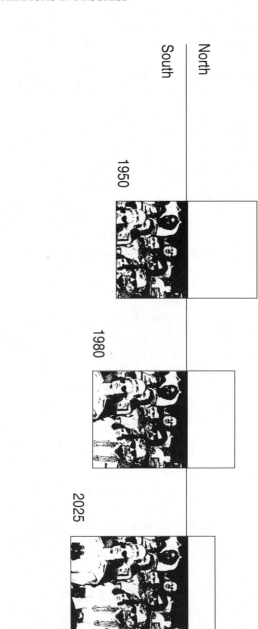

1950

1980

2025

Source: World Paper, Boston, MA 1991

PLATE 4-24

slowly refocused toward women's concerns: education, pre-and post-natal health care, well-baby care, prevention of low birth weight, breast-feeding as the most effective natural contraceptive method and prevention of early childhood diseases and unnecessary infant mortality.

This 20-year evolution of population policies is typified by the shift in focus from Paul and Ann Ehrlich's 1968 book, *The Population Bomb*, written when the world's population was 3.5 billion, to that of their 1990 book, *The Population Explosion*, with today's population at 5.3 billion. While the Ehrlichs still believe that population is the world's number one problem, they have adopted their own Indian Equivalents formula called IPAT: Impact (I) = product of Population size (P), times per capita Affluence (A), times the damage done by Technology (T) used to supply each unit of consumption. Here again a new paradigm was emerging that saw the *problems* created by technology as well as the opportunities. This debate focused around scale, environmental and social impacts and whether specific technologies were undemocratic, centralizing, or decentralizing (such as solar technologies, bicycles, and sewing machines). Schumacher's *Small is Beautiful* catalyzed the debate internationally in 1973. He was one of my mentors and wrote the foreword to my first book, *Creating Alternative Futures* (1978).

While the hawks and doves, the North and South (Plate 4-24: World Population Trend and North-South Distribution), have at last reached some common ground, such as IPAT-like approaches to controlling population growth, there is still a long way to go. Women are still pawns in most of the policies and children are still the victims as the U.N. "State of the World's Children, 1991" report so tragically documents.

The report underlines the unequal development patterns of industrialization which simultaneously marginalize rural people, women and children while over-using resources. Meanwhile only 3 percent of industrial countries' aid in 1986-87 went to health, family planning, education and sanitation programs that are the key priority areas to control population growth. Of course, there is still a body of intellectual opinion, particularly in the United States—typified by columnist Ben Wattenburg, as well as by Julian L. Simon in his latest book, *The Economic Consequences of Immigration* (Basil Blackwell, 1991)—that sees increasing population as a positive, particularly to "spur" economic, GNP-measured growth. These views were much favored by the Reagan administration, supported by the religious right, and led to the U.S. sabotage of many population-stabilization initiatives in the world community during the 1980s. Today, many economists still take the view that a growing population is beneficial to a country's economic progress (see for example *Business Week*, March 12, 1990, "Does America Need More Huddled Masses? Yes").

"The surest way to achieve a sustained decline in fertility is to give a new priority to social or 'women's resources' investment," says Dr. Nafis Sadik, executive director of the U.N. Population Fund, "to improve mother and child health, women's status and education and to make family planning as widely available as possible to both women and men." In the 1990s, the main stumbling blocks to population control in many countries are paternalistic policies which still focus most resources on unsustainable GNP-measured industrial growth, international competition and concomitantly high defense budgets. The troubled situation in the Middle East augurs the shift of conflicts to new levels of struggle between haves and have-nots on a shrinking Planet. Budding international women's policy groups and NGOs believe that today's male-dominated, competitive, international threat systems can never achieve population control—or sustainable, equitable forms of human development.

The November 1991 Women's World Congress of parliamentarians and other leaders, as well as such groups as Africa's Greenbelt movement, India's Chipko movement, the Self-Employed Women's Association, Women's World Banking and many other grassroots organizations advocated restructuring hierarchical national and international institutions to include fuller participation and partnership models. Gender-balance at all decision-making levels is also urgently needed to provide better feedback on impacts of policies on "target" groups. Today, from the World Bank and GATT circles to investment groups, the message is being heard, if not yet heeded: "trickle-down" GNP-growth policies are failing while "trickle-up," micro-enterprise-based, rural development with locally controlled technologies and resources are succeeding.

Even more common ground is emerging. In many statistical offices, it now appears that the status of women is an important overall indicator of development as we see in Chapter Seven, correlating highly with literacy rates, infant mortality declines and advances in life expectancy in new indicators of overall development now vying with GNP. These include the U.N. Development Program's Human Development Index, the Physical Quality of Life Index, World Bank economist Herman Daly's new Index of Sustainable Economic Welfare (ISEW) and my own Country Futures Indicators. Many of these new indicators include status of women and minority populations, human rights and democratic participation, as well as resource depletion and pollution.

Today's cutting edge of population policy will also need to include assessment of the past decade's successes and failures. A key will be found in China, where the greatest human demographic experiment in history has been under way for over a decade: the one-child policy. During the 1980s, as the policy took hold, China was the darling of the population hawks. Now in the 1990s, the social impacts and long-term consequences must be understood. Relatively minor social effects of this program are often reported in popular magazines, such as the new generation of single children, the "little emperors and empresses" and the new breed of psychologists and psychiatrists that are helping parents cope with these children's whims. The more serious consequences of this huge, unprecedentedly swift, demographic transition are still underreported. For example, how will China's current small cohort entering the work force cope with the enormous burden of supporting millions of additional older Chinese citizens with life expectancies of 70 years? What will motivate each of these young "emperors and empresses" to work so hard to support not only both parents, but all the additional surviving elders? In just over a decade, China—still a developing society herself—has taken on the same kind of burdens as the countries of post-industrial West Europe, North America and Japan, where intergenerational conflicts are emerging and social security systems are facing huge strains as few active work force participants must support growing numbers of the aged dependents.

Surely only new global agreements on population control can assure that leaders such as China, as well as Singapore (another early experimenter), will not fall off the population control wagon, as is now beginning to happen. An approach might be a North-South Population Credit Bank, where successful policies could be rewarded. Using IPAT, or similar measures, new "sustainable development credits" could be extended to such countries for reducing their impact on global resources. Hopefully, many hawks and doves can find such new common ground in the 1990s as we humans learn that managing our global commons will require many such win-win negotiations.

Concerning the media: redefining progress

Lastly, we need to remember that our mass media is the nervous system of our body politic and here too, there are serious paradigm problems. The problem with economic news today is that most of it comes from economists. And economists are trained to deal with statistics, not with people.

To give us a true and whole picture of world—or national—development, media need to go beyond the numbers to serious consideration of what constitutes human development. Journalists need to think about development and human needs in the context of other disciplinary frameworks, because the economic framework is so inadequate. If I were an editor of a network news program covering economic issues, I would be exploring all of the other figures that would be much better indicators of human well-being. For example, I would want to know what the World Health Organization had to say about comparative life expectancy and childhood mortality in various countries. And then I'd check with the U.N. Environment Program on how well various countries protect citizens' water and air quality. I would go to Amnesty International and look at comparative data on political freedom, and to educational organizations for literacy rates and other measurements of individuals' development.

All of these indicators of societal progress are readily available—it's just that they are overlooked by most editors or considered less important than GNP statistics. Even more significant, editors would understand that economists were not collecting this data. They would consult multidisciplinary researchers, including anthropologists, ecologists and sociologists. In fact, sociologists often collect the most significant economic data in a society, because they study the number of productive hours people actually work, whether paid or unpaid. They measure time spent parenting, volunteering in a community, homemaking, in subsistence agriculture, as well as paid labor.

In fact, to spot and interpret trends editors must think through what kind of existing quantitative statistics actually measure whether a society is making progress. In almost every case, economic data had very little relevance, and per capita income, which is what the GNP is all about, proved to be a very weak indicator of the quality of life. In fact, trying to run a complex society on a single indicator like the Gross National Product is literally like trying to fly a 747 with only one gauge on the instrument panel. There would be nothing there to tell you whether the wing flaps were up or down, whether the fuel tank was full or what the altitude was. In effect, you'd be flying blind. Or imagine if your doctor, when giving you a check up, did no more than check your blood pressure!

Of course, on television and in most general media you find almost nothing but the standard measures, which thanks to inflation and currency fluctuations are worse than useless—they're meaningless. Perhaps the most serious paradigm problem with U.S. media is their dedication to commercialism. Funded as they are by advertising, it is hard to see how messages about conserving, *and reducing* consumption are going to get through. Many of our drug problems and other dependencies are exacerbated by constant messages which tend to feed these addictions.

The Center for the Study of Commercialism in Washington addresses these issues head-on, as does, the crusading magazine *Media and Values* in Los Angeles.

Chapter Four Footnotes

1. Hazel Henderson, *The Politics of the Solar Age: Alternatives to Economics,* Chapter 13, current edition from Knowledge Systems, Inc., Indianapolis, 1988.

2. See for example, *Opening the Marketplace To Small Enterprise*, Ton de Wilde, Styntje Schreurs with Arleen Richman which describes this "Small is Beautiful" approach, Kumarian Press, W. Hartford, CT, 1991.

3. *State of the World's Children, 1991*, UNICEF, United Nations, NY.

4. *Business Week,* "America's Income Gap," April 17, 1989.

5. *Business Week,* "What Happened to the American Dream?," August 19, 1991, page 80.

6. See for example, *Rethinking the Future: The Correspondence between Geoffrey Vickers and Adolph Lowe*, Foreword by Robert Heilbroner, Editor Jeanne Vickers, Transaction Publishers, New Brunswick, NJ, 1991.

7. See for example, Severyn T. Bruyn, *A Future for the American Economy: The Social Market,* which explores the growth of awareness of problems caused by blind adherence to profit and markets. Stanford University Press, CA, 1991.

8. For examples of the application of this criterion to diverse fields of inquiry see *Healing the World . . . and Me*, edited by Mark Macy, Knowledge Systems, 1991.

9. *Global Warming Watch*, Public Health Institute with the Oil, Chemical and Atomic Workers Union, NY, Volume 1 Number 4, August 1991.

10. "Business climate" models include those developed by accounting firms for their corporate clients, such as those of Grant Thornton Inc. of Chicago, IL. These are now giving way to more realistic models by other firms, such as SRI International of California and the Corporation for Enterprise Development of Washington, DC.

11. Katsumi Yokota, *I Among Others* (1991) in English, from Seikatsu Club Seikyo Kanagawa, Kawaasa Building 3F, 2-11-5 Shin Yokohama, Kohoku-ku, Yokohama, Japan, 222.

12. *The Informal Economy* (see notes, Chapter Six) and Plate 1-5: Three Layer Cake With Icing.

13. Orio Giarini, *Dialogue on Wealth and Welfare*, Pergamon Press, London and NY, 1980.

14. See for example, the boom in guidebooks to help "electronic cottagers" with making their home-based enterprises successful: Three 1991 titles by the "gurus" of home business and self-employment, Paul and Sarah Edwards are *The Best Home Businesses for the 90s, Making It On Your Own,* and *Getting Business to Come To You* (all from Tarcher Press, Los Angeles, CA).

Ode to the Life Force

A pair of butterflies
Pollinating, propagating,
Flitting above
The long procession of cultures
Find themselves on pious, glorious day
Scanning the vast blue Bay
That Drake "discovered"
For the English.

Today it teems
With myriad sights, sounds and smells
Cable cars and seafood-sated pilgrims,
Multitudes of sails and wings.
Traders all—
Some human-scaled, warm vendors
Schooled in China's ancient way.
Some grown monstrous,
Dinosaurs drably-garbed
In faceless buildings
In a dark canyon
They call "Montgomery."

An odd couple
Meeting in mythic space.
This Isis and Osiris
Wend a way named "Grant"
Dodging firecrackers,
          and dancing sneakered dragons
Right at home, trading, scenting,
          feeling out the nectar.
Finding Holy Pollen in a treasure trove
Of old earrings and long-lost
Oriental silks.
Homely treasures these,
Celebrating the Human Family
To stash away, re-form and then
Re-offer to the world.

These butterflies in friendly hoardes
Dance ahead of cultures
Up and down history's colonnades
Attracting and seducing,
Pointing to new ways,
Beckoning new Elysian Fields.
Clouds of gentle, happy warriors,
Transmuting raw power to songs
And visions of Becoming.

Many follow, some curious,
Some with nets
Seeking to capture and
Impale the flitting wings.
But the alchemists elude—now
Slippery FISH!
Their enzyme mission asks
That they be free.
Free to love the universal Grail
Free to weave the sacred threads
That bind all life
On many-splendored GAIA.

So they flutter on
Dancing, sipping earthly joys and fears
Dreams and nightmares,
Swimming in the dark
Cycling and re-cycling seeds, ideas,
Earth gems and flowers
Arrowheads lost in burial grounds and strife
All blooming unseen.
Re-arranging Earth's treasures
Planting feather flags
Of Universal Life.

These two are humble creatures yet,
Decked not in gorgeous monarchs' wings,
But in simple guise
As common yellow butterflies.
To better attune to other
Mortal beings.
Commonsense for all
Who can hear their call:
A simple song in praise of beauty
And evolution's
Ever-lasting faith.

New Adam and New Eve,
Ever sifting cultures of the past
In awe and wonder
Re-discover the sacred scriptures
In a Polynesian Boat,
A Hopi Ceremony.
Wild Man and Wild Woman.
At home in many jungles:
Of culture, concrete or greenery.
Both strong and fragile
Forever loving and
Forever Free.

New Man and New Woman
Fierce in their pledge to care
To nuture the future's rare
Unfolding.
Both praise Change and
Sing Mutation's ode
While honoring DNA's stable living code.
They sing anew of the Divine Child
For babies everywhere anew,
For all the world's eternal young
For ever-changing GAIA, blue
Earth Mother
Orbiting in our hearts
And in Eternity.

Beyond the Battle of the Sexes

Today, not surprisingly, the rich new yeast of alternative ideas—cultural, spiritual, and action alternatives—are coming from "wild card" scientists not intimidated by their peers, and precisely those groups suppressed or subordinated during the industrial era, which demanded more and more conformity. Every culture is a system of expressions and repressions of the full spectrum of human ways of being and behaving. Today we see these alternatives emerging from the world's ethnic and indigenous peoples, subsistence cultures and from traditional wisdom, from the world's women and from the rising female principle and its nutrient energies seen in the new breed of gentle men.

Their quest has begun in earnest in the United States, spurred by poet Robert Bly and by Bill Moyer's popularization of the works of Joseph Campbell. The "men's group" phenomenon rated a cover story in *Newsweek*, June 24, 1991, entitled "What do Men Want?" It portrayed the "new man," bare to the waist, with a business tie still round his neck, a baby on one hip and an African drum on the other. These men are throwing off the shackles of industrial "macho," the need to compete with each other and the fearful need to control, dominate and "own" not only each other, but women, children, animals, plants and all of Mother Nature. Psychologists know that these unhealthy drives are rooted in the fear of death, the sense of alienation from the natural world produced at the breakdown of the bi-cameral mind and reinforced by Western, dualistic culture. As Ken Wilber notes in *Up From Eden* (Anchor Books, 1981), "Whenever there is *other*, there is fear." Any separate, egoistic consciousness, to the extent that it feels separated from all life, will fear its individual death as a final extinction, a total loss of meaning that must

133

lead to existential anxiety. This fear has underlain thousands of years of dualism in human cultures. It has shaped Western art, literature and scholarship from Aristotle and his either/or logical axiom—the Law of Excluded Middle (A cannot be equal to not-A). These same fears of death and loss of meaning led to the neurotic notion of scientific objectivity, eventually laid to rest, if not taken to heart, by the physics of Werner Heisenberg and his Uncertainty Principle. We see fear in the long saga of patriarchal literature, from the Greek myths of the hero and the hero's journey to the angst and alienation from Nature echoed from Hegel, Marx and the Frankfurt School to Hermann Hesse, the existentialists and Sigmund Freud and his followers.

My belief is that this kind of scholarship of separation and "objectified" mode of experience, together with reductionist Cartesian science is now becoming another cul-de-sac: mental games of infinite regress terminating in a logical double-bind. This may be one more aspect of the dilemma of patriarchal societies. For this anxiety about "alienation" is, I venture, a somewhat more masculine experience. Since biologically, humans do come in two asymmetrical bodily forms, it is obviously different to experience life in a male and a female body. Biologically, most women in the world do still vividly experience their embeddedness in Nature, and can harbor few illusions concerning their freedom and separateness from the cycles of birth and death. Men's experience may give them a sense of having somewhat more freedom and individualism, and for the past 6,000 years this sense, together with the alienation it brings, has been amplified. All patriarchal culture, scholarship, institutions and history have reflected and amplified male experiencing and then universalized it as if it were human experience. Of course, it is not, as sensitively explored by Mark Gerzon in *A Choice of Heroes* (Houghton Mifflin, 1982). But women, until quite recently have been relatively silent about their own experience, and herstory, which as we know from feminist literature and art is radically different. Women's spirituality is coming to the fore, as for example with Barbara Marx Hubbard's radical re-visioning of the Christian tradition in *The Book of Co-Creation* (1992). Women's spirituality affirms and celebrates human embeddedness in Nature and confirms it by researching the early matrifocal cultures and humanity's great universal religion, that of the Great Mother Goddess. Philosopher Charlene Spretnak reinterprets major wisdom traditions in her brilliant new book, *States of Grace:*(HarperCollins, 1991).

Today's eco-feminism is restoring this earlier pre-history, and its art and rituals celebrating Nature as an order that is, in principle, not fully-knowable because humans are a part of it. The most influential study of this pre-historical period is *The Chalice and the Blade* by Riane Eisler (HarperCollins, 1987) which also drew on the groundbreaking research of the University of California archeologist Marija Gimbutas. Eco-feminism resacralizes Nature. It understands the heuristic value of uncertainty, which allows each generation to reformulate its experience, cognition, epistemology and value-systems in light of new conditions. Uncertainty is valuable because it keeps us awake and aware, whereas certainty and exactitude allow us to "hard-program" our responses to our environment, become rigid or mentally fall asleep. Eco-feminism also values motherhood and the parenting and raising of children and the maintaining of comfortable habitats and cohesive communities as the *most highly productive* work of society—rather than the most devalued— as under patriarchal values and economics, where these tasks are taken for granted and unpaid.

Patriarchal scholarship is now arriving at an understanding of many of these more subtle patterns of society, sometimes experientially, as many of the support systems provided by women break down. In traditional science, it is also arriving at the understanding that alienation and the ego-individualist, dualistic view may have been a trick of the mind. These insights of indigenous science are networked around the Planet by such scholars as lawyer, Riane Eisler; biologists Lynn Margulis, (co-researcher of the Gaia Hypothesis) and Elisabet Sahtouris, author of *Gaia: The Human Journey from Chaos to Cosmos*; and anthropologist Pam Colorado, founder of The World Indigenous Science Network. Amazingly these new insights of holism are now being reached through the anomalies and paradigm shifts in patriarchal science itself, as *intellectual* exercises, in new theories embracing these subtle indeterminacies. They include concerns as expressed by physicist, David Bohm, with the *implicate* order rather than the *explicate*, and the new, open view of a surprising, living, autopoetic, evolving universe, as in the work of Sheldrake and Prigogine, as well as that of David Peat, Karl Pribram, Gregory Bateson, Erich Jantsch, E.F. Schumacher, Fritjof Capra, Humberto Maturana, Francisco Varela, Heinz von Foerster, James Lovelock, Ludwig von Bertalanffy, Ken Wilber, René Thom, Manfred Eigen, C.H. Waddington, Kenneth Boulding, Henryk Skolimowski, and others.

This new stream of scholarship, together with the enormously rich body of knowledge grounded in ecology, can be summed up as *eco-philosophy,* and it represents the simultaneous culmination, miniaturization, compression and transcending of Cartesian forms of representation and

Changing Views of "Human Nature"

Traditional View :

human nature as immutable, e.g. in economic theory : greed, selfishness, competition insatiability as fundamental (Darwin, Hobbes, Bentham, etc.)

Emerging Views :

"human potential", self-development, growth, under-utilized brain-power, physical-power bio-feedback, exploration of "yogic" feats, etc.

e.g.

The Possible Human (Houston)
   Paradigm Shift (Bateson, Capra, Thompson, Henderson)
   New Ethics and Lifestyles (Todd, Rodale, Jackson, Lovins)
   New Communities (Davidson & McLaughlin)
   New Brain-Mind Research (Pribram, Ferguson)
   New Spirituality (Soleri, Thompson, Morton, Spretnak, Daly, Marx-Hubbard)
   Morphogenetic Fields (Sheldrake)
   Psychotectonic Shift (Fuller, Weiskopf, Sorokin)
   (shift in moral understanding, e.g. slavery repealed)
   (from conforming to critical reason, "idea whose time has come")

Interactions Between:

1. perceived critical issue
2. technology
3. change in human awareness

Plus :

STRESS
COGNITIVE DISSONANCE
CULTURAL CONFUSION

BREAKDOWN
(of disabling
belief-system)

→

BREAKTHROUGH
(new personal
cultural visions)

→

EVOLUTION

PLATE 5-25

represented by *eco-feminism* documents precisely the same set of insights, but, as in Oriental modes of cognition and representation, eco-feminism has arrived at them ***experientially***. Thus, there has been up to now, almost no communication between eco-philosophy and eco-feminism, because they have approached the same phenomena, but from different directions. Eco-feminism has considered the glittering cathedrals (abstract, mathematical, rational, patriarchal exposition of this human oneness) as *intellectual* labor about the banal and almost trivial. ("What's all the fuss and debate about? Doesn't *every*body know/feel that in their bones?") On the other hand, eco-philosophy senses this disinterest, and assumes that women are just not up for such heroic scientific strivings. ("After all, the hero's journey is a male trip.") Besides, those feminist books are so "fuzzy" and unreadable, not to mention threatening, with their celebration of goddesses, trees, orgies, circles, vibrations, dances, sexuality, analogy, songs, witches, spirits, fertility, baals, devas, mystery, hedonism, and letting-go, in acceptance of our bodies, pain, decay, entropy and the endless cycle of birth and death.

I believe that these two separate streams of scholarship and world views are now beginning to flow together and augur a new cultural synthesis, as well as a more androgynized consciousness flowering in men and women. The communication is still halting and fraught with old fears, resentments and insecurities. Younger men try hard to manifest their feminine qualities, take more responsibility for children and deny their wilder "macho" urges. For these efforts they are often scorned by peers and older men and sometimes by the women in their lives as well. Unreconstructed patriarchal men take refuge in Rambo images and male pursuits, while ambivalent men try to find their submerged "wild man" and learn to channel, rather than fear, his drives. Women escalate their denouncements of patriarchal society and sue more frequently for date rape and widespread sexual harassment on the job. Never has the battle of the sexes become quite so bitter. The highly charged Clarence Thomas confirmation hearings for the U.S. Supreme Court have made it clear that males and females still largely inhabit two different cultures. The communications have only just begun. We must deal not only with the nature of harassment, but also with the broader social ramifications of the battle. Some men retaliate with escalating domestic violence, and others leave their partners to parent offspring alone. The cycles of blaming and victimizing between men and women may signal yet another paradigm shift: women must move beyond their "instinctive" maternal drive while men must move beyond the familiar animal male drives of mutual competition, female conquest, and territoriality. If we are to prescribe for today's almost terminal illness of human societies, we must dig deeply for our diagnoses. We can no longer skate around observing surface manifestations, such as those offered by economists: unemployment, inflation, declining productivity, the need for national security, stopping communism, restoring the free market, more innovation, supply to meet demand, and all the rest of the *psychotic* language of alienation, fear and insecurity.

Emerging from the age of the phenotype

The most enduring tensions in the human pysche have concerned alienation and fear of death of the ego, and the conflict these feelings generated between the perceived individual will and the requirements of the group or society. These fears not only led to what I have called the "Kilroy Was Here" syndrome often mistaken for crude, "macho" behavior or patriarchal urges, where immortality is attempted via leaving one's mark on the environment, whether in the urge to create monuments or clear-cut a forest. These drives have always been part of the fundamental conflict that has preoccupied all political science, social control theories and governance, as well as views of what constituted "Human Nature," its goodness or evil, and various mixes around the spectrum of anarchy and authoritarianism.

I believe there is a deeper layer underlying these old power issues, whether between males and females or the *individual* versus the *state*. Today, we may explore these power issues so as to shed more light on why matrifocal cultures and religions were overthrown and led to the rise of patriarchal culture, itself now collapsing. Perhaps the deeper and biologically irreconcilable conflict is that of the individual human *phenotype* versus the species *genotype*. Nature is always profligate with phenotypes, since diversity and range of experimentation requires a profusion of these fresh generations of finite forms interacting with every successive set of unique environmental conditions. Only a statistically insignificant number of phenotypes ever produce a genetically useful innovation of form or function that survives and is incorporated into the human gene pool. From the perspective of the genotype (the species as a whole) the fate of each individual phenotype is irrelevant. Now for *other* species, this ignominious fate may not produce a psychological conflict in the phenotype. At least, we have not sufficiently learned to communicate with other life forms (such as whales, dolphins or chimpanzees) to know, one way or the other. But we do know that humans possess this unusual bicameral mind, which is aware of being aware of ourselves. We live as phenotypes with will and purposes beyond that of our species genotype and move beyond the pre-human embedded consciousness of our ontological experience as well as the phylogenetic infant experience of oneness with the mother and the world.

I believe that the matrifocal period of human development may have had at its core a value-system tilted toward the genotype, in its celebration of the *processes* of life—its change cycles, seasons, and subtle forces, as well as the positive value of decay, entropy and death—which allows the grand experiment of evolution to unfold. Phenotypes whether males or females *must* die if each new generation—our children—are to have their chance. But the dying of the body on the material plane of existence is also one more transition (if we have a larger view of ourselves as an integral part of the creation, temporarily constituted as a sensory cell of the body of Gaia) and also has a transcendent dimension, as our spiritual traditions describe. I believe that the early revolts, often by males, against the Mother Goddess-worshipping societies were partly the agonized scream of the phenotypes' newly-individuated ego-awareness rebelling against the great implacable Goddess/Mother/Earth—the genotype's metaphor that decreed its sacrifice and death-sentence. Much folk-lore suggests that matrifocal cultures existed before sexual intercourse was recognized as causally-related to the birth of children. Naturally, women would have been viewed with wonder—as goddesses with the power to bring forth life—particularly if they could guard this secret by ritualizing intercourse via group orgies. In this way males may have been kept in intoxicated ignorance of their role in procreation. This hypothesis may explain the very deeply-buried fear of women, mother and Earth and its mythic connection with decay, entropy and death, which has preoccupied mythology and has recently been examined in male psychology.[1]

We may now be leaving this period of the revolt of the individuated ego-awareness of both males and females alike. The Age of the Phenotype, when individuated men and women explored the world together with their upright postures and opposing thumbs, was naturally a period of experimentation with the natural world—"moving the furniture around." Today, this individuated, manipulative consciousness in both males and females has become amplified into untenable forms of dualism driving the patriarchal epoch. This Age of the Phenotype with its brilliant creativity in manipulating Nature and human culture and biology, is now culminating in the explosion of Cartesian science, technology, explicitly-managed institutions and governance and the global spread of industrialism. The human species learned much in this extraordinary period—almost too much in this individuated ego/mental/manipulative mode for our own good, as we now face the possibility of accidentally annihilating ourselves.

Reintegrating the genotype

The emerging culture is rebalancing by including repressed ways of being, based on the heart as well as the mind: feeling, sharing, intuition, acceptance of uncertainty, decay as well as growth, transcendence of ego-death fears and letting go of the need to control and "own" each other and the world around us. This emerging culture seems also to be rebalancing toward concern for the genotype and evolution (for example, in the concern over nuclear radiation, mutagenic chemicals and other inter-generational transfers of risk about which economics and political science can say little). Therefore, there seems to be no going back to rugged individualism, or the frontier self-sufficient lifestyle of which the survivalists dream, with their shelters, dried food, Geiger counters and guns. Nor can we return to the individualistic, private property-based security promised by the Libertarians, who would repeal government but do not seem to notice that the Fortune 500 would still be there to take over our government overtly.

However, many Libertarian proposals for repealing oppressive, bureaucratic restrictions and laws on personal behavior of and between consenting adults are very useful—whether in facing down the Moral Majority's efforts to control our private sex lives and lifestyle preferences, or the Catholic church's anti-abortion campaigns and their far-out definition of when human life begins, which if enacted, would mean the risk of jail for millions of Americans. But all this too smacks of the same fears of the old patriarchs who still send their sons to fight and die for them and seek to "own" their women and children in male-authoritarian families (now revealed as rife with violence, repression, wife-battering, incest and child-abuse). Hilkka Pietila and Jeanne Vickers, *Making Women Matter, The Role of the United Nations* (Zed Books, 1991), document how far even the United Nations must still progress if it is to genuinely champion women's rights. The patriarchs also want to continue dominating the Earth, exploiting its forests, minerals and land. They are also correct in being fearful of the rising, ecologically-aware, androgynized concern for the future and the species as a whole: the remembering of the Genotype in the context of new planetary culture. Fear underlies the Politics of Denial, the strip-mining and exploitation, the mean-spirited, sexist economics of George Gilder's *Wealth and Poverty* (1980), and the rearguard actions of the Moral Majority as it attempts to put totalled women back in the kitchen, gay people back in the closet and Blacks and Hispanics back at the end of the line. The Heritage and Coors foundations both fund the new right's assault on "political correctness" as today's multi-ethnic campuses wrestle with race and gender, North and South, and Eurocentric versus pluralistic global curricula. U.S. right-wing efforts to parody the concerns in communities and on campuses to incorporate America's new multi-ethnic needs as "political correctness" bore fruit. Mass media dutifully picked up the paradigm. *Time* and *Newsweek* as well as pseudo-sophisticated TV shows including McNeil-Lehrer News Hour agonized over the issue as framed—rarely pointing out its genesis in the always resourceful conservative think tanks. Yet the genie will not go back in the bottle—the cultural revolution has already occurred.

Politics only ratifies social change after at least a ten-year lag. Even more terrifying for the old patriarchs and their female dupes is the knowledge that the whole culture is "up for grabs." For example, it could shift fundamentally in less than a generation IF women simply took back their reproductive rights, endowed by biology and Nature. All that women would need to do to create a quiet revolution is to resume the old practice of keeping the paternity of their children a secret. As Margaret Mead always stressed, motherhood is a biological fact—fatherhood is a social convention. In one stroke, the male-dominated family, the institutions of inheritance, of property rights in wives and children would be undermined. Accumulation of great landholdings and estates would be less likely and land trusts and different, more consensual, democratized families and social groups might emerge. Children, in whatever group settings they were raised would have rights as persons, rather than being "legitimized" by a marriage contract. Indeed, we now have to face up to the fact that the traditional nuclear family with breadwinner father, homemaking mother and two children only comprises 12 percent of all U.S. families, and the 85 percent of welfare payments to support children in Aid to Dependent Families goes to women and children of divorced fathers, who refuse to pay child support ordered by the courts. Already the case for defending the nuclear family is becoming a lost cause. Indeed, it is this explosion of the nuclear family that is now ripping through our society with megaton force—another dimension of change that we are forced to face, along with the build-up of CO_2 in our atmosphere, the destruction of the planet's great equatorial forests, the sacrificing of the Amazonian basin to Brazil's desperate need to pay its foreign debts, and the instabilities in the global monetary system.

Only biological, morphogenetic models of change can encompass and help us see the planetary transformation now occurring in so many dimensions simultaneously. Further, the United States is now revealed as a country where neglect of its children is almost pathological as noted in the previous chapter. The faithful work of Marian Wright Edeleman and her Children's Defense Fund of Washington, DC, has kept a lonely vigil on Capitol Hill addressing this neglect. Both eco-philosophy and eco-feminism have shown the capacity to deal with such dimensions of breakdown and breakthrough. Their synthesis—together with insights from ecology and general systems theory, as well as many of the spiritual traditions and the perennial philosophy they share—may provide the ethics and the value-systems for the Solar Age.

The synthesis of eco-philosophy and eco-feminism, as I have tried to show, is now being midwived by both women and men, many of whom I am honored to call my friends, in works such as William Irwin Thompson's *The Time Falling Bodies Take To Light* (St. Martin's Press, 1981); Fritjof Capra's *The Turning Point* (Simon & Schuster, 1982); James Robertson's *The Sane Alternative* (River Basin Press, 1980); Philip Slater's *Wealth Addiction* (1981); Theodore Roszak's *Person/Planet* (1979); Kirkpatrick Sale's *Human Scale* (McCann & Hagan,1981); Mark Gerzon's *A Choice of Heroes* (1982) and *Coming Into Our Own* (1991); and Philip Slater's *A Dream Deferred* (1991). The brilliant and extraordinary outpouring of eco-feminist literature in the past two decades has opened a rich vein of alternative social analysis, from Gloria Steinem, Adrienne Rich, and Mary Daly, summarized in Charlene Spretnak's *The Politics of Women's Spirituality*. (See also the further reading list at the end of this chapter.)[2]

Love—our most renewable resource

Because billions of years ago the Earth's living organisms progressed from cell division to the extraordinary innovation of sexual reproduction, humans are forever trying to come to terms with its consequences: sexuality and death. These two great issues have provided a continual challenge to philosophers, scientists, and almost every member of our species (and we also have assumed that our particular form of self-awareness made them exclusively human problems).

With the arrival in 1987 of the five billionth member of the human family, together with the postwar innovation of reliable birth control, our range of responses to our sexuality has expanded with bewildering rapidity in varying spheres—from medical ethics and religion to political and economic choices as well as art, philosophy, and myth. The last several decades have been ones of upheaval, experimentation, and, above all, confusion, producing excitement and joy at the new freedoms as well as much pain, misunderstanding, loneliness, and fear. Deep religious beliefs are challenged; families are divided; economic institutions are restructured and laws changed. The farthest reaches of sexual behavior and all forms of pornography and commercial exploitation have been explored; sexuality has been explicated with such clinical detail as to become banal.

The new technical means of reproduction, from *in vitro* and *in vivo* fertilization to surrogacy, have changed the definition of parenthood, while immortalists with cryogenic dreams of future lives have joined the medical professionals in redefining death. For all these reasons, we are forced to reconsider our most basic feelings: love, fear, and the meaning of life itself. Deep existential questions reemerge in books and art, even in Madison Avenue consumer surveys. Will we take refuge from our fear by tightening traditional bonds of family and romantic love? Or will we leap into the unknown—by redefining love in this Age of Interdependence as planetary citizenship—and learn to celebrate our common bonds as members of the whole human family?

Many of us will have no choice but to continue to explore these new frontiers of relationship. National boundaries and identities are blending in a new global melting pot. Seven great globalization processes (as mentioned in Chapter Two) are steadily increasing our interdependence— technology and production; work and migration; militarization and the arms race; environmental degradation; finance, trade, and debt; and consumption and culture, produce the seventh, realignment and domestic restructuring of nations in response. Thus, these globalization processes are highly interactive, dynamic, nonlinear, irreversible, and therefore accelerating. This planetary change is taking place in what I called in Chapter Two the three zones of human experience: the Breakdown Zone, where national and institutional restructuring occurs amid pollution and cultural confusion; the Bifurcation Zone, where individuals, families, and communities are trying to reframe their values and career choices; and the Breakthrough Zone, where successful adjustments occur and old ideologies give way to new social terrain, new goals, and new criteria for success.

One critical shift will entail a new view of love. Romantic love between men and women entered Western culture in fourteenth-century Europe, and perhaps earlier in other cultures. Obviously, this form of male-female relationship has served humanity well—providing for stable child-rearing beyond the primeval tribe. However, today in many industrial and postindustrial societies this dyadic form is failing. Divorce is increasing, giving rise to ever-more single parent families (most often headed by women). Gay and lesbian couples and intentional living groups of unrelated individuals are more common. The traditional Western ideal of finding "Mr. or Ms. Right" and settling down to lifelong monogamy has been fading since the sixties.

The emotional security of monogamous marriage came at the price of narrowed horizons, boredom, and lack of educational stimulation. As shown in many thousands of case studies, if one partner experiences a spurt of growth, the relationship can rupture. Other stresses on dyads have been exposed by women's movements in many countries, where traditional marriage has too often proved to be the breeding ground of violence, incest, and child neglect—far from its benign image.

In today's social upheavals, it behooves us to redefine what we mean by "love" as we examine new and extended expressions of caring, as well as the nurture of both children and the increasing number of elderly adults. Will it remain an almost exclusively dyadic term with its ubiquitous sexual and parental overtone? Or can its definition be broadened so as to expand our abilities to care for each other as a whole—in a new, global, interdependent, multicultural sense of the human family? The exclusivity associated with love implies that it is a scarce commodity, which if bestowed too widely will be "watered down" and lead to shallow relationships, lack of commitment, or promiscuity.

It's time to reexamine such assumptions. It is not love that is scarce. In fact, many people in modern societies suffer from frustration of their loving expressions, due to alienation and technologically mediated isolation deriving from TV, computer terminals, and highrise, anonymous architecture, and, in the West, the cults of individualism and competition. Certainly our time is limited by death, but we need not hoard our love, or give it to only one other of the opposite sex and to our immediate family. Viewing love as a scarce commodity puts us in a state of anxiety, fear of abandonment, and jealousy.

Suppose we change our premise and view love as something abundant and natural that we can call forth in ourselves and others by changing our attitudes. We can gradually move beyond both the purely procreative stage of sexually-focused love between men and women and the recreationally-focused sex of the sixties and seventies with its immaturity and lack of commitment.

We humans must escape the prison of gender, with its often immature baggage of romantic love, sex, rivalry, and fear, and learn the deeper lessons of unconditional love—the only love worthy of the name. A conscious effort to expand and exercise our capacities for loving and altruistic, cooperative behavior is now crucial if we are to survive in this Age of Interdependence.

Today, individualist greed and competition are failing us. Rebalancing toward our equal—but unrewarded—abilities to build community is now vital. We can no longer hope to "own" each other, or hang on to "entitlements" to love that are not freely and reciprocally given and renewed in loving community. Caring is, in fact, already a burgeoning new industry—with daycare, medical and counseling services, and home helpers—which has grown up almost by default. Millions of women who used to provide these services free in the home have already moved into the job market to obtain recognition and income. The monetarizing of caring work recognizes formerly unaccounted productivity that subsidized the official, money-dominated, GNP-measured sector (see Plate 1-5: Three Layer Cake With Icing).

All that is required is to recognize our existing cooperation and altruism, ignored by economists since it is invisible to their models. Indeed, economic theory assumes altruism is irrational! (Sociologists have measured unpaid productivity, as mentioned earlier; and while in industrial countries, unpaid work accounts for some 50 percent or more of all productive work, in traditional societies, the percentage is much larger.) When unpaid, caring work is made visible and accounted for in law and custom, then the expansion of our altruistic capabilities becomes possible and measurable. The caregivers in society will be accorded appropriately high status and be rewarded by recognition and emulation.

Thus we may begin to see how love was made artificially scarce by our social and economic arrangements (along with so many other commodities). A new sense of genuine abundance can nurture human development and move us toward an end to the battle of the sexes. In fact, living more fully in widening circles of creative, loving relationship can extend our life spans and make death less fearful. We have, at last, reached the stage of evolution when altruism has become pragmatic.

Chapter Five Footnotes

1.Wolfgang Lederer, MD, *The Fear of Women*, Harvest Books, Harcourt Brace Jovanovich Inc., New York, 1968.
2. Also recommended highly:
Linda E. Olds, *Fully Human*, Spectrum Books Prentice Hall, NY, 1981.
Eva Keuls, *The Reign of the Phallus*, HarperCollins, NY 1985.
Mary Daly, *Pure Lust*, Beacon Press, Boston, 1984.
Elise Boulding, *Women in the Twentieth Century*, Halsted Press, John Wiley, NY 1977.

Country Futures Indicators™

beyond money-denominated, per-capita averaged growth of GNP

Re-formulated GNP to Correct Errors and Provide More Information:

- **PURCHASING POWER PARITY (PPP)** corrects for currency fluctuations
- **INCOME DISTRIBUTION** is the poverty gap widening or narrowing?
- **COMMUNITY BASED ACCOUNTING** to complement current enterprise-basis
- **INFORMAL, HOUSEHOLD SECTOR PRODUCTION** measures all hours worked (paid and unpaid)
- **DEDUCT SOCIAL & ENVIRONMENTAL COSTS** a "net" accounting avoids double counting
- **ACCOUNT FOR DEPLETION OF NON-RENEWABLE RESOURCES** analogous to a capital consumption deflator
- **ENERGY INPUT/GDP RATIO** measures energy efficiency, recycling
- **MILITARY/CIVILIAN BUDGET RATIO** measures effectiveness of governments
- **CAPITAL ASSET ACCOUNT FOR BUILT INFRASTRUCTURE AND PUBLIC RESOURCES** (Many economists agreed this is needed. Some include environment as a resource.)

Complementary Indicators of Progress Toward Society's Goals

- **POPULATION** birth rates, crowding, age distribution
- **EDUCATION** literacy levels, school dropout and repetition rates
- **HEALTH** infant mortality, low birth weight, weight/height/age
- **NUTRITION** e.g. calories per day, protein/carbohydrates ratio, etc.
- **BASIC SERVICES** e.g. access to clean water, etc.
- **SHELTER** housing availability/quality, homelessness, etc.
- **PUBLIC SAFETY** crime
- **CHILD DEVELOPMENT** World Health Organization, UNESCO, etc.
- **POLITICAL PARTICIPATION AND DEMOCRATIC PROCESS** e.g. Amnesty International data, money-influence in elections, electoral participation rates
- **STATUS OF MINORITY AND ETHNIC POPULATIONS AND WOMEN** e.g. Human rights data
- **AIR AND WATER QUALITY AND ENVIRONMENTAL POLLUTIONS LEVELS** air pollution in urban areas
- **ENVIRONMENTAL RESOURCE DEPLETION** hectares of land, forests lost annually
- **BIO DIVERSITY AND SPECIES LOSS** e.g. Canada's environmental indicators
- **CULTURE, RECREATIONAL RESOURCES** e.g. Jacksonville, Florida

PLATE 6-26

The Indicators Crisis
Toward Post-Economic Policy Tools
for Post-Industrial Societies

As described in the preceding chapters, we now can see that most of today's global crises—the arms race, famine, pollution, crime, addiction and social breakdown—are symptomatic of deeper crises of human perception. Many futurists, philosophers and leaders now can see this deeper crisis as nothing less than the shifting of the entire belief-system that undergirded the Industrial Revolution, as we approach some as yet ill-defined "post-industrial" future.

Such shifting of a culture's belief-system is not new in human affairs; in fact, such paradigm shifts occur with great regularity as even more fundamental shifts in our climate, environment and resources have forced humans to change and respond with new ideas, behavior and technical inventions. These interacting shifts in our circumstances and behavior, (see Part II of *The Politics of the Solar Age*) are, of course, the stuff of all human history. One of the key elements in all such transition periods and changing worldviews is the shift in perception of *what is important, what is valuable, the goals* to be pursued and *the ways to measure* collective progress toward these goals. The old slogans of economic progress, industrial modernization, and a growing GNP now compete with the emerging slogans of the new paradigm: quality of life, human potential and the search for ecological balance, social justice and global citizenship on our small, fragile Planet Earth.

No wonder economics is in a crisis of its own, since it developed along with the Industrial Revolution, as a study of rational human choice under conditions of scarcity, but in the vastly different context of eighteenth-century England. Economics attempted to keep pace with the changing pattern of industrialization but, understandably, fared better at

147

describing such changes after the fact than in monitoring them, let alone forecasting them. As technological change accelerates, economics is now merely backing us into the future looking through the rear-view mirror.

Economists of all ideological stripes, from Marxists to supply-siders, have attempted with some success to operationalize the goals of industrial cultures wherever they developed: West, East, North or South. These goals involved expanding production of material goods with efficiency both of technological means and social organization, with the admirable goal of creating paradise here on Earth.

Thus, as social goals have shifted, the debate in economics now concerns *what* to measure, rather than merely *how* to measure. The once pre-eminent measure of an industrial society's success, the GNP, is now under daily challenge. Its U.S. inventor, Simon Kuznets, never intended it to be used as such an overall measure of progress. Economics as a profession has thus far been unwilling to clarify the limited applicability of the GNP or to warn the public against its widespread use as an indicator of overall human betterment. Most countries use GNP and the additional measure of Gross Domestic Product (GDP) in accounting for their "progress." GNP refers to the total per capita money income of its citizens, whether from domestic or foreign earnings. GDP measures the total money-denominated, domestically-produced goods and services. Most countries use both GNP and GDP, at times substituting whichever one shows their economies in the most favorable light. For example, in the second quarter of 1991, the GNP in the United States fell by 0.8 percent (annualized). The Department of Commerce, which issues these indicators, decided in November 1991 to focus more attention on the GDP. [1]

Happily, new indicators are proliferating to challenge the GNP, amidst the understandable groans of economists and statisticians whose intellectual investments in it are illiquid (textbooks, data series, computer models, not to mention research programs, high-paying jobs and tenure). Many of these new indicators were developed in the Sixties and began deducting some of the social costs of urbanization, congestion, crime, traffic delays, etc., from "gross" GNP, thus arriving at slightly more sober assessments which drew attention to the "bads" as well as the "goods" of industrialization. They included the Measure of Economic Welfare (MEW) proposed by James Tobin and William Nordhaus and Japan's Net National Welfare (NNW), which also deducts some kinds of environmental damage and depletion of the Earth's natural "capital."

As early as the 1950s there had been many efforts by U.N. statisticians—for example the 1954 report, *International Definitions and Measurement of Standards of Living*—calling for alternative measurement standards in recommendations of the Economic and Social Council (ECOSOC), the International Labor Organization (ILO), and the Food and Agricultural Organization (FAO). (A good summary of this early work is the October 1988 Discussion Paper Number 6, "Some Reflections on Human and Social Indicators for Development" by Dharam Ghai, Michael Hopkins and Donald McGranahan.) Most efforts relied too heavily on trying to force such indicators into the economics framework, or to relegate them to lesser status as "social satellite accounts." Former Senator Walter Mondale was a champion of social indicators use in the U.S. government in the late 1960s and early 1970s, while some economists, including Robert Eisner of the National Bureau of Economic Research, were working on keeping better accounts of capital accumulation, consumption and depreciation (still not done today!) which would include the value of "human capital" as well as unpaid and household production. Needless to say, with no clear lobbying pressure, funds were never found for these improvements. In 1972, the American Institute of Certified Public Accountants took up the cause, and published a book exploring the issues, *Social Measurement,* which is no doubt still lying on many library shelves. The issues it explored are as relevant as ever.

Social indicators have been a theme of discussion in many mature industrial societies for years, but their application has been thwarted by bureaucratic resistance; intellectual vested interests in methods, textbooks, etc.; and cultural biases (for example, against accounting for the work of women in parenting, housekeeping and subsistence agriculture). No one "correct" method will emerge, since multiple models and indicators will be more closely fitted to local situations and the different "cultural DNA" of diverse societies. The social indicators debate is about disaggregation, revealing overlooked detail, locally and sectorally, and adding a whole row of additional gauges to the societies' "instrument panels," so as to plug feedback into decision levels with more precision and timeliness. For example, an in-house audit evaluated 1000 World Bank projects and found that none of them had met their projected goals—even in traditional *economic* terms. Thus no easy formulae are available for even addressing the needs of developing countries for the new culturally sensitive, egalitarian and sustainable development. The first order of business for development officers is to be able to "decode" the cultural DNA of a recipient country and determine what values and goals it is optimizing, which may *not* be goals with which the development officers are qualified to assist.

It has been pointed out that traditional indicators such as GNP and GDP were actually developed for military mobilization purposes in the

United Kingdom and the United States, and their materialistic view of "progress" cannot guide humanity beyond consumerism toward moral growth and sustainable development. The crucial role of the informal economy and the unpaid productive work of subsistence agriculture is now the subject of a small, but growing, body of literature. In addition, there is the inability of national accounts to distinguish between goods and "bads" (i.e., wealth and 'illth') since liquor, tobacco, auto accidents, cleaning up pollution and the multi-billion dollar "stress industry" are all included as "progress." It might well be that in the United States these growing social and environmental costs—as well as the increasing monetarization of cooking, childcare and other formerly unpaid work— are the main "growth" sectors of the GNP. Yet efforts to add "sin" taxes to harmful products are fiercely resisted by industry lobbies.

In the 1970s the debate was joined by such development economists as Irma Adelman and Cynthia Taft Morris,[2] Grace Chichilinsky and others, who focused on the propensity for income disparities to increase right along with the GNP in developing countries, leading to the now familiar, widening gap between rich and poor, both within and between nations. Such debates and new indicators were fostered by the more fundamental and encompassing works of Barbara Ward and her study of the economics of *Spaceship Earth* published in 1966, and similar paradigm-shifting efforts by Kenneth Boulding in *Beyond Economics* (1968), and the work of Sweden's Gunnar and Alva Myrdal, to name a few. The Society for International Development joined in with the Physical Quality of Life Indicator (PQLI),[3] which shifted attention to new measures of success in maintaining the quality of life in liveable environments, housing, health care, education, as well as money-denominated income. Another early set of social indicators was developed in the 1970s by Prof. Richard Estes at the University of Pennsylvania. During the same period, the U.N. Environment Program developed the Basic Human Needs (BHN) indicator, which shifted attention toward measuring how these broader indicators of quality of life affected all income groups, and particularly focused on measuring the success of a nation's economic policy by how well it met the basic human needs of its poorest citizens. This touched a raw nerve in all countries committed to the goals of industrialization, since most economists from Marxists to laissez-faire traditionalists seemed to share the view that the early processes of capital accumulation to the magic "take-off point" would be socially messy and unfair, or as Marx saw it: socialism would have to grow out of the womb of capitalism. Focusing on how well governments served their poorest citizens was not popular in market-oriented or centrally-planned societies.

In the "stagflation" of the late 1970s, the idea dawned that perhaps industrialization was not to be the global panacea. Misgivings arose that perhaps it might only work for some people at the expense of other people, for some countries at the expense of other countries, and worse, that it might only be sustainable in the short-run—to be bogged down by domestic strife, nationalistic competition for the world's raw materials and capital, and the degrading of resources and pollution. The Organization for Economic Cooperation and Development's (OECD) paradigm-breaking 1978 report warned that the 1980s might be an "era of jobless economic growth," with simultaneously rising levels of GNP, automation, capital investment, unemployment and poverty. In the same period, the spate of new post-economic policy tools proliferated—environmental impact statements, social impact assessments, technology assessments, cross-impact analyses and future studies—and were joined by employment impact statements as fears of automation and technological change grew and unemployment levels rose.

In the 1980s, attention shifted to another, more fundamental issue clarifying the difference between wage-labor and work: how to measure all the productive work, consumption and investment carried on in the *non-money* sectors of both industrial and developing societies, i.e., the "informal economy" composed of all the work people do for each other and themselves—subsistence agriculture; building bridges, irrigation canals, schoolhouses; storing seed; caring for the young, the old and the sick; maintaining the household; volunteering for community service; and all the vital cooperative work that subsidizes the "official" GNP-denominated half of industrial societies. (See Plate 1-5: Three Layer Cake With Icing.) Originally, this debate had been carried on by non-economists, since economists are usually preoccupied with money-denominated activities and data. Non-money economies had been studied for decades by such anthropologists and social scientists as Marshall Sahlins, Karl Polanyi, and Thorstein Veblen, as well as political philosophers of the Enlightenment from Alexis de Tocqueville, Rousseau and Weber to Marx and, later, by economists Barbara Ward, E.F. Schumacher, Kenneth Boulding and Nicholas Georgescu-Roegen. But by the 1980s, GNP-focused, macroeconomic management policies were becoming erratic enough to embarrass the entire economics profession and "economist jokes" were becoming standard humor.

In the early 1980s a rash of new economic studies emerged on the underground, subterranean economies, by Peter Gutman, Edwin Feige and others, summarized well in a cover story in *Business Week*, April 5, 1983. Predictably, all these studies took the "statist" view that most of these cash and non-money activities were illegal and should be reported, taxed and added into the GNP—thus improving the picture of overall economic performance and leadership, and showing that unemployment and poverty had been overestimated. Rather than separating out the colossal illegal activities of drug-trafficking, multinational corporate barter deals estimated to account for some 25 percent of all world trade, under-reporting of interest, cash moonlighting and tax-dodging as the undocumented underbelly of the GNP-denominated sector, these economists often lumped these illegal activities with all the traditional, loving, unpaid work in the subsistence, household and community sectors described earlier by Sahlins, Polanyi, et. al., and more recently by myself and others as the cooperative "love economy," the "informal economy" (James Robertson), the "dual economy" (Joseph Huber), the "barefoot economy" by Manfred Max-Neef, and Orio Giarini's *Dialogue on Wealth and Welfare* (1980).

In the 1980s, many began to focus attention on how leaders used indicators selectively and, when necessary, manipulated their formulations in order to show voters "economic progress" at election times. George Orwell warned us in his book, *1984*, of leaders "newspeak," where "war is peace" and "love is hate" and how unwanted history would be shredded and "deep-sixed" into "memory holes." Often in history leaders endeavor to focus the attention of voters via diversionary tactics, not only the whipping up of foreign wars and domestic scapegoating as of yore, but even more subtle rhetorical diversions. In the 1960s, leaders could keep voters happy by focusing on two seemingly manageable indicators of performance: *inflation* and *unemployment*. As both of these indicators proved more embarrassing during the Stagflation Seventies, they were reformulated and "corrected," as I discussed at length in my earlier books.

In the "Orwellian Eighties" new diversions were necessary, since the situation had become even more unmanageable. Three new, unwanted indicators emerged in most industrial societies: alarming *government deficits*, *high real interest rates* and unruly *trade balances*. Many leaders, including Mr. Reagan and Mrs. Thatcher, tried to focus attention on lowering the inflation indicator and then holding this up to the voters as evidence of economic success—diverting attention from the other four indicators: *unemployment, deficits, trade balances* and *high real interest rates*. They promised that these latter four indicators would "improve in due course" as the deflationary medicine "took hold." Voters found all this less believable each year as similar pronouncements were made at successive economic summit meetings (see Plate 3-20, pg. 94).

Clearly, it is possible to push inflation down at the expense of making these other four indicators worse. The pressure must flow somewhere, as spending—primarily on the arms race, space, nuclear, high technology, medical care, etc., accelerates. Here we saw more "newspeak" diversions as development of Star Wars and new weapons systems were ordered to increase "national security." Mr. Reagan even called for a constitutional amendment for a balanced budget while racking up more deficits in his eight years in office than all previous U.S. Presidents put together! Many conservative U.S. economists are now asking how long all this can go on—bailing out our savings and loans, the banks and insurance companies at the same time that the United States is now the world's largest debtor nation.

Thus, willy-nilly, new indicators on which attention is focusing are deficits, trade balances, savings rates and real interest rates (i.e., corrected for inflation). Most leaders can now use economics and economic indicators as diversionary factors to mystify voters and keep them from participating fully in national debates. Today there is a growing awareness among voters in most industrial societies that economics is not much more than politics in disguise. Leaders most often have governed by managing ignorance, and as feminist theorists point out, power is inherent in the ability to *name* things and events and goals, and to choose the indicators by which they are judged.

Part of the demand for new indicators in all the quality-of-life areas where economic measures are inappropriate may be a natural desire to see real results that can hold politicians accountable. Voters are also demanding measures of social costs of production that can be estimated, with the goal of at last, filling that empty box marked "externalities" (costs producers pass on to consumers, taxpayers and future generations) in so many traditional economic models. Typical are recent studies of the social and environmental costs of energy now required of electric utilities by California's Public Utilities Commission (*Business Week*, July 15, 1991, page 136). Further, fundamental premises need to be addressed relating to the globalization of economic patterns and whether the underlying logic of "comparative advantage" can continue, based on global economic competition for markets, technology, capital, human and natural resources. Clearly it cannot, since it leads to unacceptable social and environmental costs and seems to be a war-prone system of winners and losers that becomes more horrifying with each day's news headlines. Obsolescent indicators still buttress this dying logic of national economic competition, even while covert protectionism is rampant everywhere. Understandably, politicians can no longer manage their

domestic affairs in today's roller-coaster, global economy, since most of
the variables are beyond their national boundaries, and the best-laid
domestic investment and technological strategies can be upset each
morning when the currency exchange markets open.

The last play of this globally-disordering system is currently facilitated
by economics and its hypnotic focus on money. Today, as I have detailed
elsewhere, money is fast losing all meaning as a measuring system for
real-world production and value. Manipulated by politicians and central
banks, and now speeded up by electronic funds transfers in a multinational
banking system and abstracted by global, 24-hour asset management,
money bears little relationship to reality. Smart investors everywhere
know that it is easier to "make" money by speculating, arbitraging currency,
playing interest rate differentials and other forms of paper entrepreneurship
than to invest in a real factory employing real workers and producing real
products in the real world. Even the staunchest upholder of this old order,
for example U.S. Treasury Secretary James Baker, proposes a money unit
backed by a "basket" of real commodities, e.g., gold, oil, or grain.

With so much footloose capital and "funny money" sloshing around
the global system, the world's "smartest" investors may keep the U.S.
deficit financed quite well, and it is a testament to the hold over our minds
of narrow economic indicators that the United States is still viewed as the
investment capital of the world in spite of our growing inability to
manage our domestic affairs. Were it not for the mystifications of the
global economic system and its current indicators veiling the reality,
average voters everywhere might see today's anarchic trade system as
nothing short of global economic warfare.

Financial reporters could help by continually reminding their
audiences of the political strategies behind all economic policies, studies
and indicators, and that economics is not a science but a profession which
is useful for limited and often political purposes.

More indicators are needed that build on the very important work of
contrasting weapons budgets with what similar-size expenditures could
achieve in health care, housing and education, etc., such as that of Ruth
Leger Sivard of World Priorities, Inc. in her "World Military and Social
Expenditures Reports."[4] Such indicators need to be broken down in many
ways and publicized for the use of diverse constituencies to force political
change. Similarly, economic conversion studies and detailed conversion
plans for orderly shifting to peacetime production (such as research by
the Council of Economic Priorities of New York and the Center for
Economic Conversion in California) are needed particularly to foster
these conversion processes as the USSR and the United States reduce

their arsenals. One of the first efforts to bring Soviets and Americans together to plan conversion of both economies from weapons to civilian production was the Swords into Plowshares Conference, September 1990, in Boston. The brainchild of three women—Rena Shulsky, a real estate and media entrepreneur; Vivian Day, a high-level citizen-diplomat and expert on Soviet affairs; and Randall Forsburg, Executive Director of the Institute for Defense and Disarmament Studies—the conference brought 40 high-level Soviets into contact with U.S. business and government executives. Ripple effects include a $1 billion fund of Battery March Financial Management of Boston to invest in the conversion of Soviet arms factories to passenger jets, lasers, microscopes and other civilian uses.

The Worldwatch Institute's *State of the World* [5] reports represent excellent models for monitoring crucial trends in population control, grain production, aquaculture (which now provides one seventh of world seafood consumption), water and soil management, materials recycling, renewable energy, world carbon dioxide emissions from fossil fuel combustion, and future-conscious government policies. Many heads of state and top business and government executives rely on these reports, which were started in 1984 and are published annually. Similar global assessments based on the *Global 2000* report issued by the Carter Administration in 1979 are now in process in many countries. But we must act and think *locally*, as well as *globally*, and therefore we need to keep our attention on and publicize all of the models and indicators of holistic, ecological, equitable approaches to human progress. Such approaches must be spelled out in detail for regions, localities and cities, which all need their own kinds of indicators of progress toward local goals, such as those used in Jacksonville, Florida (Plate 6-28: Life in Jacksonville: Quality Indicators for Progress) and elsewhere. Much of the data needed has already been compiled by diligent statisticians.

Recent efforts to redefine indicators of national wealth and progress beyond the GNP index are gathering momentum and may eventually depose economics from its current catbird seat in the policy arena. In 1990 the U.N. Development Program's Human Development Index (HDI) took a step in challenging the narrow economic definitions of progress that make up the GNP index. The HDI, by incorporating widely available statistics on literacy, life expectancy and purchasing power, has energized the debate on reforming national indicators (Plate 6-27: Human Development Index 1990 Scorecard).

Many politicians in the less-developed countries believe the GNP scorecard is rigged in favor of industrial countries. They cite perverse, no-win effects of trying to please the International Monetary Fund by boosting their GNP growth: increasing environmental depletion rates, increasing unemployment and, often, uneven income distribution. We already see similar effects in Eastern Europe where GNP-oriented economic reforms are creating dangerous economic backlashes, such as soaring unemployment in Poland and Hungary, as well as the other travails of restructuring in all these countries. It is in Eastern Europe that the oversimplifications of "Left or Right" economic models are clearest. As one magazine editor in Hungary noted, "People here are still sitting around waiting for the magic of market forces to start working." The truth is that markets were never a natural state of affairs but must be *legislated* into existence by *human hands* rather than an invisible hand. This fact was neatly underlined by none other than the usually orthodox editors of *The Economist*, in their article entitled "Creating the Invisible Hand" of May 11, 1991. It described some of these legislated efforts toward privatizing former state industries in Poland and Czechoslovakia. Since there were no buyers for these state companies, both countries came up with various schemes to give citizens "vouchers" to "buy" them, i.e., to give these companies away. The Hungarians think these vouchers are "crazy." In Czechoslovakia vouchers will be offered to all citizens over 18 years of age for a nominal 2000 korunas ($17.00), while in Poland every Pole will be given these vouchers free and expected to put them into "privatization" funds (similar to mutual funds). Such new realities finally allow us all to see some of the "blue smoke and mirrors" in economic theories on which GNP is based.

In the emerging global village, the study of national economies has become increasingly combined with the study of social and ecological issues that are far too important to be left to the economists' realm. Until recently, industrialized nations' governments and their economic bureaucracies have helped perpetuate the legitimacy of the GNP, since changing these comparative scorecards might show them in an unfavorable light. So, depending on what assumptions are made in national accounting methods, a national deficit can be made to look even larger than it is or a budget to be in surplus (by treating education, for instance, as investment rather than expenditure as it is currently treated).

But each government puts its own spin on national economic statistics. For example, in the 1970s and 1980s the USSR systematically over-stated its GNP growth (generally measured in terms of material consumption). Similarly, the OECD countries have downplayed unemployment figures by redefining "full employment" from two percent unemployment in the 1960s to seven percent in the late 1980s. Virtually all countries ignore environmental costs and natural resource depletion rates and, oddly, add into the GNP as useful production the costs of environmental cleanups. The important alternative statistics, such as those included in HDI, are still viewed by the old guard at the United Nations, World Bank and IMF as incidental data to real economic statistics.

The most obvious crack in the GNP is its reliance on money-denominated per capita incomes in an era of wildly fluctuating currencies. Thus, GNP statistics cannot give comparisons of the hours a Russian must work to buy a loaf of bread to how long it takes a Japanese to earn a bowl of rice. But because the HDI takes into account purchasing power parity, among other non-traditional economic indicators, it ranked the United States 18th as opposed to its GNP ranking of second behind Switzerland. Meanwhile, countries that are usually considered poorer by GNP standards, such as Sri Lanka and Costa Rica, rank much higher under HDI indicators (Plate 6-27). Another inadequacy of the GNP is its narrow, at times ethnocentric, view of wealth and progress. By definition, the GNP ignores diverse visions of the goals of development—not to mention cultural differences that lie far beyond the scope of most economists' concerns.

The Country Futures Indicators (Plate 6-26) which I have advocated over the past decade are deliberately open-ended to encourage the much needed multi-cultural debate about definitions of development and progress. Beyond the North-South debate about who is developing and who is developed, we need to recognize that all countries are developing in different ways—and developing in a world of increasing interdependence. Thus, I believe that new indicators measuring so many diverse paths to development must first be unbundled to avoid the GNP's mistake of simply piling obsolete economic formulas on top of one another to come up with an aggregate score. These traditional economic measurements assume a certain degree of agreement on development goals and are predicated on outdated notions, such as immobile capital.

The Country Futures Indicators (CFI) are of greater interest to most people than the many arcane economic indicators that seem to be of interest only to investors and the readers of financial pages. Unlike the GNP, the CFI assume that users will not necessarily be governments but millions of average citizens in all countries who are yearning for greater democracy, freedom and participation. Today, citizens everywhere wish to hold all their institutions, including governments, more accountable for their promises and performance.

The intrinsic value in devising new types of national wealth indicators is that they often spark more discussion in the ongoing and necessary

Human Development Index (HDI) 1990 Scorecard

Rank by HDI		Life Expectancy at birth (years) '87	Adult Literacy rate (%) '85	Real GDP per head (PPP-adj'd) '87, $	Rank by GNP per head	HDI
1	Japan	78	99	13,135	5	0.996
2	Sweden	77	99	13,780	6	0.987
3	Switzerland	77	99	15,403	1	0.986
4	Holland	77	99	12,661	14	0.984
5	Canada	77	99	16,375	7	0.983
6	Norway	77	99	15,940	3	0.983
7	Australia	76	99	11,782	17	0.978
8	France	76	99	13,961	12	0.974
9	Denmark	76	99	15,119	8	0.971
10	Britain	76	99	12,270	18	0.970
11	Finland	75	99	12,795	10	0.967
12	West Germany	75	99	14,730	11	0.967
13	New Zealand	75	99	10,541	22	0.966
14	Italy	76	97	10,682	19	0.966
15	Belgium	75	99	13,140	15	0.966
16	Spain	77	95	8,989	26	0.965
17	Ireland	74	99	8,586	25	0.961
18	Austria	74	99	12,386	13	0.961
19	USA	76	96	17,615	2	0.961
20	Israel	76	95	9,182	23	0.957
21	East Germany	74	99	8,000	16	0.953
22	Greece	76	93	5,500	33	0.949
23	Hong Kong	76	88	13,906	20	0.936
24	Chile	72	98	4,862	58	0.931
25	Czechoslovakia	72	98	7,750	29	0.931
26	USSR	70	99	6,000	30	0.920
27	Bulgaria	72	93	4,750	32	0.918
28	Costa Rica	75	93	3,760	54	0.916
29	Uruguay	71	95	5,063	45	0.916
30	Hungary	71	98	4,500	44	0.915
31	Yugoslavia	72	92	5,000	41	0.913
32	Argentina	71	96	4,647	42	0.910
33	Poland	72	98	4,000	48	0.910
34	South Korea	70	95	4,832	39	0.903
35	Singapore	73	86	12,790	21	0.899
36	Portugal	74	85	5,597	37	0.899
37	Trinidad/Tobago	71	96	3,664	31	0.885
38	Panama	72	89	4,009	43	0.883
39	Cuba	74	96	2,500	65	0.877
40	Mexico	69	90	4,624	50	0.876
41	Romania	71	96	3,000	47	0.863
42	Venezuela	70	87	4,306	36	0.861
43	Kuwait	73	70	13,843	9	0.839
44	Jamaica	74	82	2,506	69	0.824
45	Colombia	65	88	3,524	59	0.801
46	Malaysia	70	74	3,849	51	0.800
47	Albania	72	85	2,000	70	0.790
48	Sri Lanka	71	87	2,053	93	0.789
49	North Korea	70	90	2,000	64	0.789
50	Mauritius	69	83	2,617	56	0.788
51	Brazil	65	78	4,307	46	0.784
52	Paraguay	67	98	2,603	66	0.784
53	Thailand	66	91	2,576	76	0.783
54	UAE	71	60	12,191	4	0.782
55	Iraq	65	89	2,400	35	0.759
56	Ecuador	66	83	2,687	63	0.758
57	Peru	63	85	3,129	57	0.753
58	Jordan	67	75	3,161	55	0.752
59	Turkey	65	74	3,781	60	0.751
60	Nicaragua	64	88	2,209	77	0.743
61	Mongolia	64	90	2,000	74	0.737
62	Lebanon	68	78	2,250	53	0.735
63	South Africa	61	70	4,981	49	0.731
64	Libya	62	66	7,250	28	0.719

PLATE 6-27a

Rank by HDI		Life Expectancy at birth (years) '87	Adult Literacy rate (%) '85	Real GDP per head (PPP-adj'd) '87, $	Rank by GNP per head	H D I
65	China	70	69	2,124	109	0.716
66	Philippines	64	86	1,878	85	0.714
67	Saudi Arabia	64	55	8,320	24	0.702
68	Dominican Rep.	67	78	1,750	80	0.699
69	Syria	66	60	3,250	52	0.691
70	Iran	66	51	3,300	34	0.660
71	Tunisia	66	55	2,741	61	0.657
72	El Salvador	64	72	1,733	75	0.651
73	Botswana	59	71	2,496	62	0.646
74	Algeria	63	50	2,633	40	0.609
75	Vietnam	62	80	1,000	115	0.608
76	Guatemala	63	55	1,957	68	0.592
77	Indonesia	57	74	1,660	90	0.591
78	Lesotho	57	73	1,585	96	0.580
79	Zimbabwe	59	74	1,184	86	0.576
80	Honduras	65	59	1,119	78	0.563
81	Burma	61	79	752	120	0.561
82	Bolivia	54	75	1,380	87	0.548
83	Oman	57	30	7,750	27	0.535
84	Gabon	52	62	2,068	38	0.525
85	Laos	49	84	1,000	122	0.506
86	Egypt	62	45	1,357	82	0.501
87	Morocco	62	34	1,761	83	0.489
88	Zambia	54	76	717	112	0.481
89	Kenya	59	60	794	101	0.481
90	Cameroon	52	61	1,381	67	0.474
91	Kampuchea	49	75	1,000	129	0.471
92	Papua New Guinea	55	45	1,843	81	0.471
93	Madagascar	54	68	634	117	0.440
94	India	59	43	1,053	106	0.439
95	Pakistan	58	30	1,585	98	0.423
96	Tanzania	54	75	405	119	0.413
97	Namibia	46	30	1,500	71	0.404
98	Congo	49	63	756	72	0.395
99	Cote d'Ivoire	53	42	1,123	79	0.393
100	Yemen, PDR	52	42	1,000	92	0.369
101	Ghana	55	54	481	94	0.360
102	Haiti	55	38	775	97	0.356
103	Uganda	52	58	511	110	0.354
104	Togo	54	41	670	107	0.337
105	Liberia	55	35	696	89	0.333
106	Yemen Arab Rep.	52	25	1,250	84	0.328
107	Nigeria	51	43	668	95	0.322
108	Bangladesh	52	33	883	125	0.318
109	Angola	45	41	1,000	73	0.304
110	Rwanda	49	47	571	105	0.304
111	Zaire	53	62	220	126	0.294
112	Ethiopia	42	66	454	130	0.282
113	Senegal	47	28	1,068	88	0.274
114	Nepal	52	26	722	123	0.273
115	Cen.African Rep.	46	41	591	102	0.258
116	Sudan	51	23	750	99	0.255
117	Malawi	48	42	476	124	0.250
118	Mozambique	47	39	500	121	0.239
119	Bhutan	49	25	700	128	0.236
120	Burundi	50	35	450	113	0.235
121	Benin	47	27	665	103	0.224
122	Afghanistan	42	24	1,000	114	0.212
123	Mauritania	47	17	840	91	0.208
124	Somalia	46	12	1,000	108	0.200
125	Guinea	43	29	500	100	0.162
126	Chad	48	26	400	127	0.157
127	Sierra Leone	42	30	480	104	0.150
128	Burkina Faso	48	14	500	118	0.150
129	Mali	45	17	543	116	0.143
130	Niger	45	14	452	111	0.116

Countries are listed in descending order based on their Human Development Index (HDI) score which was figured by UNDP researchers by combining life expectancy, adult literacy and purchasing-power parity. The other column shows the ranking by unadjusted GNP per person.

PLATE 6-27b   Adapted from The Human Development Report 1990, UNDP New York debate about which economic indicators are useful and what existing definitions of progress are valid. Traditional economic indicators such as productivity and unemployment have lost their meaning and usefulness since they've become the property of media consultants and "spin doctors" who use them to blatantly obscure economic issues at election time.

New results-oriented indicators will help citizens decide if governments are delivering the best services for the specific quality they are seeking and will make politicians much more accountable for progress toward specific goals of the electorate. For example, the British Green Party produced its own *"Green Budget"* in 1991, with many proposals for overhauling and "greening" the British economy. The plan's first order of business is the need to reformulate GNP as well as GDP (Gross Domestic Product). It notes sarcastically, "If GDP or GNP show an increase from one year to the next, economic growth is said to have been achieved. It simply means that more money has been exchanged for goods and services rendered in the last year, often allowing for price increases." One conclusion the *Green Budget* reaches is that GNP and GDP need to be replaced by a whole range of more specific indicators already available, such as life expectancy and infant mortality, which already tell us more about human progress than how much money changes hands in a society each year.[6] And politicians will need better information to deliver those services more effectively.

Beyond economics—new indicators for culturally specific, sustainable development

As the so-called Fourth Development Decade of the United Nations unfolds, the lessons of the previous three decades are becoming clear. Traditional models equating industrialization and per capita-averaged, currency denominated GNP and GDP growth—which are enshrined in the U.N. System of National Accounts (UNSNA), have proved failures in most of the countries of the Southern Hemisphere. At last, in its 1991 World Development Report, the World Bank addressed some of the sorry realities, a break from its usual upbeat style. In Chapter Two it notes:

> Thinking on development has undergone a sea of change during the past forty years. . . . Economists have traditionally considered an increase in per capita income to be a good proxy for other attributes of development. But the weakness of income growth as an indicator is that it may mask the real changes in welfare for large parts of the poor population. Improvements in meeting the basic needs for food, education, health care, equality of opportunity, civil liberties, and environmental protection are not captured by statistics on income growth.[7]

This historic admission was the result of increasing pressure from grassroots groups and alternative development practitioners who saw the failures firsthand in the villages, rural areas and urban slums and, in recent years, from the anti-World Bank campaigns of environmentalists highlighting the environmental destruction caused by the Bank's policies.

In fact, the entire development process not only derailed in the 1980s but, tragically, in most of Sub-Saharan African countries it went into reverse. This was also the conclusion of a group of experts on problems of measuring development, convened by President Perez of Venezuela in Caracas in August 1989. The final report of this meeting co-sponsored by the South Commission was titled "Toward a New Way to Measure Development."[8] It concluded that this traditional development model involved a one-time, historical process—unrepeatable in any case. This is particularly true in today's crowded, polluted world where natural resources are depleting rapidly and Northern industrial countries are now demanding that Southern countries actually forego this industrial development model as too polluting and instead, change their courses to pursue only "clean" or "green" technologies and "sustainable development."

The ironies of this about-face, after decades of pushing the old prescriptions for GNP-measured economic growth as the path to progress, still seem to be lost on most development economists. For example, the World Bank now glosses over past theoretical errors by stating disingenuously in its 1991 *World Development Report*, "Economic development is defined in this Report as a sustainable increase in living standards that encompass material consumption, education, health, and environmental protection." This is a highly political redefinition which avoids addressing the fact that all of the Bank's statistical methods require changing, if indeed the Bank *has* now redefined economic development in the above-mentioned way. But, clearly, it has not! Neither has it retrained its staff of economists and statisticians, nor, significantly, has it made any changes in GNP, GDP accounting or even incorporated the changes advocated by its own staff, such as valuing infrastructure and human capital and environmental assets in GNP accounts as part of a capital assets budget. Nor has the Bank adopted the new Index of Sustainable Economic Welfare (ISEW) developed by its own staff economist, Herman Daly, in his *Toward the Common Good*[9] co-authored with John Cobb. This index is possibly the best that can be made from within the single discipline of economics and could help serve as a basis for a full-scale debate on new indicators within all the relevant agencies at the United Nations, the International Monetary Fund (IMF), the U.N. Development Program (UNDP) and all the rest.

Curiously, even the Report of the World Commission on Environment and Development[10] does not advocate, among its many useful recommendations, correcting the GNP—even to require valuing environmental resources at something more than zero (the current practice). The Report merely calls for countries "to develop criteria and indicators for environmental quality standards and guidelines for the sustainable use and management of natural resources"—apparently leaving the rest to the global markets. Yet in an interdependent global commons the key variable is government intervention, i.e., whether, when, where and how to set up markets and use them, or when, why, whom and how to regulate or devise state or local plans. In other words, the success or failure of development policies seems to boil down to whether any given government intervened expertly, stupidly or has been just plain lucky! Economists, from left to right, are being forced to admit that all economies are "mixed" and that they have, as yet, no theories of mixed economies. It is now clear that "economies" are simply sets of rules, based on the vastly-different goals, values and public priorities of each specific culture. There is more acknowledgment today of this cultural factor by economists, since it is the only way of explaining the "Japanese miracle" (homogeneous cultures, "cronyism," good conflict resolution, hard-working, well-educated people) and the very different factors that fueled the growth of the "Four Tigers" of Asia: Singapore (a benevolent dictatorship), South Korea (heavy state intervention), Hong Kong (free-market oriented, almost no natural resources), and Taiwan (much state intervention, hardworking people).

These broader analyses show the shallowness of purely economic development formulas regarding "correct" rates of capital accumulation and investment (an insane generality since the key problem is to make *wise* investments!), or the old formula of taxing agriculture to invest in industrialization. For example, the influential economic journal *The Economist* now equates good economic growth policies with investments in people, their health and education—not a free-market idea (in fact, markets tend to fail in such social goals). Yet free-market ideologues in the private sector generally oppose such government investments as "unaffordable" or as "socialism" and naturally, if the society's scorecard remains the GNP, they will be vindicated (since people are not included in GNP as assets, as are machines and capital investments in technology or plants and equipment).

Therefore, we can only trust this sudden change of heart by economists about the value of people and the environment if we see them also crusading to correct the GNP. When goals change, any citizen knows that the scorecard has to change too to reflect the new goal and measure results in progressing toward it. The Human Development Index (HDI)[11] has done precisely that, by measuring educational investments of governments (as a ratio of their military expenditures) as well as measuring health goals (life expectancy and infant mortality). Another example of this persistent schizophrenia among economists is that the U.N.'s own statistical office has not yet adopted even the HDI.

Decoding the cultural-DNA

Thus as the debate about development has become more fundamental—involving the need to decode specific "cultural-DNA" patterns, ideals and goals in very different societies and to define "basic human needs"—it has now shifted toward more realistic and results-oriented indicators of progress toward these various visions of an "ideal society." A good example of this new approach is *The Middle Path for the Future of Thailand: Technology in Harmony with Culture and Environment*[12] (East-West Center, 1991) by Sippanondha Ketudat, former Minister of Education of Thailand and President of its National Petrochemical Corporation. This exercise in building scenarios for Thailand's future employs an "ethnographic futures" approach developed with Robert B. Textor, which uses the culture and values of a society as its starting point. While not rejecting a "high-tech," traditional export-oriented economic model, it chooses technology based on the Buddhist values of harmony, maintaining a rich rural tradition and preventing further growth of Bangkok through focusing on small regional towns. The study does *not* reject import substitution (now an article of faith among most development economists), for example, where Thailand's own natural gas can serve as fuelstock for domestic plastic production capability, rather that the heavy foreign exchange cost of importing plastics. Import substitution is being rediscovered in many areas, even in small U.S. towns, whose locally-generated capital is drained off in unnecessary imports of oil or electricity—local solar power, small dams, and wind-generators can keep dollars at home to lend to local small businesses and construction.

As noted, GNP, GDP, inflation, interest and unemployment rates, all are loaded with biases and ignore structural issues of power and prior distribution of wealth and foster an unrealistic view which equates real wealth (natural resources and the skills, specific cultural assets, local conditions and creativity of resourceful human beings) with mere money. The international journal *Culture and Development* in Brussels, Belgium, covers these issues well. A whole treatise would be necessary just to elucidate the difference between money and true wealth. It suffices to remind ourselves that money, i.e., currencies, are virtually worthless in themselves and only acquire value inasmuch as human beings use and trust money and it tracks accurately and keeps score of human transactions and production or real wealth as described in *Politics of the Solar Age*. It became clear to me in the 1970s that sooner or later Eurocentric models of economic development—from Left to Right—would be too narrow and one-dimensional to serve as a framework for truly human, ecologically-sustainable, culturally-specific models for development. I was persuaded by Mohandas Gandhi who said, "Should India ever resolve to imitate England, it will be the ruin of the nation," as well as the unforgettable quote that "There is enough in the world for everyone's needs, but not for our greeds."

Today, we still suffer in the North and South from international systems of finance, debt and currency manipulation invented in the northern Hemisphere which even the respected U.S.-based magazine *Business Week* referred to as "The Global Casino." However, this inequitable global casino, unreal as its worldwide electronic funds transfer systems are, has become a structural element blocking the aspirations for real and sustainable development of most of the countries of the South. In his new book,[13] *Debt and Environment: Converging Crises* (United Nations, 1991), insider Morris Miller, former Executive Director of the World Bank, gloomily assesses the false assumptions concerning World Bank and IMF policies, the Structural Adjustment Loans which continue to exact a heavy social price on developing countries. Miller had warned in his earlier book on the debt crisis, *Coping is Not Enough* (1986), that the entire structure of international finance, debt and official development aid (ODA) had become a cruel farce, with Third World debt doubling from 1982 until in 1990 it stood at $1,340 billion.

As mentioned earlier, this perverse global financial apparatus, buttressed by institutions put in place in the North after World War II— the International Bank for Reconstruction and Development (IBRD) or the World Bank, the International Monetary Fund (IMF), the General Agreement on Trade and Tariffs (GATT), the Bank of International Settlements (BIS), etc.—is now operating at odds with its original purposes and generally well-meaning ideals. For example, the deepest dogma of economics is that free trade is always good, thus GATT must move to speed opening up markets everywhere. However, when unequal bargaining power exists, as say between New Zealand's farmers and those in the United States or the European Community, the open market conditions demand a loser, i.e., New Zealand farmers will be slaughtered along with their sheep. These problems are exacerbated in developing countries whose products face trade barriers in Northern countries while simultaneously GATT negotiators demand they open up their own industries, which would then be decimated by more powerful foreign competitors. Fundamentally, this global financial apparatus and its institutional underpinnings cannot be reformed until its deeply-coded system of accounting of national "wealth" and "progress" is brought to light, challenged and reformulated to account for true wealth, rather than currency flows and exchanges and per capita-averaged income statistics, such as GNP and GDP.

Yet we are faced with a tragic situation today where the United Nations statistical system still uses GNP, GDP, and other traditional indicators and thus they became virtually the "lingua franca" defining the whole global debate about "economic development" and its theoretical and operational approaches. Thus, the IMF calculations that required Venezuela to hype its GNP growth in order to service its debt in 1989 resulted in riots over the "belt-tightening" (higher food prices, etc.) in which hundreds died. No social indicators were able to outweigh the monetary-denominated GNP indicator. This colossal epistemological error which has already caused so much human misery and starvation was then fed back by the United Nations aid agencies into criteria used by the World Bank, which in turn promulgated rules *requiring* developing countries applying for loans to set up systems of national accounts which perpetuated and proliferated these tragic errors.

Even though in May 1990 the U.N. Development Programme first released its own newly-formulated Human Development Index (pioneered by Mahbub Ul Haq), it still remains to be seen whether this will influence the more entrenched U.N. System of National Accounts, since the non-monetary data included in the HDI has usually been viewed by traditional statisticians as "soft." The highest status is accorded to the "hard" economic data both at the United Nations and the World Bank. Social statisticians are considered well-meaning but of peripheral importance. In *Debt and Environment* Morris Miller notes that in 1974 Robert McNamara, the World Bank's President, called on the Bank to shift its focus from macrodevelopment (assumed to trickle-down to the poor) directly to the "bottom 40 percent" of the world's poor. The Bank did shift its focus in a series of policy papers on land reform, nutrition, health, education, populations and "integrated rural development." In 1975, a "special projects division was established," Miller recalls, "but the whole effort soon fizzled and the division was abolished a few years later."[14] I remember being invited on many occasions to address a small caring cabal of World Bank officers at their Tuesday breakfasts to consider "values in development." I soon realized that these unpaid presentations were quite irrelevant to the Bank's main focus on GNP-growth. Since then several of these conscientized Bank officials have left to pursue independent work more relevant to genuine development goals. An example is Turid Sato, a Norwegian economist who now heads her own firm. Organizing for Development Institute, Inc. (ODII), which takes a grassroots approach.

Exposing the politics of economics

This appalling, circular tangle based on faulty epistemology proved impervious to all the efforts of the Group of 77 over the past fifteen years to bring about the badly-needed New International Economic Order (NIEO). Indeed, part of this imperviousness and the general blindness to the looming debt crisis was precisely a problem of inability to *perceive* the dimensions of the crisis, due to the prevailing "economism" paradigm! Of course there has already been a de facto default of massive proportions, requiring not only political resolutions but also a shift of paradigms beyond "economism" and toward a new global realism that acknowledges that both "debtors" and "creditors" are in the same global boat and will eventually sink or swim together. The only question that remains is *in what manner* these often inequitably-negotiated debts will be written down or off—securitized with the aid of surplus countries, such as Japan and Germany, and agencies including the World Bank and the IMF—or failing these strategies, repudiated en masse. Even today, the *net* transfers of funds between industrial and developing countries are still reversed. From 1983 to 1989 the flow of funds from poor countries to rich ones was $200 billion. In 1990 this drain was estimated to be more than 50 percent of their total new external debt.[13]

Facilitating the achievement of a more stable, equitable development world order will require that faulty accounting systems be corrected and expanded to reflect the difference between money and wealth. It has now become clear that today's outmoded GNP, GDP and other money-denominated statistics now best serve the world's currency arbitrageurs and stock market speculators. In fact, *Euromoney* magazine (September 1988) "refined" these indicators further. Their new Country Risk Ratings treat whole countries as "statistical black boxes" reduced to one "key" indicator—Ability to Service External Debt! No further case need be made for responsible politicians within these countries to redefine their own internal goals, values and priorities for their own specific development path, since it is now clear that economics is merely politics in disguise.

The time has ripened for this urgent task since all the United Nations member countries conducted census-gathering operations in 1990 and 1991. Census questionnaires need redesigning in several respects, particularly to change the "head of household" model which distorts and shortchanges the productive work of women in families and family enterprises. The new indicators based on households will need to document the economic productivity of men and women sharing the credit for production for sale as well as production for home use and the work of household maintenance and raising children. Because GNP does not account for unpaid work (mostly of women, raising food, producing crafts, etc., as well as household maintenance), it has simply "subsidized" the apparent economic production of the "head of household"—presumed to be a man. Today, 30 percent of all households worldwide are headed by women and women worldwide work longer hours than men (from 2 hours more per week in Japan and 5-6 more hours per week in Western Europe to Africa and Asia where women work 12-13 hours more per week than men). Wherever women's non-market economic activity is taken into account in statistics (for example, in Cote d'Ivoire and Nepal) it is comparable to that of men. Some countries have estimated the additional contribution of unpaid housework to their GNP accounts: Denmark estimates an added 50 percent, Norway 41 percent, the United States 30 percent, Pakistan 35 percent and the Philippines 11 percent. This wealth of new statistics is in the 1991 United Nations survey, *The World's Women: Trends and Statistics, 1970-1990*. As U.S. economist John Kenneth Galbraith stated in *Economics and the Public Purpose* (1973), "The household, in the established economics, is essentially a disguise for the exercise of male authority."

Even more damning of the worldwide dimensions of mysogeny is *If Women Counted* by Marilyn Waring (1989) which documents the ways in which economics has functioned to oppress women. Venezuela, because of the initiatives of President Carlos Andres Perez, continues to provide leadership in operationalizing a new Index of Social Welfare. Perez hosted a follow-up meeting for statistical office heads in Venezuela and other Latin American and Central American countries in October 1989. Such new indexes can provide a sounder basis for the World Bank and other aid agencies in their current search for new models of "sustainable development," the widely-adopted term of the World Commission on Environment and Development in *Our Common Future* (1987). New future-oriented social indicators can help operationalize emerging and traditional values, even though they will never be sufficient to the task since there will always be important values and issues which can never be quantified and must remain within the realm of democratic debate and political resolution.

As mentioned, this debate over development measures puts the statisticians of the U.N.'s official System of National Accounts with those working in agencies like UNDP, both signalling a shifting of conventional thinking. Comparing the GNP and the 1990 HDI measures of human progress changed the ranking of many countries in surprising ways, as real purchasing power (rather than money income) is also taken into account. For example, Sri Lanka whose GNP is only $400 per person actually offers its citizens purchasing power equivalent to $2,000 per year and has a life expectancy of 71 years (similar to Argentina and Hungary and higher than the USSR) while its literacy rate of 87 percent outstrips the United States (which has fallen to around 80 percent). Costa Rica with purchasing power of $3,760 per head, 93 percent literacy and life expectancies of 75 years streaks ahead of several European countries while the United States drops from second (after Switzerland) in the GNP stakes to 19th in the HDI scorecard. The average purchasing power of the G-7 country members is approximately $14,000 per head per year, while this average among G-15 member countries is about $3,500.

Clearly the first Caracas meeting on New Indicators in August 1989 helped trigger much of the accelerated interest in new indicators, as well as the UNDP's release of its HDI in 1990. As shown in Plate 6-27, the HDI included literacy and life expectancy rates, two of the measures recommended by the South Commission Report.

The Caracas experts noted that, in fairness, GNP and other macroeconomic statistics and indicators were never intended to be used as overall measures of welfare. Yet the power of statistics is that they are powerful attention-getters, and when widely disseminated over mass media they focus public concern, thus sometimes distorting political debates and issues. This power of statistics to shape and sometimes misshape social awareness of issues was underlined at the almost simultaneous August meeting in Washington, DC, of the American Statistical Association whose Executive Director, Barbara Bailor, drew attention to these ways in which "statistics affect all our lives." They narrowly focus the attention of mass media and political leaders at all levels, as well as voters, on GNP growth, inflation, interest rates and currency exchange rates, which in turn further skews public concern away from the vital human, social and environmental issues which are short-changed. This circular process is amplified by the workings of the global electronic trading and financial system, where these economic indicators become ever more arcane and of interest mainly to speculators and currency arbitrageurs, such as the new Country Risk Index of *Euromoney* magazine, already mentioned. In media-dominated societies, polls and indicators shape politics. The split between economic and money-based indicators and those of human, social and environmental quality is ubiquitous, due to the over-specializing of the statistics and the mandates of governmental departments. Thus it was not surprising that the some 4000 attendees at the American Statistical Association meeting were unaware of the Caracas meeting and vice-versa.

Lastly, the Caracas group called for a range of specific social indicators, such as those collected in many countries in areas including health, shelter and other vital services—education, democratic participation, the status of women, and other concerns—and giving these adequate attention by releasing them to the mass media with the same regularity and emphasis as those on GNP and other economic concerns. The group acknowledged that these kinds of indicators would be specific to the various countries and cultures of the world and their own special goals for development. The group added that all indicators should be gathered with the participation of those being surveyed so that these new indicators could serve both as feedback tools to enhance government and local decision-making, and the communities themselves. In June 1990 the South Commission launched the new Group of Fifteen Economic Summit in Kuala Lumpur to continue its work and help engender a new global debate about alternative economic, technical, social and cultural paths to development.

As this debate leads to inclusion of more of the quality-of-life factors proposed by the South Commission Report, many highly-polluted industrial countries may find that their rankings fall behind more pristine, resource-rich ones in the South.

Toward the fourth development decade

With the advent of the G-15, the fundamental rethinking of what is meant by "development" will likely continue, leading to divergent definitions, as the differences between money and real wealth are clarified. Many countries of the South now wish to develop along their own specific, cultural paths, rather than slavishly following World Bank and IMF formulas to hype economic growth whatever the human or environmental costs. The end of the Cold War also signals the end of ideological, mutually-exclusive, capitalist or socialist paths to progress and enhances the awareness that, in fact, most of the world's economies are various mixtures of both.

Even the London-based journal, *The Economist*, has joined the search for broader, less simplistic indicators of development—both in giving broad coverage to the advent of such new indicators as HDI and in utilizing such criteria in its reporting. Its own *Book of Vital World Statistics*[15] (Random House, 1990) also widens its perspectives. While economic, trade and production data still predominates, a few pages have been included on health, infant mortality, life expectancy, "family life," poverty and inequality, crime, religion, and even eight pages at the end focus on the state of the environment: deforestation, air pollution, water use, recycling and nuclear power. The realities of the U.N.'s Fourth Development Decade of the 1990s are likely to be more complex, where the development process will be seen in its wider cultural and global ecological contexts—requiring interdisciplinary policy tools beyond macroeconomic analyses. The G-15 can only enrich this debate as countries revalue their own "cultural DNA" and innovative potential. Furthermore, the G-15 member countries (Algeria, Argentina, Brazil, Egypt, India, Indonesia, Jamaica, Malaysia, Mexico, Nigeria, Peru, Senegal, Venezuela, Yugoslavia and Zimbabwe) comprise combined populations that total 29.6 percent of the world's peoples, compared with only 12.7 percent represented by the G-7 Economic Summit countries (the United States, Britain, Germany, Italy, Canada, France and Japan). Up to now, the world's press have covered the G-7 summit meetings, and their pronouncements have dominated and defined the global debate about both means and goals of economic development, which were equated with human progress. Although journalists from the South covered the G-15 Economic Summit in Kuala Lumpur, it was widely ignored in Northern media.

Today, these anomalies are clearly emerging into public awareness in many countries similarly beset by poverty, malnutrition, illiteracy, homelessness and lack of other basic needs, as well as acid rain, desertification and a myriad of other environmental threats. Such avoidable realities are behind the recognition of the need for new indicators in Germany, France and Norway, as well as in the countries of the Southern Hemisphere. The Green Party in Germany, although it lost power during unification, had already pushed the Bonn government to agree that it would, by the mid-1990s, include environmental costs in its national accounts. However, like many other national accounts officials, the Kohl government still plans to use two separate statistics, i.e., continue with GNP and publish the environmental indicator separately.

Thus most of the debates over the past century about whether "economies" should be market-driven, centrally-planned or a mixture of the two (as most are in reality) are more generally-stated; *debates about rules and regulations* of one kind or another are no longer clarified by ideological positions, whether from the left or right. The more important question is the extent to which they are functioning cybernetically at all levels of the society, from family and village to the state level. The essential role of feedback in governing cybernetic systems has been proven scientifically throughout many systems studied, as well as, once again, in the democratization and defeat of the authoritarian conservatives in the USSR. Economics recognized the importance of feedback provided by the price system. But, as noted earlier, prices are only one form of feedback, and often distorted in reality, by power and unaccounted "external" costs. Systems theory allows a more generalized framework and the recognition of many other feedback loops just as or more important than prices. The task of constructing new indicators of social welfare is precisely that of designing additional feedback mechanisms to our societies of how well they are performing according to their own established criteria, rules and goals.

Each country will need to delve into its own traditions and cultural heritage so as to optimize its own primary values and goals. Only then can a country decide for itself which of its cultural, human and ecological riches can provide the basis for sound exports. This process underlies all the transformations occurring in East Europe and the USSR, where the original charitable ideals of socialism are still alive. Some states in the U.S. as well as some countries are now taking this kind of approach to rethinking what development means and how to balance a more stable, exporting stance with a more locally oriented homegrown economy.

Rethinking social indicators

As this type of rethinking proceeds, new indicators will emerge and can be tested and then highlighted in mass media to foster a broad democratic understanding of the shift in focus. In many cases these indicators by themselves can engender new pride, such as Costa Rica's continual emphasis on its own social values and goals: peace, justice, health and education as well as biological diversity. Costa Ricans know that per capita income is not the whole story and point with pride to their social and cultural achievements, such as almost universal literacy, which compares well above the United States. Costa Rica is still taking leadership (via its former Minister of Natural Resources, Energy and Mines, Alvaro Umana, Ph.D.) in defining new indicators for sustainable development by hosting many international seminars, as well as in developing its system of protection of bio-diversity in its national parks and through the National Bio-Diversity Institute.

When countries shift beyond GNP, they will not be flying blind. Statistics on a full range of many-dimensional aspects of social progress are readily available to fill out the government's "instrument panel":

Life in Jacksonville: Quality Indicators for Progress

These are the categories through which Jacksonville, Florida, has chosen to measure its Quality of Life. Statistical data has been recorded in these categories since 1983.

THE ECONOMY
includes individual economic well being and community economic health.

Total unemployment rate
Black unemployment rate
Teenage unemployment rate
Annual retail sales per capita
Effective buying income per capita
Average price of previously owned, single family home
Revenue generated by the Bed tax
Taxed taxable value of real estate
Cost of 1,000 kw hours of electricity (DEA)
New housing starts

PUBLIC SAFETY
includes the perception of public safety, and the quantity and quality of law enforcement, fire protection and rescue services.

Index crimes per 100,000 population
Percentage who have been victims of a crime
Percentage who feel safe walking alone at night
Rescue call response time
Fire call response time
Police call response time
Motor vehicle accidents per 1,000 population
Fire and rescue operating expenditures per capita
Law enforcement operating expenditures per capita

HEALTH
refers to the physical and mental health of residents and the local system of health care.

Age-adjusted deaths per 100,000 population
Infant deaths per 1,000 live births
Deaths due to heart disease per 100,000 population
Suicides per 100,000 population
Deaths due to cirrhosis of the liver per 100,000 population
Packs of cigarettes sold per capita
Percentage who exercise three times per week
Percentage who rate the medical health care system good or excellent
Percentage who rate their own health good or excellent

EDUCATION
includes the system of public education (kindergarten through 12th grade), higher education, including adult education, and the overall literacy and educational attainment of the population.

K-12
    Standard Achievement Test Scores
    Student dropout rate
    Educational expenditure per student
    Average public school teacher salaries
    Percentage of teachers holding advanced degrees
HIGHER EDUCATION
    Percentage of faculty holding terminal degrees
    Average faculty salaries at public institutions
    Total student enrollment
    Academic degrees awarded
EDUCATIONAL ATTAINMENT
    Percentage who are high school graduates or above
    Percentage who are college graduates or above

NATURAL ENVIRONMENT
includes the natural elements of the earth's ecosystem, the quality and quantity of water, air, green space, and landscaping and visual aesthetics.

Days when the Air Quality index is in the Good range
Frequency of compliance of St. John's River with water quality standards
Frequency of compliance of tributaries with water quality standards (desolved oxygen)
New sewer permits issued
Sign permits issued
Environmental public employees per 100,000 population
Per capita tons of solid waste

MOBILITY
refers to opportunities for people to travel freely within Jacksonville and between Jacksonville and other locations.

Total weekday commercial flights in and out of JIA
Direct flight destinations to and from JIA
Average weekday ridership on JTA buses
Average miles of JTA bus service per weekday
Commuting time from downtown along J. Turner Butler/I-95
Commuting time from downtown along Atlantic Blvd.
Commuting time from downtown along San Jose Blvd.
Commuting time from downtown along Roosevelt Blvd.
Commuting time from downtown along I-95 North

GOVERNMENT/POLITICS
includes an informed and active citizenry, professionalism and performance of local government.

Percentage of population eighteen and over registered to vote
Percentage of registered voters who voted
Percentage of households purchasing local Sunday newspaper
Percentage who can name accurately two City Council members
City capital outlay expenditures per capita
Total City revenues per capita
Percentage of City Council members who are blacks
Percentage of City Council members who are female
Rate of Planning Department/City Council concurrence on rezoning petitions
Percentage who rate the quality of local government leadership good or excellent
Days from arrest to disposition of criminal cases

SOCIAL ENVIRONMENT
encompasses collective or group concerns such as equality of opportunity, racial harmony, family life, human services, philanthropy and volunteerism.

Child abuse and neglect reports per 1,000 children under 18
Employment discrimination complaints filed with the Jacksonville Equal Opportunity Commission
Percentage of white persons who believe racism to be a problem
Percentage of non-white persons who believe racism to be a problem
City government human services expenditures per capita
Contributions per capita to the United Way and its member agencies
Percentage who volunteered time during the past year
Licensed day-care spaces per 1,000 children under 5 years

CULTURE/RECREATION
includes the available supply and use of sports and entertainment events, the performing and visual arts, public recreation, and leisure activities.

Annual expenditures of major arts organizations
Public parks acreage per 1,000 population
Public parks and recreation facilities per 100,000 population
Public library materials per capita
Public library book circulation per capita
Days of bookings of major City facilities
Zoo attendance per 1,000 population

PLATE 6-28   Jacksonville Chamber of Commerce, Jacksonville, FL.

- *Indicators of investment in human resources* include World Health Organization statistics on life expectancy, infant mortality, and low birth weight (differentiation by gender will also be needed). Much can be built on the Physical Quality of Life Index, developed by David Morris for the Overseas Development Council in the 1970s and outlined in *Politics of the Solar Age*. UNESCO and many other national organizations devoted to education can provide literacy statistics (many will need sex differentiation). As mentioned, we already know much comparative data in this area. It may only need to be adopted as an official indicator and publicized. Amnesty International and other human rights organizations collect data on political participation, as do U.N. agencies. Investments in early childhood stimulation and development can be gauged in many different ways which we can explore.

- *Human Resourcefulness and Productivity* (paid or unpaid, see Plate 1-5: Three Layer Cake With Icing). The Organization for Economic Cooperation and Development (OECD) has many studies (usually performed by sociologists) of total social production, based on number of productive hours worked, whether paid or unpaid, self employed or engaged in a family enterprise or community cooperative. Such an indicator would highlight how much greater is the true productivity of many countries, where their official cash-based, GNP-measured "economy" is still small compared with their traditional, informal sectors (see Manfred Max-Neef, Hernando de Soto,[16] Robertson,[17] Waring,[18] Shankland,[19] Nicholls and Dyson[20] and my own work).

  Another useful measure might be designed around the important value of social cohesion, i.e., the extent to which community solidarity permits local problem solving and conflict resolution, as for example, the "Social Environment" sub-index in Jacksonville, Florida's Quality-of-Life Indicators for Progress (Plate 6-28).

- *Military versus civilian budget ratios*. Here the data is available and this will be a crucial measure of government performance in diplomacy and conflict resolution. The 1990 HDI includes a ratio in each country between teachers and soldiers, but the most comprehensive and pioneering index is *World Military and Social Expenditures*, 1991, now in its 14th Edition, authored by Ruth Leger Sivard. It contains illuminating charts and a clear highlighting of priorities (e.g., it will take 125 years under current

Military Spending and Human Development Performance

When military spending takes priority, human development performance is poor

Emphasis on health and education yields good human development performance

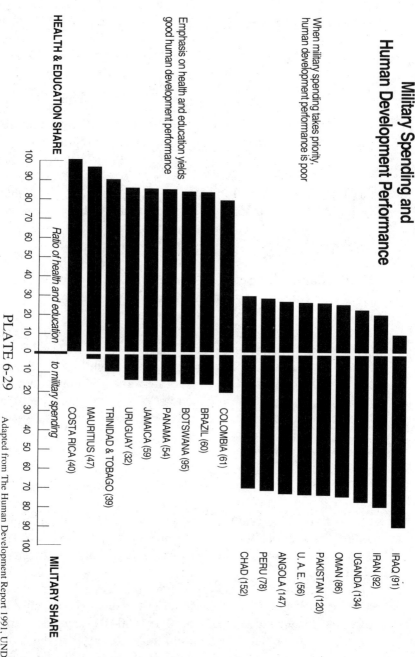

HEALTH & EDUCATION SHARE

Ratio of health and education

to military spending

MILITARY SHARE

COSTA RICA (40)
MAURITIUS (47)
TRINIDAD & TOBAGO (39)
URUGUAY (32)
JAMAICA (59)
PANAMA (54)
BOTSWANA (95)
BRAZIL (60)
COLOMBIA (61)

CHAD (152)
PERU (78)
ANGOLA (147)
U. A. E. (56)
PAKISTAN (120)
OMAN (86)
UGANDA (134)
IRAN (92)
IRAQ (91)

priorities before annual education expenditures per school-age child match the current level of military expenditures per soldier). In some categories, this Report diverges from HDI figures, since HDI only includes funds spent at national levels of government, rather that using percentage of GNP figures.[21]

- *Capital stocks of built infrastructure less depreciation.* By this kind of measure, the U.S. budget would be in surplus, and this has now begun to generate a debate among economists in the United States about the way national accounts are structured, as well as a spate of articles on whether deficits are real or if so, whether they matter.

- *Capital stocks of natural resources, parks, genetic diversity of species,* etc., as well as minerals and conventionally viewed resources such as Costa Rica's new model of natural resources (developed by Dr. Carlos Quesada and Dr. Alvaro Umana). Studies of Brazil's rain forests show that it would be twice as efficient, even in traditional economic terms, to use sustainable-yield methods of selective gathering and harvesting of these forests rather than to cut or burn them for traditional agriculture or cattle ranching (according to *The Economist*).

    U.N. Environment Programme (UNEP) is a primary source of worldwide data on *Environmental Quality*, as well as national agencies which are measuring the pollution of air, water, rates of recycling and reuse, etc. An urban air pollution index might be one of the most relevant and widely comparable indicators. The Organization for Economic Co-operation and Development (OECD) released its own Environmental Indicators in 1991.[22]

- *Energy efficiency* is another key indicator of overall production efficiency. Much data is available, some of the best is from the U.S.-based Rocky Mountain Institute in Colorado. As noted, the United States uses two and a half times as much energy to produce a unit of GNP as does Japan and many West European countries. At last, in 1991, the energy efficiency end-use paradigm was accepted into the mainstream in simultaneous articles in *Business Week* (September 16, 1991) and *The Economist* (August 31, 1991).

- *Per capita income statistics need to be reformulated* to show the relative gaps between richest and poorest quintiles of the population, between males and females, and whether the gap is widening or closing. Statistics are often available and this is another example of the need to *adopt* and *publicize* indicators that already exist.

It would be counterproductive if new indicators were to become weighted and averaged together—lending to more fetishizing of one single index, which tries to add up all the apples and oranges into a single number coefficient. This can very soon lead to the same kind of nonsense as the GNP indicators. It is better on both scientific grounds, as well as those of public education and efficient, democratic government to have a *group* of indicators covering different dimensions of development and welfare such as my Country Futures Indicators. Then, an effort must be made to "train" the news media to use them as they are, even if this may require more time and space. Only *transparent* and *tangible* indicators that people can readily understand and visualize and relate to their own lives will produce the desired political constituency for needed government policies. This has been an endemic problem with economics, and its arcane formulae, which have left people mystified, alienated and demotivated.

Human imagination and creativity are the truly unlimited resources in our new equations, bounded only by the social capital invested in developing caring, responsible citizens, whose gifts can contribute to the further evolution of their societies and the whole human family. At last, more and more countries are coming to realize that people are the real wealth of nations.

Much experimentation with formatting these new indicators of development will be needed, since although much of the raw data is readily available from traditional sources, such as the United Nations and the World Bank, it requires reformulating around the specific goals and priorities that different societies determine in their own democratic processes. Many indicators will be designed locally, such as the "Quality of Life" indicators of Jacksonville, Florida, and those of other U.S. cities collated by the Population Crisis Committee of Washington, DC.[23] Others will be designed regionally and may not be relevant internationally. However, after an experimental period of some years, it is certain that many indicators such as those already widely comparable: infant mortality, low birth weight, literacy, air and water quality, as well as data on poverty gaps and energy efficiency, will drift upward and assume the status of internationally comparable indicators of development. They will take their place alongside syntheses of the Basic Human Needs indicators which emerged out of the debates of the 1970s and 1980s.

Local indicators

While national accounts and indicators are important, local indicators provide the balance to correct overaggregation. Local indicators and methods now being tried in the United States are useful, while key experiments during the 1980s were in response to the economic and social problems experienced by many localities as a result of the laissez-faire policies and budget priorities of the Reagan administration. The local search for alternative models in many states in the United States stemmed partly from the national policies based on overaggregated "statistical illusions" such as GNP, inflation, unemployment, interest rates and all the other paraphernalia of macroeconomic management. Even mainstream U.S. economic development consultants are beginning to advise local governments not to rely on GNP led models of development, but to find local resources, talents and capital for building "home grown" economies, such as the Corporation for Enterprise Development of Washington, DC, and the Naisbitt Group founded by John Naisbitt, author, with his wife, Patricia Aburdene, of *Megatrends* and its 1990 sequel. Due to its failure at the local level, where conditions are vastly different across the North American continent, macroeconomic management has become almost as discredited in the United States as have the centralized Stalinist policies in the USSR. Both became bureaucratic, out of touch with regional needs, relying more in the United States on "single bullet" monetary and fiscal policies with very different lead and lag times, which often were in conflict with each other. As the seven great globalizations took hold during the 1980s (see Plate 3-14: Emerging Era of Global Interdependence), it was clear that *domestic* economic policy was a thing of the past, as such policies were swamped each day by the billions of footloose "hot" money sloshing around the Planet seeking interest rate advantage. No one knows how to measure these global monetary aggregates, which also began swamping bilateral trade statistics, obscuring policy options and leading to faulty trade legislation and unnecessary conflict with trading partners.

In all this national confusion, with rising domestic deficits in the United States, its states and localities were left to fend for themselves. Many, suffering severe economic disruption, unemployment, deficits, crime, social and environmental problems, turned to experiments and activist policies, in spite of their ideological commitments to the "free market" and nonintervention. Formerly, they had relied on accountant firms to assist in their economic development goals. This economic approach offered assessments of a state's "business climate" in terms of what conditions the firms' corporate clients were looking for in their location of plants. Predictably, they told states that a good business climate was one of low taxes, tax credits, cheap land and cheap labor, i.e., the "plantation model," mentioned earlier. Such a strategy in the new

Profile of Human Distress in the Industrial Countries

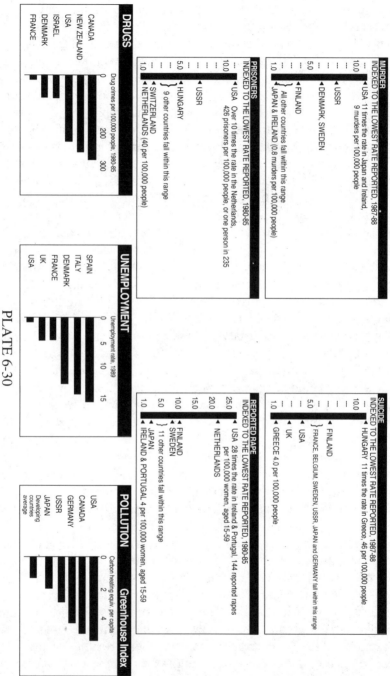

MURDER
INDEXED TO THE LOWEST RATE REPORTED, 1987-88

USA 11 times the rate in Japan and Ireland,
     9 murders per100,000 people

10.0 ▲ USSR

5.0   ▲ DENMARK, SWEDEN

      ▲ FINLAND

1.0   } All other countries fall within this range
      ▲ JAPAN & IRELAND (0.8 murders per 100,000 people)

PRISONERS
INDEXED TO THE LOWEST RATE REPORTED, 1980-85

      ▲ USA Over 10 times the rate in the Netherlands,
10.0   426 prisoners per 100,000 people, or one person in 235

5.0   ▲ USSR

      ▲ HUNGARY
      } 9 other countries fall within this range

      ▲ SWITZERLAND
1.0   ▲ NETHERLANDS (40 per 100,000 people)

DRUGS

Drug crimes per 100,000 people, 1980-85
0   200   300

CANADA
NEW ZEALAND
USA
ISRAEL
DENMARK
FRANCE

SUICIDE
INDEXED TO THE LOWEST RATE REPORTED, 1987-88

      ▲ HUNGARY 11 times the rate in Greece, 46 per 100,000 people
10.0

      ▲ FINLAND

5.0   } FRANCE, BELGIUM, SWEDEN, USSR, JAPAN and GERMANY fall within this range
      ▲ USA
      ▲ UK

1.0   ▲ GREECE 4.0 per 100,000 people

REPORTED RAPE
INDEXED TO THE LOWEST RATE REPORTED, 1980-85

25.0 ▲ USA 28 times the rate in Ireland & Portugal, 144 reported rapes
             per 100,000 women, aged 15-59
20.0 ▲ NETHERLANDS

15.0

10.0 ▲ FINLAND
      ▲ SWEDEN

5.0   } 11 other countries fall within this range
      ▲ JAPAN
1.0   IRELAND & PORTUGAL 4 per 100,000 women, aged 15-59

UNEMPLOYMENT

Unemployment rate, 1989
0   5   10   15

SPAIN
ITALY
DENMARK
FRANCE
UK
USA

POLLUTION   Greenhouse Index

Carbon heating equiv. per capita
0   2   4

USA
CANADA
GERMANY
USSR
JAPAN
Developing
countries
average

PLATE 6-30

Adapted from The Human Development Report 1990, UNDP New York global economy puts the state in direct competition with much lower wage and resource countries, *also* offering tax holidays. Indeed, most multinational corporations have financial models which can tell them on a daily basis which country is currently offering them an annual 35 percent return on their investment. Local officials can never win at such games in the global financial fast lane, since their responsibilities involve real people who must be trained or retrained and real facilities that must be built, whereas the corporate players and investors are operating at the speed of global electronic funds transfer, with no allegiance to any locality.

Quality-of-life indicators

Another approach in the desperate search for local development is the use of comparative quality-of-life indicators developed by firms such as the Midwest Research Institute of Kansas City, which rates various cities for their liveability and attractiveness to top managers, their schools, research facilities and cultural opportunities, climate, etc., as well as the more traditional factors such as trained workers, few unions, capital availability, friendly politicians, and weak environmental laws. Another new approach is that of Ameritrust/SRI (formerly the Stanford Research Institute) of Menlo Park, California. Their revised indicators of economic capacity (1986) are based on a somewhat arbitrary regional grouping of states and still geared towards traditional economic growth. However, these indicators move away from the "plantation model" and identify "quality inputs" such as an educated workforce, level of state investment in academic excellence, research facilities, quality of faculty at universities, numbers of PhDs graduated, levels of state investment in infrastructure, civic services and other quality-of-life factors, as well as capital availability.

Transforming economies leave statisticians in the dust

Everywhere in the world economies are changing ever faster. So measuring their performance is a moving target too. As new social goals, new categories of products and services, and new views of wealth and progress emerge, new questions are raised about *what* to measure.

Efforts to catch up are beginning, for example:

- Chairman of President Bush's Council of Economic Advisors, Michael Boskin, has called for an additional $36 million to modernize U.S. government statistics. "GNP data misled U.S. policy makers in 1990 by underestimating the severity of the current recession," noted Senator Paul Sarbanes, Chairman of the Joint Economic Committee.

The World's Women: Heading Households—Trends and Statistics (1970-1990)

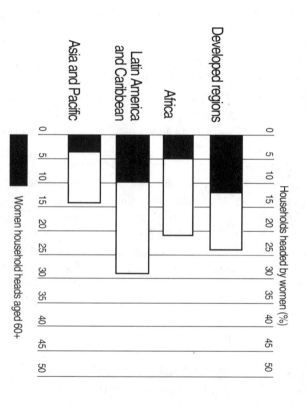

Households headed by women (%)

Developed regions

Africa

Latin America
and Caribbean

Asia and Pacific

■ Women household heads aged 60+

Up to 30 percent of households are now headed by women. Nearly half the women heading households in developed regions and at least a quarter in other regions are elderly.

Source: *The Worlds Women 1970-1990.* United Nations, New York

PLATE 6-31

• Recently, the Inter-Action Council (a group of thirty-five former heads of state) meeting in London to assess the economic transformations occurring in Eastern Europe and the USSR, specifically called for better indicators of development beyond today's GNP. [24]

• The 1991 Human Development Index[25] from the U.N. Development Program has progressed in this second edition to include new indicators measuring environmental damage and human freedom, in addition to its original focus on life expectancy, literacy, infant mortality and ratios between civilian and military budgets. The HDI is now a precision policy tool for governments to actually identify waste and improve their efficiency and performance in targeting the goals of their electorates. These popular goals of education, health, democratic participation are clearly more decisive in positioning a country for progress in the 1990s than simple GNP-growth.

• The November 1991 Second Economic Summit of the Group of Fifteen heads of states has already commissioned several studies on ways to correct errors in GNP and construct broader indices (including the 1989 Caracas Report, *Toward A New Way to Measure Development*, and the 1990 *Challenge to the South*). President Carlos Andres Perez of Venezuela, who hosted the G-15, sees development in more human terms, beyond GNP-growth and "economism."

This new ferment among a small group of statistical experts, politicians and the U.N. Development Program has still not yet spread to other U.N. agencies the World Bank, or most other development programs. Barriers to the adoption of such more realistic measures of human progress are legion: (1) economic theories are still grounded in static notions of equilibrium which cannot embrace change; (2) many governments do not want to be held so clearly accountable to their citizens for their performance; (3) academic conventions change slowly and statisticians are more comfortable with the old categories and data series and prefer measuring quantities to deciding what *ought* to be measured under new conditions.

For example, today's unprecedented trend toward democratization clearly needs measuring and HDI includes a Human Freedom Index which it finds correlated with prosperity (*Christian Science Monitor*, May 24, 1991). HDI has also become embroiled in controversy, particularly over its Human Freedom Index, since many governments, particularly in the South and the Islamic world, object that it may lead to new kinds of

The World's Women: Working Hours—Trends and Statistics

Women in most regions spend as much or more time working than men when unpaid housework is taken into account

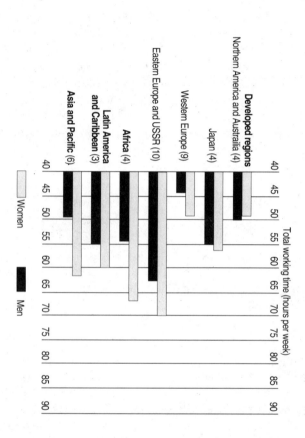

Total working time (hours per week)

Developed regions
Northern America and Australia (4)

Japan (4)

Western Europe (9)

Eastern Europe and USSR (10)

Africa (4)

Latin America and Caribbean (3)

Asia and Pacific (6)

☐ Women   ■ Men

40 45 50 55 60 65 70 75 80 85 90

Note: Numbers in parentheses refer to the number of studies in each region.

PLATE 6-32

Source: *The Worlds Women 1970-1990*, United Nations, New York "human rights conditionality," and see it as incorporating too many Western-style values for loans and development aid.[26] HDI also looks at the way this prosperity is shared (which GNP obscures) and finds Brazil, Nepal and Cote d'Ivoire with the widest gaps between rich and poor. HDI even cheekily offers a rule of thumb for measuring government inefficiency: public spending exceeding 25-35 percent of GNP with less than two percent of GNP going to human priority concerns. Here too, Brazil shares bottom ranking with Thailand and Sierra Leone. Other losers on the HDI scorecard are those with large military versus civilian budgets for education and health at the national level of governments only. The United States spends $37 on the military for every Federal Budget dollar spent on these two civilian needs, while Britain's ratio is 45-to-1 and the Arab states stand at 166-to-1. Such figures were not listed for Israel, but for comparison, Israel has 191 military personnel for every 100 teachers. Clearly, such focused "scorecards" can pinpoint areas where policy action is needed, such as the urgent requirement to limit the new arms race in the Mideast recognized by President Bush and other leaders.

Another aspect of HDI is poverty, not only that of the one billion people in the developing countries, but also the 100 million poor in the market democracies of the industrial countries of North America and West Europe, and an additional 100 million below the poverty line in East Europe and the USSR. As the Inter-Action Council report noted, the transitions of the Eastern European countries cannot be understood from the often obsolete perspectives of economic theory—as simply transitions from communism to capitalism and the "free market" of textbooks. They are social, political and cultural transformations to new mixtures of markets and regulations—indeed, all economies are "mixed" while economics, as yet, has no theories for them.

A new Human Distress Index compares industrial countries and finds that Canada, Austria, Australia and the United States lead the world in serious road injuries. In the European Community, Spain, Ireland, France, Belgium and Denmark topped the unemployment scorecard. The United States leads in divorces (with the USSR second) and in the most rapes reported (114 per 100,000 women) while Finland, Austria, France, Belgium and Sweden top the suicide statistics.

The 1991 HDI now includes some environmental indicators including inventories of radioactive wastes (Britain leads with 1,279 kilograms per hectare of land, with Bulgaria and France runners-up). Canada and the United States lead the world in industrial air pollutants (with 78 and 64 kilograms per 100 people respectively) with Australia (40 kg.) and Britain

The World's Women: Value of Unpaid Housework—Trends and Statistics

Estimates of addition to GDP if women's unpaid housework were included

Country	Year	Value of unpaid housework as % of GDP*	Sponsoring organization or researcher
A. For all women			
Developed regions			
Canada	1961	27	Statistics Canada
	1971	28	
Denmark	1949	50	Denmark Statistics
Finland	1979	31	Ministry of Social Affairs and Health
France	1975	24	INSEE
Norway	1972	41	A.L. Brathaug and A.B. Dahle
	1981	28	
United States	1929	25	National Bureau of Economic Research
	1960	29	M. Murphy
	1970	27	
	1975	30	J. Peskin
	1980	23	
Developing regions			
India	1970	33	M. Mukherjee
Pakistan	1975	35**	T. Alauddin
Philippines	1982	11	National Commission on the Role of Filipino Women
B. Housewives not economically active			
Chile	1981	15**	V.L. Pardo and N.P. Cruz
Japan	1955	11	Economic Council
	1970	9	
Venezuela	1982	22**	Central Bank

* Methods of valuation based on equivalent market wages or services were used except in the case of Japan where overall average female wage was used.

** Data from one or a small number of major cities only.

Source: Compiled by Luisella Goldschmidt-Clermont as consultant to the United Nations Secretariat. From *The World's Women 1970-1990*, United Nations, New York

PLATE 6-33

(37 kg.) as runners up. The air quality winner among industrial countries was Portugal (only 12 kg.). Hungary reports the highest level of hazardous wastes (76.7 tons per square kilometer) with the Netherlands in second place at 44.2 tons. Figures for other heavily-polluted East European countries and the USSR were not available. Canada has made great strides in developing a National Set of Environment Indicators.

- The 1991 *Report on Canada's Progress Toward A National Set of Environmental Indicators,*[27] called for following its government's Green Plan and following the initiative of the Organization for Economic Cooperation and Development (OECD). This is perhaps a state-of-the-art approach which goes well beyond efforts by economists to try to embrace so many diverse fields in their own approaches to environmental accounting or auditing. These suffer from efforts to weigh all these multi-disciplinary factors within economic scalars and obsolete models from welfare theory, e.g., "How much would people be willing to pay to keep a wilderness protected from developers?" This ignores prior distribution of wealth and power in society, and the fact that while wilderness developers will profit, ordinary people will not, and are being, in effect asked to behave altruistically—which is irrational in market economic theory. Thus, the Canadian indicators (43 in eighteen issue areas: air and water quality, solid waste, contaminants in species of birds and fish, etc.) employ experts and statisticians from mostly other disciplines than economics.

- Another recent release from the United Nations is *The World's Women: Trends and Statistics, 1970-1990,*[28] which for the first time, addresses the inequities of GNP statistics in ignoring the unpaid work of women in subsistence farming, food processing, operating household enterprises, as well as in maintaining households, parenting children and caring for old, sick and handicapped members of the community. The report calculates that if women's contribution only to the latter household tasks were accounted for in GNP and Gross Domestic Product (GDP) these would rise in all countries by 25-30 percent. Women today, as mentioned, head 30 percent of all households worldwide and everywhere they work longer hours than men.

- Other notable new approaches include the U.N.'s *State of the World's Children*[29] reports, whose 1991 edition attests to the low priority all governments put on their most precious future asset. Reversing these trends and preventing the 40,000 unnecessary child deaths each day is estimated to cost $20 billion—as much as

Women's Status in Highest and Lowest Ranked Countries

In Sweden...

(Population: 8.4 million, Area: 173,730 square miles)

- Female life expectancy is 81 years.
- One in 167 girls dies before her fifth birthday.
- One in 53 15-year olds will not survive her childbearing years. (One percent of these deaths relate to pregnancy and childbirth.)
- Fewer than one percent of 15-19 year old women have already been married.
- Women bear one to two children on average.
- Over three fourths of married women use contraception.
- Virtually all school-aged girls are in school.
- Female university enrollment is 37% of women aged 20-24.
- About half the secondary school teachers are women.
- Three out of five women are in the paid labor force.
- Two out of five women are professionals.
- Women live an average of seven years longer than men.
- Women and men have similar literacy rates.
- About half of the paid workforce is female.
- In 1988 women held 113 seats in Sweden's 349-member parliament.

In Bangladesh...

(Population: 109.5 million, Area: 55,598 square miles)

- Female life expectancy is 49 years.
- One in five girls dies before her fifth birthday.
- One in six 15-year olds will not survive her childbearing years. (About one third of these deaths relate to pregnancy and childbirth.)
- Almost 70 percent of 15-19 year old women have already been married.
- Women bear five to six children on average.
- One fourth of married women use contraception.
- One in three school-aged girls is in school.
- Female university enrollment is less than 2% of women aged 20-24.
- One in 10 secondary school teachers is a women.
- One woman in 15 is in the paid labor force.
- Only three out of 1,000 women are professionals.
- Women live an average of two years less than men.
- Some 24 percent more women are illiterate than men.
- Only 14 percent of the paid workforce is female.
- In 1988 women held four seats in Bangladesh's 302-member parliament, out of 30 reserved for them.

PLATE 6-34

Source: Population Crisis Committee, Washington, DC

the world spends on the military every ten days, and of course, this $20 billion would create thousands of new enterprises and jobs.

None of these new indicators of human development and quality-of-life have yet displaced GNP, but politicians, goaded by their voters in many countries including Germany, France, Britain, Denmark, the Netherlands, Sweden, and Venezuela are calling for their introduction. These trends, together with even more broad-based indicators (such as my own Country Futures Indicators, which include bio-diversity and species loss, cultural and recreational assets and accounting for the unpaid productive work), will mean boom times for number crunchers everywhere.

U.S. statistics badly need retooling, as Michael Boskin rightly shows. Yet Boskin himself, along with Budget Director Richard Darman and White House Chief of Staff John Sununu are themselves still part of the old guard of traditional economics, and may actually slow down the full range of changes needed to refocus our own policies for the 21st century. However, the problem with all such economists' attempts to create a single index of development is precisely the incommensurability of all these different dimensions that make up truly sustainable quality-of-life. Many now share my view that such new indicators must remain "unbundled," so that ordinary citizens can clearly understand how they relate to goals in education, health, housing, political participation, cultural goals and environmental safety, such as the Country Futures Indicators (Plate 6-26). In fact, some of the most useful new indicators are those prepared by non-governmental organizations, such as Worldwatch Institute's annual *State of the World Reports* mentioned earlier, which take an inter-disciplinary, ecological approach which identifies "threshold" problems which are likely to become irreversible if not addressed, such as global warming. Others take a local approach, such as the new *Green Index, 1991-1992*,[30] a state-by-state guide to environmental health in the United States from the Institute for Southern Studies, Durham, NC, and the State of the States Reports, published by Renew America of Washington, DC.

Searching for scorecards

Lastly, it is clear that the adoption of more realistic indicators of development is not a technical problem. Many socially-concerned statisticians, sociologists and a few renegade economists have produced good work for years, unused and underfunded by their agencies, such as those summarized in the U.N. Handbook on Social Indicators 1989. *The World Paper*, on which I serve as an editorial advisor, is published as a monthly insert in some twenty-eight influential newspapers in five languages and covers the new indicators now proliferating. Many remain pessimistic that such broader indicators will ever be accepted by governments, since they will hold politicians to much higher standards of performance. At a presentation in Budapest at the World Futures Studies Federation, I was asked, "What makes you think that governments will buy these indicators of yours?" I replied, "What makes you think that I will try to sell them to governments—or to persuade economists of their social importance?" As I have discovered over the past twenty years, one does not debate with economists—one simply hires them. Likewise, one does not entreat governments or media editors to use new indicators; it is better to find the right audiences and markets and sell them as broadly as possible. Today's movements for greater democracy and more accountable governments and corporations augur a wide new market of aware citizens and consumers. Yet another new set of "post-economic" indicators, designed by Victor Anderson has been published by the New Economics Foundation, London, U.K.[31]

Perhaps in this way, objections of governments will be end run. The main roadblocks are (1) political will, i.e., government leaders will have to require their bureaucracies to adopt them, and (2) obsolete economic and industrial ideologies still pervasive among "development" officials in the majority of aid and lending agencies whose overaggregated macroeconomic models still predominate, even as they become little more than statistical illusions. The new indicators should remain disaggregated, distinct and politically-transparent, so that average TV viewers can respond to them, especially at the ballot box during election times. This will mean that the new indicators may be dismissed by intellectuals whose main efforts have been directed toward the heroic overaggregations of statistical "apples and oranges" which constitute the GNP. Clearly, a new world debate redefining development is overdue. New scorecards are now essential to this debate, as well as in providing the necessary benchmarks and course corrections on the path toward the new goals. Further evidence that grassroots groups and citizens grasp the fact that these new indicators of real wealth and progress are needed is the 1991 Report of the North American Coalition on Religion and Ecology (representing hundreds of inter-faith congregations) on Principles for an Earth Charter (Plate 8-44) which specifically calls for replacing the Gross National Product in all countries with more correct and multifaceted indicators such as the UNDPs Human Development Index.

The proliferation and acceptance of such indices could, in itself, be an indicator of the restoration of mental health to the human species as well as to the biosphere. We must never forget that, in the most scientific sense, *reality is whatever we pay attention to!* Indicators only *reflect* our innermost core values and goals, measuring the development of our own understanding. At this point in human evolution, we can no longer avoid the consequences of our old belief systems which are threatening our survival. Post-economic policies are based on the knowledge that all our individual self interests are equated with the interest of the whole human species and all other lifeforms of this Planet.

Chapter Six Footnotes

1. *The Economist*, September 21, 1991, p. 33.
2. Irma Adelman and Cynthia Taft Morris, *Economic Growth and Social Equity in Developing Countries*, Stanford University Press, CA, 1973.
3. Hazel Henderson, *The Politics of the Solar Age: Alternatives to Economics*, current edition from Knowledge Systems, Inc., Indianapolis, 1988, pages 386-389.
4. Ruth Leger Sivard, *World Military and Social Expenditures*, World Priorities Institute (1991 14th Edition) Box 25140, Washington, DC, 20007.
A study of the costs of economic conversion in each state, *Building a Peace Economy* by John T. Marlin and Betty Lall, Westview Press, 1991, is available through the Council on Economic Priorities.
5. *State of the World Reports* (published annually since 1985) available from Worldwatch Institute, 1776 Massachusetts Avenue, NW, Washington, DC 20036.
6. *The Green Budget*, Editors Kemball-Cook, Baker and Mattingly, foreword by Sara Parkin, The British Green Party, Merlin Press, London, 1991.
7. *World Development Report 1991*, The World Bank, Washington, DC, Oxford University Press, New York, 1991. p. 31.
8. The report is now available in English, *Redefining Wealth and Progress*, foreword by President Carlos Andres Perez, Knowledge Systems, Indianapolis, 1990.
9. Herman Daly and John Cobb, *For the Common Good*, Beacon Press, Boston, 1990.
10. World Commission on Environment and Development, *Our Common Future*, Oxford University Press, New York-London 1989, page 320.
11. U.N. Development Program, *Human Development Report 1990 and 1991*, Oxford University Press, New York-London, 1990, 1991.
12. Sippanondha Ketudat with Robert O. Textor, *The Middle Path for the Future of Thailand: Technology in Harmony with Culture and Environment*. East-West Center, Honolulu, HI 1991.
13. Morris Miller, *Debt and Environment*, United Nations Publications, New York, 1991, p. 27.
14. Ibid.

15. *The Economist Book of Vital World Statistics*, Times Books, Random House, New York, 1990.

16. Hernando de Soto, *The Other Path*, HarperCollins, NY 1990.

17. James Robertson, *Future Wealth: A New Economics for the 21st Century*, Bootstrap Press, New York, 1990.

18. Marilyn Waring, *If Women Counted*, HarperCollins, San Francisco, 1989.

19. Graeme Shankland, *Wonted Work*, Bootstrap Press, New York, 1989.

20. Nicholls and Dyson, *The Informal Economy: Where People are the Bottom Line*, Vanier Institute of the Family, 121 Slater Street, Ottawa, Canada, 1983.

21. op. cit. Sivard.

22. OECD *Environmental Indicators, 1991* available from The Organization for Economic Cooperation and Development, Paris and Washington, DC.

23. The Population Crisis Committee of Washington, DC. produces a wide array of excellent charts, wallposters and reports comparing quality-of-life factors affected by population growth and density, status of women, etc., that make effective teaching materials. Available from Population Crisis Committee, 1120 19th Street, NW, Suite 550, Washington, DC.

24. Report, *Economies in Transformation,* chaired by former Prime Minister of Canada, Pierre Elliott Trudeau, April 1991, page 3, available from the Inter-Action Council, 821 U.N. Plaza, New York.

25. op. cit. UNDP.

26. New York Times, "Index on Freedom Enrages Third World," June 23, 1991, Page 11.

27. Environmental Canada, *A Report on Canada's Progress Toward A National Set of Environmental Indicators,* January, 1991, Ottawa.

28. *The World's Women: Trends and Statistics, 1970-1990*, United Nations, NY, 1991.

29. U.N. Children's Fund (UNICEF), *The State of the World's Children 1991*, Oxford University Press, New York, 1991.

30. *Green Index, 1991-1992*, Institute for Southern Policies, Bob Hall and Mary Lee Kerr, Island Press, Washington, DC, 1991.

31. Victor Anderson, *Alternative Economic Indicators,* Routledge, London, 1991. New Economics Foundation, 88-94 Wentworth Street, London, E1 7SE, U.K.

NOTE: Important additional information addressing the issues presented in this chapter can be obtained from the Office of Technology Assessment, Washington, DC 20515. Particularly recommended by the author are *Statistical Needs for a Changing U.S. Economy* (background paper, September 1989) and *Energy Use and the U.S. Economy* (background paper, June 1990) which contains an index of U.S. energy intensity.

United Nations Commission on Transnational Corporations

Recommendations preparatory to the United Nations Conference on Environment and Development, Brazil, June, 1992

- Observance of international environmental standards and guidelines, both governmental and corporate;

- Improving management and regulation of industrial processes, including the application of corporate worldwide environment and development policies and the maintenance of consistently high environmental, health and safety standards for all products, processes and services;

- Developing and providing access to environmentally sound technologies particularly for developing countries;

- Using environment and development accounting and reporting methods;

- Consideration of principles such as the "polluter pays," preventive action at the source, and the precautionary approach to environment and development issues;

- Minimizing the risks to human life, health, property and the environment, as well as the question of reparation of damage.

The commission also plans further work on the feasibility of establishing mechanisms for financial or in-kind contributions by TNCs for protecting and enhancing the environment. The findings of the research project on the "Transfer of environmentally sound technologies to developing countries on favorable terms" will be forwarded to the third session of the Preparatory Committee (Geneva, 12 August-4-September 1991).

Source: United Nations Commission on Transnational Corporations, UN, 1991

PLATE 7-35

CHAPTER 7

Greening the Economy and Recycling Economics

Environmentalism emerged as a real movement in the United States in the private sector during the 1960s. Small groups of individuals began to organize around specific, local environmental concerns—in much the same way that minimata disease victims banded together in Japan. However, there were few such horribly visible disasters here in the United States. Rather, such issues as pollution of rivers and the Great Lakes focused these early environmentalists, as well as urban air pollution, which led me to join in founding Citizens for Clean Air of New York City in 1964. Rachel Carson had written her ground-breaking, *Silent Spring* in 1962, which, though much criticized by chemical companies, alerted a whole generation to the dangers of pesticides. Today, after a thirty-year struggle, the U.S. Congress seems set to pass tough pesticide controls which industry prefers to having many different state laws.

Not surprisingly women were in the forefront of the early environmental movement, just as they pioneered Seikatsu food buying co-operatives in Japan. Since women were labelled in the role of "consumers" they took special responsibility for the safety of their families, and saw the coming environmental destruction with clearer eyes than many men, who were caught up in the industrial world as "salarymen." The first broad coalition between many of these local groups, the older conservation organizations including Sierra Club, Audubon Society, the Wilderness Society and others, took place in the late 1960s at such gatherings as the First National Congress on Population and the Environment in Chicago in 1969. For the first time, many local pollution crusaders saw themselves in a broader context as "environmentalists," a word that only came into common usage about that time.

Earth Day, organized by Senator Gaylord Nelson of Wisconsin in 1970, extended the definition of environmentalism to include groups working on population control, consumer protection, such as the Ralph Nader groups, others working for better urban design, public transportation, social equity (to try to reduce over-consumption and waste) as well as promoters of organic agriculture, preventive health care and a shift from reliance on fossil fuels and nuclear power to renewable energy and recycling. Because environmentalism was expressed in so many groups over such a range of issues, it remained misunderstood and largely unnoticed by society and was portrayed by mass media, only rarely, as an oddball movement of social utopians and malcontents. I remember being invited to Japan on a lecture tour in 1973, and finding my counterparts, such as Professor Jun Ui of Tokyo, and the "nisshoken" (solar energy) groups treated in similar ways by much of the Japanese media.

All this changed in 1990, when the second Earth Day, with its public relations and grassroots organizing efforts, at last broke through the alternative "mini-media" into the mainstream, including *Time, Newsweek,* and *The New York Times.* These dominant-culture media began reporting twenty-year old stories (long-covered in the alternative press) as if they were "news." The global warming problem (covered in my 1981 edition of *The Politics of the Solar Age*) was highlighted, along with ozone depletion, rain forest loss, desertification and all the other environmental movement's long-standing concerns. This leap in coverage, in turn, caught the attention of corporations, pollsters, marketers, and suddenly, to the amazement of environmentalists, they found their protest movement was now "trendy"! Just as in Tokyo where Suntory beer is now "Thinking About the Earth," thousands of American companies started to persuade the public that we could *consume* our way to a clean environment![1] Green marketing claims became ever wilder and watchdog magazines such as *Mother Jones* began exposing "green" frauds and environmentally-friendly labels. The environmental movement launched its own Green Seal of Approval, founded by media and real estate executive Rena Shulsky, also an environmental activist.

Until 1990, most corporations in the United States waited until some citizen activist group or stockholder campaign forced them to begin cleaning up their products and processes. For example, back in 1968 I had worked as an organizer on Campaign GM (the Campaign to Make General Motors Responsible) begun by Ralph Nader to garner proxies at GM's annual meeting to elect three new directors to the board: a prominent environmental scientist, a well-known consumer advocate and a respected African-American, civil-rights-activist and business leader. Although the

GM management resisted our campaign in many ways, they later added three new directors to change their policies on environment, civil rights and consumer issues. Even so, GM still resists high mileage laws, while Honda, in 1991 unveiled its new Civic which does 55 miles per gallon.

No one should be surprised at this corporate foot-dragging behavior. Traditional economic theory (which has changed remarkably little in the past twenty years) holds that corporate decisions should be narrowly-focused on the balance sheet and on maximizing the stockholders returns in the short-run. Furthermore, any concern for broader social issues was not only viewed as irrational, but downright wrong and even immoral, as some money managers still believe today. During this early 1970s period, I wrote many articles in such investment and business journals as *The Financial Analysts Journal* of New York, pointing out that such short-term economic theorizing was short-changing society and causing significant environmental costs as well. These hidden costs of production were being passed on to consumers (for example in ill-health and cleaning bills), taxpayers (to collect excess trash) and to future generations as these pollution problems worsened. I was proud that my analyses earned me the title among many corporate executives of "one of the most dangerous women in America!"

Today, all this has changed dramatically. Environmentalists are courted by corporations to serve on their boards and accept corporate grants for their programs. For example, one of the early environmental consumer protection research groups, the Council on Economic Priorities of New York (on whose board I have served since 1970), was considered "radical." Today, it is widely-respected, its reports hit the front pages of the big daily papers, and its *Shopping For A Better World* supermarket guide has sold over 700,000 copies.[2] In Japan, the *Asahi Journal* used CEP methods to evaluate 70 large Japanese corporations in similar areas of social responsibility.

Thus one must conclude that it is the maturing of the citizen-based environmental organizations (many now large, with millions of members), together with saturation media coverage that has produced the new environmentally-concerned businesses and large corporations. This is not to downplay corporate efforts, but only to acknowledge the constraints imposed on their managers by traditional economic theories, investment analysts, and models of pricing and marketing. (The plates in this chapter and the next clearly point out the directions in which the people are pushing their structures.)

This traditional economics, as we have seen, is destructive to the environment, focusing on continually increasing the GNP. It is this kind of distorted economic growth that both GNP and corporate balance sheets measure, while the heavy social costs incurred must be born by local governments who clean up the mess, deal with broken neighborhoods, crime, drugs, monitoring pollution levels, etc. This raises local taxes or leads to deficits in many city and provincial budgets. The next stage is when these cities and provinces begin to compete with each other to lower their regulatory standards for pollution, urban design, etc., in order to try to lure companies to move from other cities into the area to create jobs and provide new tax revenues. As we have seen, this only leads to even greater social and environmental costs more deficits or inflation—finally resulting in the politicians calling for more economic growth to "solve" the problems. The focus on money transactions and balance sheets causes erroneous decisions and even less realistic assessments of the hidden costs of this type of "economic development."

Today, we see how faulty, obsolete economics led to the "bubble" economy, both in Japan and the United States during the "economic growth" of the 1980s. Now we see the real-world "hangover" in both countries in junk bonds; failed banks, savings and loan and insurance companies; overvalued stock markets and real estate; and the loss of faith of small investors and citizens as they saw the systemic effects of greed and efforts to maximize profits and "the bottom line." We see the industrial value system splitting in many mature industrial countries, such as the United States and West Europe, where old short-term profit maximizing is giving way to older, more traditional community concerns, socially-responsible investing, and the search for a "greener," gentler economy. (See Plate 3-17: Values Bifurcating.)

Many companies are responding to the challenges of "green" marketing, "greener" products and more socially-responsible ways of doing business. The best indicator is the overall growth of the socially-responsible investment movement, up from $40 billion of assets in 1982 to $650 billion in 1991, with this type of "clean and green" investing growing faster than any other market segment. In addition, some of the socially-responsible funds out-perform the market, even though they screen companies (avoiding polluters, companies making weapons, or in nuclear energy, those unfair to workers or which test their products on animals or do business in repressive foreign regimes), which, in theory, increases their risk. The Calvert Social Investment Fund, with four portfolios (equity, bonds, money market, and balanced) is the "flagship" of the group. The oldest, and one of the most successful is Pax World Fund, which topped the performance in its class with a five-year return of 71.1 percent compared to the average of 57.4. These funds now have an

Index of their own, the Domini Social Index, a benchmark of 400 ethical stocks which gained 19 percent in 1990 compared with the Standard and Poors 500 Index, which was up 18 percent. Franklin Management and Research put out a list of the fifty most promising ethical stocks, including blue chips (such as Dayton Hudson Company, Digital Equipment and Minnesota Mining and Manufacturing), small new companies (Apple Computer, Ben and Jerry's and Wellman, which recycles plastics), utilities (Ameritech, due to its solar products; Energen; and Sierra Pacific), mutual fund groups (Calvert Social Investment Fund, Pax World and Parnassus), and money markets (South Shore Bank, which lends to neighborhood enterprises; Vermont National Bank; and Working Assets Money Fund).[3]

Electric utilities for many years rejected pressure from environmentalists to clean up and shift from simply building ever more power plants of low efficiency, to increasing overall efficiency and helping their customers purchase less wasteful appliances, light bulbs, shower heads and insulate their homes. Today, utilities are jumping on the environmental bandwagon and realizing that it is cheaper for them to even *give* their customers efficient light bulbs and shower heads and give them low-interest loans to install good windows and other insulation than it is to build new power plants. Typical of the new wave are Pacific Gas and Electric of California and even New York's old-fashioned Con Edison has turned around. It will now offer 80 percent discounts on compact fluorescent bulbs (the most efficient), free energy audits and a huge new rebate program for its business customers who replace energy-wasteful machinery and equipment, even up to covering its full cost.

Conservation is at last recognized as seven times more cost-effective than adding new supply. The much-touted "pollution licenses" discussed in Chapter Three, have, so far, been of little interest to utilities—in spite of the Chicago Board of Trade's decision in 1991 to trade them. Energy analyst Amory Lovins of the Rocky Mountain Institute estimates that the average cost of saving three quarters of all the electricity Americans now use would be about 0.6 cents per kilowatt hour (several times cheaper than just *running* a coal-fired power plant). The American Council for An Energy-Efficient Economy estimates that it would cost 1-2 cents per kilowatt hour. If either of these estimates prove correct, the justification for building *any* new power plants or transmission lines would vanish. Iowa Public Service Company has decided to test Amory Lovins' estimate in the town of Rock Valley, Iowa, where its 2700 people will have their homes, apartment buildings, factories, public buildings equipped with the very latest in electricity-saving devices. A similar test is planned by

Business Charter for Sustainable Development

International Chamber of Commerce's Principles for Environmental Management

1. Corporate priority
To recognize environmental management as among the highest corporate priorities and as a key determinant to sustainable development; to establish policies, programs and practices for conducting operations in an environmentally sound manner.

2. Integrated management
To integrate these policies, programs and practices fully into each business as an essential element of management in all its functions.

3. Process of improvement
To continue to improve corporate policies, programs and environmental performance taking into account technical developments, scientific understanding, consumer needs and community expectations, with legal regulations as a starting point and to apply the same environmental criteria internationally.

4. Employee education
To educate, train and motivate employees to conduct their activities in an environmentally responsible manner.

5. Prior assessment
To assess environmental impacts before starting a new activity or project and before decommissioning a facility or leaving a site.

6. Products and services
To develop and provide products or services that have no undue environmental impact and are safe in their intended use, that are efficient in their consumption of energy and material resources, and that can be recycled, reused or disposed of safely.

7. Customer advice
To advise and, where relevant, educate customers, distributors and the public in the safe use, transportation, storage and disposal of products provided; and to apply similar considerations to the provision of services.

8. Facilities and operations
To develop, design and operate facilities and conduct activities taking into consideration the efficient use of energy and materials, the sustainable use of reusable resources, the minimization of adverse environmental impact and waste generation, and the safe and responsible disposal of residual wastes.

9. Research
To conduct or support research on the environmental impacts of new materials, products, processes, emissions and wastes associated with the enterprise and on the means of minimizing such adverse impacts.

10. Precautionary approach
To modify the manufacture, marketing or use of products or services or the conduct of activities consistent with scientific and technical understanding, to prevent serious or irreversible environmental degradation.

11. Contractors and suppliers
To promote the adoption of these principles by contractors acting on behalf of the enterprise, encouraging and, where appropriate, requiring improvements in their practices to make them consistent with those of the enterprise; and to encourage the wider adoption of these principles by suppliers.

12. Emergency preparedness
To develop and maintain, where significant hazards exist, emergency preparedness plans in conjunction with the emergency services, relevant authorities and the local community, recognizing potential transboundary impacts.

13. Transfer of technology
To contribute to the transfer of environmentally sound technology and management methods throughout the industrial and public sectors.

14. Contributing to the common effort
To contribute to the development of public policy and to business, governmental and intergovernmental programs and educational initiatives that will enhance environmental awareness and protection.

15. Openness to concerns
To foster openness and dialogue with employees and the public, anticipating and responding to their concerns about the potential hazards and impacts of operations, products, wastes or services including those of transboundary or global significance.

16. Compliance and reporting
To measure environmental performance; to conduct regular environmental audits and assessments of compliance with company requirements, legal requirements and these principles; and periodically to provide appropriate information to the Board of Directors, shareholders, employees, the authorities and the public.

PLATE 7-36

Source: International Chamber of Commerce

Pacific Gas and Electric. Energy-use is the key to environmental quality, and when all the social and environmental costs are included in the price · of energy, we find that the environmental solution is also the economic solution. More and more countries are now also seeing that energy-efficient, environmentally-sound economies are necessary for truly sustainable development in the long-term. (See Plate 3-19: Restructuring Industrial Economies.)

Yet it is the private sector, especially global companies, which will have to understand all this and the design revolution that must take place. Some of them are appointing Vice Presidents for the Environment, including Dow Chemical, Exxon, Union Carbide, Chevron, Scott Paper and Walt Disney Company, while others including du Pont and Occidental Petroleum have created Vice Presidents for Health, Safety and Environment. Companies such as Minnesota Mining and Manufacturing (also known as 3M) have taken more systemic approaches: changing their production processes in their almost ten-year old program Pollution Prevention Pays. These twin lessons of energy-efficiency and preventing pollution at the source are the most important. This can only happen when prices are corrected to reflect their full cost and investments are costed out over their full useful life, so that the most ecologically benign technologies win out. The latest report on the social performance of 100 U.S. companies is the Council on Economic Priorities *Better World Investment Guide*.[4] Another newer approach is the social responsibility survey of the 1,000 largest industrial companies by Covenant Investment Management of Chicago. The survey ranked the group and found that the "Top 200" had not sacrificed returns, but had out-performed Standard and Poor's 500 in total 5-year returns by almost 15 percent.

Cutting-edge companies are moving beyond recycling into re-manufacturing and re-use. Hercules Aerospace Company now re-uses its huge rocket booster cases, which are buried upright in desert areas in Utah for water storage tanks. Other companies are getting into environmental enhancement rather than just pollution control. For example, Groundwater Technology, Inc. tackles formerly impossible tasks of restoring soils and underground water contaminated with oil or toxics by injecting naturally occurring micro-organisms which digest these contaminants harmlessly. And Israel's Weizmann Institute of Science has a new approach to solar energy which could at last, be a key to large scale application.[5] The British-based Body Shops International (now with 56 stores in the United States) is the pre-eminent pioneer, since its founder, former school teacher, Anita Roddick uses the stores to educate the public about environmental values. The stores sell natural, simple toiletries, soaps, toothpaste, etc., which are produced by indigenous people in developing countries, thus providing them with a living and showing them how to harvest in a sustainable way their land and forests. The store franchises are often owned by environmental activists, so that their cause can also provide them with a job and income. The stores are bases for environmental activism and campaigns and feature educational window displays and promotions to help customers understand current global environmental issues. The Body Shops are one of the most successful companies on the London Stock Exchange and Anita Roddick says she is *still* an educator.[6] Indeed, the Body Shops have changed the business paradigm forever and redefined what can be done by entrepreneurs in the private sector to make the world a better place. In Japan, similar creativity is shown by the Citizens Bank, a joint program of Tokyo's Koto Ward's Eitai Credit Union and Press Alternative, as well as the Shimin Bank, spearheaded by Masaru Kataoka, an irrepressible young entrepreneur who recently conducted an acid rain survey, mailing out hundreds of testing kits, so that people could not only test their own area's rainfall, but also contribute to an accurate statistical map analyzed by scientists. Perhaps, the most creative idea yet in energy is the conversion of old nuclear plants to natural gas which is cheap and as mentioned emits only half the CO_2 of oil or coal. CMS Corporation made its first purchase of an old nuclear plant in Midland Michigan and the plant was "recycled" in April 1991. William McCormick, CMS Corporation's chairman says that there are $20 billion worth of half-completed or abandoned nuclear plants as his "market." He says, "We are in the business of turning lemons into lemonade."[7]

Many consulting companies are growing up around the new environmental awareness of the big multi-nationals, offering "green" ideas, marketing, promotions, etc., while many advertising agencies now have special departments offering "green" campaigns. A recent Gallup poll taken around Earth Day found that 77 percent of adult Americans now define themselves as environmentalists. Many large accounting firms offer new environmental audits (although they go little beyond checking mere compliance with existing regulations). Several hundred small firms in the United States and Europe now offer environmental auditing services. The latest private sector thrusts in the environmental field include the many chief executives planning to attend the U.N. Conference on Environment and Development to be held in Brazil in June 1992. The International Chamber of Commerce has already drawn up a Business Charter for Sustainable Development (Plate 7-36). Hopefully, they will be looking for business opportunities in greener, more organically designed and ecologically-sound technologies: solar and renewable energy, wind, biogas, tidal and ocean thermal technologies, desert-greening and re-forestation. The Global Environment Fund, a limited partnership which invests in the best of environmental and energy efficient or "green" technologies wherever then can be found worldwide was founded by H. Jeffrey Leonard, author of *Pollution and the Struggle for World Product* (Cambridge University Press, 1988) and *Environment and the Poor: Development Strategies for a Common Agenda* (Transaction Books, 1989). All these efforts will need to be joint-ventured with entrepreneurs and governments in the countries of the Southern Hemisphere. The first Global Environmental Investment Conference was held in New York, September 1991. Co-sponsored by the Investment Management Institute, the United Nations and the International Finance Corporation of the World Bank, several hundred institutional investors, bankers and venture capitalists attended. Unless the private sectors get involved, the shift to environmentally-sustainable technologies and companies will be slow indeed, forced only by government regulators. Another interesting group in Tokyo is the new Global Infrastructure Fund Research Foundation described in Chapter Eight.

Many environmentalists have understandable misgivings about big, multinational corporations and such large scale environmental projects, and indeed, they must be assessed very carefully beforehand, to determine their effect on local people, cultures and ecosystems. However, we humans have already intervened so massively in the planet's ecology that there is no way that we will not have to learn to undo the damage and remediate the destruction as well. Thus, bio-remediation and ecological restoration are new industries of the 21st century. Already, in the United States the "trade association" for the new ecological remediation business, the Society for Ecological Restoration has held its third annual meeting in Orlando, Florida, May 1991. Projects were described by the thousands of participants, ranging from restoring rain forests and re-creating lost wetlands, freeing rivers whose flows had been channeled, to greening desert areas, replanting waste land around power facilities and introducing lost species into their former habitats. The group can be contacted at the University of Wisconsin-Madison, 1207 Seminole Highway, Madison, WI 53711 (fax 608-262-5209).

The cold war between economists and ecologists still rages, but there are signs of detente. A step forward is the 1991 report, Project 88-Round Two on Designing Market-Based Environmental Strategies, sponsored by Colorado Senator Tim Wirth and the late Senator John Heinz of Pennsylvania. Round One of Project 88 was reviewed in

Chapter Three. As outlined earlier, the bitter struggle has been over whether economic management tools, like the GNP, will continue to reign supreme over the affairs of nations, or whether broader social and ecological values will expand the policies of business and government beyond the traditional "bottom line." This 20-year paradigm war has progressed very little since 1973 when my article "Ecologists versus Economists" first appeared in the *Harvard Business Review*.

Since Earth Day 1970, environmentalists have challenged economists' definitions of progress, wealth, and development—pointing out that economic theories and models shortchange Nature as well as future generations. They highlight absurdities of GNP accounting such as in Alaska, which posted gains after the Exxon Valdez oil spill because the additional costs of the clean-up are added to GNP instead of being subtracted (as environmentalists advocate). GNP ignores the value of clean water, fish and pristine, scenic environments like Prince William Sound.

As we have seen, economists are responding to growing pressure to correct such skewed national accounting by adopting gauges like the Human Development Index (HDI) and the World Bank's Index of Sustainable Economic Welfare (ISEW). However, many are skeptical of economists, once more, applying their assumptions to weighting values such as the environment into narrow economic calculations. The Project 88-Round Two report is light years ahead of the first version, which pushed the debate along, but which many environmentalists viewed as an effort by economists to put new labels on their old wine bottles and claim their share of the lucrative new environmental policy turf. The first report, in 1988, did make many useful proposals, including taxes on the big four "environmental sins": (1) use of non renewable resources, such as that encouraged by today's oil depletion allowances; (2) waste, such as over-packaging and making inefficient cars and appliances; (3) planned obsolescence, such as producing hosiery that runs on the first wearing; and (4) polluting emissions and environmentally unsound manufacturing processes and products. Only by levying taxes, fees and return deposits, etc., can the market correctly reflect in prices the full social and environmental costs these "sins" inflict on us and future generations.

The 1991 version of Project 88 corrects some of Round One's weaknesses, including its inattention to issues of social equity and fairness. Traditional economic theory ignores the existing maldistribution of incomes, the growing gap between rich and poor, and assumes that everybody has equal power and information. As a consequence, most economists tend to favor "incentives" and subsidies to ease the pain of restructuring wasteful old industries rather than backing a "greening" of tax law to level the playing field for new and budding enterprises in the emerging sectors: energy conservation, efficiency, recycling and renewable resources. The new report would, however, have made a better case had it taken note of German studies showing that "greening" national tax codes with environmental "sin taxes" would raise so much money that, merely to remain "revenue neutral," income taxes would have to be slashed! Leading congressional Democrats like Wirth could do the nation a favor by proposing revenue-producing "sin taxes" that discourage such unhealthy behaviors as smoking, drinking and destroying the environment, while encouraging useful employment and environmentally sound products, jobs, profits and investment in sustainable forms of development. Once politicians on the Republican side saw the potential for such "greener" forms of taxation, there might, at last, be a way out of the federal budget stalemates without the need to impose higher income taxes.

Project 88-Round Two no longer argues its case in the cold war terms of the earlier study. Instead of using tired and tiresome arguments about "socialism vs. capitalism," about the only choice being *either* "the free market" or "command and control regulations," the report tacitly acknowledges that all workable economic approaches are mixtures. It focuses on our need to redirect wayward incentives that today encourage pollution and depletion. It covers a host of new mechanisms to identify hidden social and environmental costs, which can be quantified and added into prices, while showing the explicit limits of such market based policies in dealing with longer-term, less quantifiable values. It also acknowledges that economic approaches are not a panacea and that all these new markets must, in fact, be legislated into existence rather than being derived from God or the "invisible hand" so beloved by traditional economists. Further, these "green" markets, like all others, will not be "free" or even cheap, since they will require complex regulation and standard-setting, monitoring and enforcement.

Nor will they necessarily be fair, a point glossed over in the Round One Report. As Round Two clarifies, although many "green" markets will be more efficient overall, they will produce winners and losers. All this makes the new report more credible and useful as it discusses how impacts can be mitigated and "losers" (often workers or low income citizens) can be compensated or retrained. Perhaps Round Three can advance the debate even further by identifying the "win-win" strategies beyond economics: building political coalitions to support healthy, "green" tax codes and adoption (as in various other countries including Canada, Germany, the Netherlands, Venezuela, Denmark and Norway) of new "scorecards" to redefine development and progress beyond GNP. A July

1990 poll by Martilla & Kiley/Market Strategies suggests the public may understand all this. Eighty-two percent said that by creating a cleaner environment, we can actually help create jobs and raise income levels, as mentioned earlier.

The social equity issues glossed over in economic theories were also challenged in one of the first salvos of the new 1990s North-South debate over the redefinition of development (no longer associating the word "economic" which has been replaced by the word "sustainable"). This new debate was joined in Kuala Lumpur in June 1990 by former president of Tanzania, Julius Nyerere, and Malaysia's Prime Minister, Dr. Mahathir Mohamed, who hosted the G-15 summit. President Suharto of Indonesia was in Kuala Lumpur, as was India's Prime Minister, V. P. Singh, who felt G-15 would enhance cooperation between southern countries. The summit's final communique included references to a new post-cold war global economy, and a need for North-South sharing of responsibility.

The new G-15 country-group accepted responsibility for their own development and change, and cautioned the industrialized nations on "their formation of economic groupings . . . that could lead to a fragmentation of world trade." Key issues included unresolved external debt problems and the ongoing transfers of resources from poor to rich countries. The "alternative" summit, The Other Economic Summit (TOES), held in London in 1991, called for a reversal of this ghastly on-going flow of funds from poor countries (interest and loan repayments) to Northern banks. TOES also called on the G-7 to discuss the damage done to Third World countries as a result of policies of the World Bank, International Monetary Fund (IMF) and the GATT. TOES supports the adoption of new indicators to replace GNP and opening up the G-7 process, making it and all the U.N. global financial institutions more democratic and replacing the G-7 with a World Economic Council.[8]

The G-15 has pledged to continue to meet and form common approaches to debt problems. A new study of the debt crisis and World Bank and IMF "structural adjustment" policies toward repayment and debt service shows how women, children and the poor become victimized by these "belt-tightening" measures. The report *Beyond the Debt Crisis* offers many new approaches.[9] The G-15 reaffirmed a commitment to "a balanced and successful conclusion to the Uruguay Round of GATT negotiations which takes into account the concerns and needs of developing nations." The group called for new approaches to funding environmental protection that will be presented at the 1992 U.N. Environment Conference. G-15 will likely continue the work of the South Commission whose report, *Toward a New Way to Measure Development*, called for new economic models and measures of progress. The report concluded that more realistic "scorecards" of development were needed. New indicators would include such non-monetary indexes as literacy rates, life expectancy, unpaid productive work—along with indicators of energy efficiency, military versus civilian budget ratios, and environmental depletion.

It is my hope that the Report of the U.N. Commission on Environment and Development, *Our Common Future* (1987), which promotes "sustainable development" will be debated together with the Report of the South Commission, *Challenge to the South* (1990), since the power of the Northern industrial countries many otherwise overwhelm the discussion with their far-larger, better-financed participation in all the world's forums and conferences. As Dr. David Brooks of Canada's International Development Research Center noted in his evaluation of the *Our Common Future* report, it does put the issue of North-South equity back onto the world's agenda, but Brooks fears the term "sustainable development" has been too-glibly co-opted by the World Bank, without much analysis and commitment, since it will *require* that Northern industrial countries consume *less* if the countries of the South are to achieve the levels of development sufficient to their need.[10] World Bank economist Herman Daly echoes the need for limits on consumption of energy and materials in the rich countries, and maximum allowable incomes as well as minimum incomes for the poor.[11]

The G-15 will cause a rethinking of "development." New definitions will emerge as differences between money and real wealth are clarified. Many southern nations now seem ready to develop along their own cultural paths, rather than slavishly following World Bank and IMF formulas. The G-15 will enrich this debate as countries find their own innovative potential in an era of global interdependence.

The final report of the three-year deliberations of the South Commission—a prominent group of dignitaries from the Southern hemisphere—was released in Caracas at a widely-covered ceremony hosted by Venezuelan President Perez, in August 1990, the day after Saddam Hussein marched into Kuwait. The resulting preemption of media coverage by the Middle East crisis all but blacked out news of the attendees such as Malaysian Prime Minister Mahathir Mohamed, former Prime Minister of Tanzania Julius Nyerere, the Commission's Chairman and the foreign ministers of the newly formed Group of Fifteen Economic Summit—Algeria, Argentina, Brazil, Egypt, India, Indonesia, Jamaica, Malaysia, Mexico, Nigeria, Peru, Senegal, Venezuela, Yugoslavia, and Zimbabwe. This new economic summit "Group of Fifteen," held its second meeting in Caracas in November 1991, as mentioned.

The 1990 report, *Challenge to the South,* is a distinct departure from much of the usual rhetoric of former collective statements from what used to be called the "third world." But in light of global changes, the new U.S.-Soviet relationship, the regrouping of Warsaw Pact countries toward a more united Europe, the old terminology of first, second and third worlds has become obsolete—as has that of the Non-Aligned Movement, now facing a newly consolidating industrial Northern hemisphere and its proliferating trade blocs. Most of the issues concern the still-widening gap between North and South. These rich versus poor issues will be much in evidence in the 1990s as augured by the Gulf War. The South's views are typically underreported in the North and the reception of the *Challenge to the South* report was no exception. Whereas its counterpart, the report of the Brundtland Commission, *Our Common Future,* has sold hundreds of thousands of copies, received wide publicity and is taught in hundreds of college courses; *Challenge to the South* has received no such attention.

New realism

Challenge to the South clearly accepts a new level of responsibility for the South's own development, and a new realism and self-reliance in fostering its own human resources and still unexploited natural wealth. President Perez and Chairman Nyerere also both emphasized that the report fully acknowledges past mistakes, missed opportunities and other errors of omission, as well as facing such problems as corruption.

Perez noted that in today's global climate, many countries, including the USSR and those of Eastern Europe are making restitution for their past mistakes: forthrightly admitting errors in government policies, planning and macroeconomic measures. He noted that this new report was offered in the same spirit of *glasnost* and *perestroika*, and called on industrial countries of West Europe and North America to join this spirit and admit their own imperfections—rather than sing the chorus of ideological claims that their systems have "triumphed" over those of other countries.

An article entitled "That Let Down Feeling" in *The Economist,* July 13, 1991, underlines the declining economic clout of the United States vis-a-vis the European Community and its G-7 partners, where Treasury Secretary Brady was rebuffed in calling for lower interest rates to help the indebted, recession-beset U.S. economy. Even more frankly, President Jacques Attali of the new European Bank for Reconstruction and Development dismisses the United States as a "failed country."[12] *The Economist* also surveyed mounting U.S. domestic problems, homelessness as an indicator, noting that "George Bush's 'kinder, gentler nation' had actually become 'rougher and tougher.'"[13] *The Economist* also covered the plight of U.S. unemployed workers compared with European workers, noting that while 6.8 percent of U.S. workers were unemployed in 1991, only 42 percent qualified for unemployment benefits. Although Congress passed a law in August 1991 to extend these benefits, President Bush did not activate it.[14] The U.S. Administration, still flush with its Gulf "victory" seems unaware that even the dollar's days as a world reserve currency are running out, as more and more countries tie their economies to the yen or the new European currency, the ECU.[15] Meantime, as Washington budget cutters shifted social costs of crime, drugs, homelessness, illiteracy and medical care to the states, Governors were forced to balance their budgets by raising state taxes and less orthodox means, such as "creative accounting" for their deficits, selling off state assets or trying to "raid" state employee pension funds. California's Governor Peter Wilson was caught "red-handed" by some of the pension fund's trustees.[16] The federal government started these "raids" by balancing the federal budget with the Social Security Trust Fund.

The inability of the Reagan and Bush Administrations to see the decline of the United States in the world, its increasing indebtedness, not only internationally, but in every major domestic sector, can be understood best as a paradigm problem. Most of the Reagan and Bush advisors are devotees of conventional market economics and GNP watchers. As we know this is a narrow "productionist," supply-side approach, which ignores both the social costs incurred and the problems of demand. Ignoring the demand-side allowed them to ignore energy efficiency's potential for making America more competitive with Japan and Europe, at the same time ignoring problems of under-employment, falling real incomes, needs for retraining the workforce and the rising indebtedness of consumers (on whom they rely, contradictorily, to keep spending to support 60 percent of America's GNP). The transition to sustainable, renewable energy will cause initial disruption and job losses, which also must be cushioned by grants and retraining. Balanced, solar-based economies will be more labor intensive, as spelled out in many studies on which I reported in Chapter Nine of *Politics of the Solar Age*. For example, a 1983 report to the Minnesota Department of Energy pointed out the greater local job "multiplier effect": a dollar spent on renewable energy would generate $2.33-$2.92 of local economic activity versus only $0.64 for imported oil. A useful new look at this issue is *Jobs in a Sustainable Economy*, Worldwatch Institute Paper #104, September 1991.

The same paradigm problem of this narrow "economism" allowed Bush to pursue the Free Trade Agreement with Mexico, even though cheap Mexican labor will pull U.S. wages down—making it harder for these workers to support the U.S. GNP with adequate purchasing power. Instead, the "production, supply-side" paradigm sees the economy from a top-down business perspective which assumes that low wages and disinvesting-investing in "human capital" (i.e., education, retraining, etc.) will boost profits. Supply and demand do not *oppose* each other, but in a systems view *interact*—where producers must also have workers and customers with enough wages to consume their products. The "market" cannot become too arrogant. Indeed, many others have also become surfeited with such arrogance, because humans have been using markets since they came down from the trees. They were not *invented* by Adam Smith, and in any case are rarely as "free" as Western textbooks suggest.

The South Commission report takes a sober look at these old dogmatic debates between capitalism and socialism, and while acknowledging the need in many countries to substitute government bureaucracy with more use of markets, also recognizes the truth that most economies in the world are regulated—and that some government intervention is necessary. *Challenge to the South* focuses on the need for immediate action on furthering South-South cooperation, and aims at last for operationalizing the rhetoric of the past two decades. It acknowledges the failure of the much-awaited North-South dialogue—emphasizing that the only option left for the South is more concerted action on its own behalf. Such concerted new policies are realistic, as the United States is forced to deal with its own problems. South action plans covered trade, finance, debt, environment and charting new paths toward their own specific forms of development. Blind imitation of Western-style wasteful, mass consumption patterns were seen as impossible and counterproductive, as well as slavishly following prescriptions for hyping growth of their Gross National Products like those from the International Monetary Fund and the World Bank.

New indicators of a more balanced kind of development were advocated, based on the South Commission's earlier report, *Toward a New Way to Measure Development*, in order to challenge GNP and other conventional measures of wealth and progress.

Debtors' forum

Some other groundbreaking recommendations include the forming of a debtors' forum, to guide concerted policies for relief of debts. Also a new South Bank to make export credits and investments more available to expand South-South trade and technological development, augmented data networks for information sharing, as well as many programs for increasing investments in human resources and education.

The paradigm of "productivity" as measured in "per capita" terms led inevitably to increasing the capital intensity of industrial societies and to the drive for technological innovation and automation. The debates of the 1970s around "appropriate technology, scale and centralization" have shifted the development paradigm in the 1990s, particularly in the South. Technological choices are more critically examined as to whether they will dis-employ people, widen income disparities, draw populations from rural food production into already burgeoning cities, as well as for their environmental impacts. Not yet well covered in the new debate is the "mindless automation" syndrome—particularly in the United States, where billions have been invested in computerization, robots, etc., in the drive to cut costs and labor. The horror stories include General Motors $80 billion investment in automation and how it derailed as told in "When GM's Robots Ran Amok."[17] Lester Thurow, Dean of MIT's Sloan School of Management asks the $64,000 question: in spite of all the computerization, no productivity gains are showing up in a roundup *Business Week* ran August 12, 1990, on the future of personal computers. In my own bulging file marked "computer SNAFUs" are many stories about perfectly healthy companies being actually put out of business by inappropriate computerization. Another paradigm problem here is economists' sloppy category "investment" where the issue is: was it *wise* investment.[18] The failure of the Uruguay Round of GATT highlighted some of the structural inequities and procedures hampering fair participation in such areas vital to the South as equitable terms of trade— which has been expanded to include intellectual property—clearly rigged in favor of transnational corporations and industrial countries. Such burning issues at the GATT which must be addressed by the North are covered in depth in a new book by famed Indian journalist Chakravarti Raghavan entitled, ominously, *Re-colonization 1990*.

In a world of shuffling trade blocs among the most powerful industrial nations, it is little wonder that the countries of the South are learning yet another lesson from the North—that they too, must organize, form tighter links and cooperate, for their very survival. These developing countries are also watching Eastern Europe closely, as the interest of the North is continuing to be diverted away from the South and toward trade with these former Comecon countries—now wildly swinging back to laissez-faire forms of unbridled free market capitalism and kneejerk privatizations as in Poland, for example—creating social backlashes as unemployment and inflation rise.

Challenge to the South adopts many of the suggestions of the Brundtland Commission report, *Our Common Future*, for a more ecologically sustainable, people-centered and equitable form of development—although it is understandably hardnosed concerning global bargaining around issues such as global warming and ozone depletion. It calls for a Planetary Ecological Fund, so that the costs of shifting to more benign, "green" technologies will be born fairly by the North—which is responsible for 80 percent of these problems—as well as the South. The World Bank now has such an Environmental Facility, but little expertise in finding such "green" investment opportunities.

Indeed, *Challenge to the South* is a major new policy statement which may well redefine what we mean by development, providing leadership in many policy areas on the cutting edge of efforts to outline a just, ecologically sane world for the 21st century. *Challenge to the South* seeks to level the global playing field by placing an ethical floor under it and raising it up to new standards of corporate and government responsibility. The South and its new voice, the G-15 Economic Summit, should be heeded carefully—it seeks to acknowledge this new era of global interdependence, change the world game, the rules and scorecards of "progress."

The most highly-articulated plan for the new, people-centered ecological paradigm of development is the Economic White Paper presented by Green Forum-Philippines which represents a breakthrough in many respects. I was honored to write the foreword since its authors and developers had invited me in 1989 to see its process of exhaustive grassroots consultation, fact-finding and research.

Firstly, this Economic White Paper is built on one of the most cogent critiques of the conventional economic development paradigm, and the particular ways in which it has failed in the Philippines, as it has in other countries (always for many of the *same* and many quite *different* reasons). At last, it is now possible to see in so many countries, the clearly misguided effort to industrialize the Planet by extrapolating a simple set of highly abstract formulas and overaggregated statistics gleaned from the experience by which Britain and much of Europe industrialized almost three centuries ago! These Eurocentric ideologies of industrialism and economic "development" (as measured by GNP), were not only one-time historical processes, but also deeply culturally imbedded—not to mention based on inadequate scientific understanding of the Earth's ecosystems. It has taken the rest of the world over a hundred years of attempts to imitate this process, supported by the proselytizing of generations of well-meaning economists, to realize that this discipline of economics which rationalized the European industrialization experience was not generalizable in other cultures and eco-systems. Indeed, at last, economics' claims to status as a science have been exposed as fraudulent, as documented in *The Politics of the Solar Age* and elsewhere.

The so-called U.N. Third Development Decade at last revealed the gigantic hoax of Euro-industrialism and its siren song of GNP-growth as a measure of real progress. In Europe this "progress" was won at the expense of colonial exploitation, stripping agricultural assets and peasants of their rights to farm the "commons." Furthermore, the Earth's population then was not yet stressing ecosystems, and we are only now beginning to calculate the "pollution indebtedness" of these early industrial "winners." These Northern Hemisphere industrial countries, typified by the Economic Group of Seven (G-7: the United States, Canada, Britain, France, Germany, Japan, Italy) today have created most of the world's pollution, contributed the lion's share of carbon dioxide now leading to global warming, and most of the chlorofluorocarbons that are destroying the Earth's ozone layer, while they still talk of the "indebted" countries of the developing world! Calculations of these social and environmental costs (clearly in the trillions of dollars) that were the price the world has paid for this industrial development, make it clear that it is the industrialized countries that are most in deficit and furthest in arrears!

It now remains for countries of the Southern Hemisphere to negotiate their money debt on this basis, as they begin to teach the world about another model of development. The Green Forum Model is based on scientific understanding of how eco-systems function to support human activities: stabilize carbon, oxygen and nitrogen balances; recycle wastes; and is based on meeting real human needs, not only for income, but health, education, nutritious food, adequate housing, meaningful cultural and spiritual lives, and sharing the fruits of their labor in equitable, cohesive communities. This Economic White Paper addresses just this kind of healthy development so many countries and peoples now need and to which they aspire. The Paper documents with careful research how the whole macroeconomic, GNP-oriented "development" process has devastated the Philippines, and how it continues each day (tied as it is to the inequitable workings of world trade and the current financial system) to marginalize ever more rural Filipinos while destroying the productivity of their land, water and forests.

Most significantly, the Green Forum White Paper is a carefully-researched, *tested* plan to reverse this decline, re-invest in rural communities, raise agricultural productivity and reduce the rampant poverty which is now tearing the country apart. The main aspects of this new plan to develop the skills and lives of the Filipino people and restore the fertility and productivity to their lands in an equitable and sustainable way, are eminently practical, even *unremarkable*. But it is this kind of tested, hands-on common sense that eludes economists with their computerized macroeconomic models and with which "development" officers are unfamiliar. It doesn't fit the formulas, and therefore can't be evaluated by their quantitative yardsticks: GNP-growth doesn't tell whether the poverty gap is widening (as it most often has), or whether children are healthier or better educated or how much topsoil has been sacrificed to hyping short-term productivity. Not that this new plan isn't quantitatively measured or computerized—it is. But it starts from the ground up, and with different assumptions: that *households* (some 30 percent of which are headed by women) are the basic units of production (rather than corporate enterprises) and that villages composed of these productive households can be viewed as enterprises in a system of Community Centered Capitalism, rather analogues to the worker-ownership model now sweeping the United States and Europe. The principle of "subsidiarity," i.e., problems that can be solved at a lower level of governance need not concern higher levels (a principle also of the European Community and clearly of the new republics of the old Soviet Union), governs the plan. Indicators of performance will provide feedback to producers at all levels from households to villages to the larger communities which will act as "hubs" to market produce and add value to products via processing, etc. Most importantly and almost unique, each of these Community Enterprise areas will be nested within an Ecological Zone, 225 of which have been identified for their unique ecological features, natural resources, bio-diversity, rates of sustainable yields, etc.

Thus, the main parameters of development will be sustainability within ecological tolerances and the household-based "trickle-up" features, founded on local equity, rather than the top-down, macroeconomic models of the now failed "trickle-down" approach. Similar approaches to incorporating whole villages so as to allow everyone to share in the productivity increases and motivation have been successful, such as the Sarvodya Shramadana movement founded by A.T. Ariyaratne in Sri Lanka, mentioned earlier, which uses principles of development based on the Buddhist concept of "awakening of all," and has raised the development levels in 8000 villages. Of course, powerful vested interests in Sri Lanka opposed this development, which required rich landowners and industrialists to curb their greed while politicians feared the loss of their old patrons, and A.T. Ariyaratne has had numerous threats on his life.

The time is ripe for Green Forum's bold new plan, even though it will depend on the foresight of the Philippine Parliament and of the Aquino and successor administrations, and on the determination to finally deliver on promises of real land reform. Yet today, even the World Bank is trying to get back to its original mandate of the Presidency of Robert McNamara in the 1960s to foster rural development among the "poorest of the poor" in agricultural areas. We are witnessing shifts in the World Bank's understanding of ecological science, which economists everywhere are being forced to learn. The Bank's priorities were skewed in the 1980s by pressure from the United States and other industrialized countries and their commercial banks' exposure to the mountain of unsound petrodollar loans. This dragooned the Bank into guaranteeing much of the securitizing and discounting of these debts and accelerated its shift to structural adjustment loans (SALs) which would keep indebted countries servicing the interest payments on their debts. Agricultural project loans were slashed because their payout periods are longer and results were more difficult to assess.

Clearly, the 1990s must be the decade where the debt crisis, now exacerbating the environmental crisis must be put behind us—by securitization, swaps, and in many cases where the loans were illegitimately incurred, by repudiation. In the case of many countries that are already in de facto default, these debts must be forgiven. This is only a necessary, but not sufficient condition for a new era of genuine development. Let us hope that the Philippines can summon the wisdom and leadership in both its government and private sectors to embark on this sensible new model offered by Green Forum-Philippines. Certainly, it is already clear that a broad grassroots coalition from all over the country is ready and willing to put its shoulder to the wheel—motivated by this vision of equitable, homegrown, people-centered, ecologically-sustainable development— which they can have a stake in creating. Who knows, this new model of human development might yet make the Philippines show that the other "Tigers" of Asia are as endangered a species as other industrial societies will soon become, unless they change their ways. The United States is now the world's laggard in shifting to new paradigms of progress— preferring to send its young men and women to fight and die for "cheap" oil rather than restructure its wasteful economy and old alliances.

American *people* ahead of the U.S. government

The Gulf crisis again highlighted America's Achilles' heel of energy profligacy. Yet President Bush's and Energy Secretary James Watkin's public campaign to urge Americans to conserve, with initial focus on lowering highway speeds, inflating tires properly, and improving the gas mileage of cars was something of a joke. Tragically, the burning Kuwaiti oil wells have been adding to the world's atmosphere as much pollution

each day as all of the world's automobiles according to the World
Meteorological Organization (WMO) in an April 1991 study—contributing
to global warming as well.

Longer-term solutions must be set in motion now, enabling the
United States to shift its economy to an energy-efficient, sustainable
base. Several opinion surveys show that large numbers of Americans are
willing to make the needed changes. So what is missing? There is a lack
of leadership in laying out all the options, coupled with the large, rigid
industrial sectors still running on waste, and still slowing the transition
from polluting economies based on fossil fuels to the dawning solar age
of economic and environmental sustainability. After the oil shocks of the
1970s, the United States achieved steady energy efficiency gains through
better standards for appliances and auto mileage, the 55-miles-an-hour speed
limit, and tax credits for solar and renewable energy technologies. But in
the 1980s we faltered, reverting to even greater reliance on foreign oil.

Yet even in the 1980s, a survey by Americans Talk Security showed
that Americans were ahead of their "leaders," according to Alan Kay,
director of the ATIF which sponsored the survey. In October 1988, 90
percent of Americans thought our dependence on oil imports was a
serious threat to our national security. By wide margins they approved of
strategies to decrease dependency on Mideast oil, ranging from building
up our strategic reserves to further developing domestic and alternative
sources. In the same 1988 poll, 41 percent of Americans were even
willing to pay more for oil from non-Mideast suppliers.

Now is the time for Americans to face the future; the dream world of
cheap oil may never return. The world's present demand for oil, 64
million barrels a day, is growing 1.5 percent per year, adding another 10
million barrels a day to demand by the year 2000. A bipartisan survey by
ATIF in September 1990, found that 81 percent thought that the Gulf
crisis might have been avoided if we had waged a campaign to increase
energy efficiency in autos, homes, offices and factories.

The long delayed transition to solar-age economies is now at hand.
Although it will not be painless or cost-free, this new course is the best
and most palatable prescription for Americans and all other industrial,
fossil fueled economies. Yet in early 1990, the Bush Administration at
last unveiled an energy "plan" that still assumed that no plan was really
necessary. That old magic of market forces would once again, produce
the right mix of policies. Thus, no real conservation strategies were
forthcoming while paradoxically, it was deemed all right to plan for more
nuclear power and to exploit the Arctic National Wildlife Refuge. The
policy could only be understood by deciphering the underlying paradigm

of traditional economics: i.e., the millions of individual decisions Americans would make in the "free" marketplace (where the theory says that all buyers and sellers have equal power and information and that no side effects harm others) *was* the best of all possible plans. Invisible to the economism paradigm are global interdependence, globally mobile capital markets, large oligopolistic producers with pricing power and Washington lobbies—not to mention the uncounted social and environmental costs of our fossil-fueled economy.

The transition to sustainable solar-age economies includes:

- "Greening" our tax code—levying fees and charges on the new economic "sins": pollution, waste, obsolescence, and resource depletion. Such levies might include a carbon tax to prevent excessive buildup of carbon dioxide in the atmosphere and global warming. Already 70 percent of the American people approve such a carbon tax, according to a June 1990 survey by Martilla & Kiley/Market Strategies.

- Increasing energy efficiency standards for appliances and cars. Here the same survey shows Americans sharply critical of foot dragging by both industry and government.

- Restore tax credits and government programs to encourage investments in alternative, renewable-energy technologies, and remove subsidies that currently favor non-renewable energy, such as oil depletion allowances.

- Encourage, subsidize, and where necessary, mandate waste recycling programs. Fifty-three percent of Americans are now separating cans and bottles for recycling. By a margin of 55 percent to 43 percent, Americans already believe that recycling should be mandatory.

- Strengthen pressure for a genuine national energy policy. Entrenched interests in existing energy systems are still blocking the emergence of budding renewable-energy sectors and companies in wind, solar, biomass, hydrogen, and tidal energies. Yet in the United States today, less than six cents of every dollar in energy research and development goes to renewables. Scott Sklar, Executive Director of the Solar Energy Industries Association warns that other nations are seizing the lead. "The European Community is outspending the United States thirty times on renewable energy export promotion, while Germany, Italy and Japan already outspend the United States on photovoltaics, wind and other renewable energy. During the 1980s the U.S. share in the world wind energy market dropped from 27 percent to 5 percent."

- Widespread debate and public opinion surveys are needed, based on alternative options. As more surveys spell out the conservation and renewable-energy alternatives and relate these options to the future health of our economy and to expansion and job opportunities in the rapidly growing sustainable, environment-enhancing sectors, Americans can stay abreast of needed policy changes.

A hopeful sign of such shifting opinion was the June 1990 poll by Martilla & Kiley/Market Strategies: The conventional wisdom that we must choose between economic growth and a clean environment was rejected. While 72 percent of Americans said that they would be willing to sacrifice economic growth in order to preserve the environment, as noted earlier, fully 82 percent said that by creating a cleaner environment, we can actually help create jobs and raise income levels. Furthermore, in May 1991, a bipartisan Environmental Opinion Survey found that 80 percent of Americans believed that environmental protection would require difficult changes in national policy and our personal lives. All this seems to show that Americans are more ready to move beyond oil dependency to a solar-age economy than are their leaders. And, as we have seen, a Solar Age economy is, by definition, a green economy.

While not much progress has been made by the U.S. government, pollution levies, or "green taxes" as they are called in Europe, are approved by governments and most businesses. The Paris-based Organization for Economic Cooperation and Development (OECD) which represents the world's 24 major industrial nations, recently surveyed the 85 different kinds of "green" fees on polluting already on the books in Europe. These taxes both speed cleanups *and* increase revenues. For example, carbon taxes, previously mentioned, are now levied in Norway, Finland, Denmark, Sweden and Holland. The European Community as a whole began discussing a carbon tax on all twelve country members in August 1991, according to a useful survey of "green" economic policy issues by Frances Cairncross, author of *Costing the Earth*. In the *The Economist*, August 31, 1991, Cairncross says, "The new greenery represents perhaps the biggest opportunity for enterprise and invention the industrial world has ever seen."

These "green" fees can include deposits on returnables, car exhaust taxes, depletion taxes, and levies on such pollutants as carbon and sulfur dioxide. *The Economist* applauded all these measures as good economics and urged their passage: "The environment could be a way to cut public spending and to generate a whole new source of revenue."

While governments in Europe are now seeing "green" fees as a major source of new revenue, business executives see them as much more palatable than bureaucracy and regulation. Most economists approve of "green" levies, since they provide correct price signals and improve markets' functioning. Some continue to offer more dubious proposals to institutionalize the right to "trade" such pollution licenses in the market-place. While markets cannot achieve the whole job, there are many cases when they can be effective—if fees for polluters are set high enough. Economists like "green" charges because they help pay for the costs of pollution. Polluters are now "free riders"—passing on the costs of their activities to others. At last, after much resistance, this principle is being applied in many countries, including the United States. Now is the time to fully extend it to our tax system.

Greening our tax code would also help correct our national accounts. GNP figures include the costs of cleaning up pollution and repairing damage and adds them into our accounts—instead of subtracting these costs to give a "net" GNP as in Japan. A 1991 study by the World Resources Institute of Washington, DC, estimates the distorting effects of current tax policy (which ignores environmental costs) as 4-7 percent a year in lost GNP. Replacing some taxes with pollution levies would make the U.S. economy more efficient. Adding the cost of the cleanup of the Valdez oil spill to the GNP of Alaska, made 1989 look like a bumper year! Such costs should not only be subtracted from GNP, but the bills should go to the polluters. One doesn't have to be an economist to understand this. Polluting products would include costs of disposal and recycling. New markets for cleaner, recyclable products would be able to compete more fairly. A May 1991 opinion survey found that 92 percent of those surveyed were either already buying (35 percent) or willing to buy more environmentally friendly products—even at higher cost. *Business Week* says the "Green Market" will grow from $56 billion in 1990 to $174 billion by 1995—creating new jobs.

A "green" tax code should include four environmentally expensive activities: pollution, waste, depletion of non-renewable resources and deliberately planned obsolescence, (an example: disposables, like throw-away lighters and cameras). The need to protect low incomes is addressed in Germany by reducing taxes on personal incomes proportionately as the "green" fees are raised. This shifts the burden from low-income individuals to those activities which pollute and deplete the Earth—while remaining "revenue neutral" overall. Americans already approve the fairness of "sin" taxes (tobacco, alcohol) to pay for their effects.

Most companies that pollute see the writing on the wall. Consumers and employees of such companies are bringing law suits for damages, and companies are being found liable for a wide range of new claims. The same May 1991 Environmental Opinion Survey found 80 percent of Americans were either already (14 percent) or willing to boycott the products of companies with bad environmental records. Another benefit of "green" charges would be to promote the less-polluting, substitute products and services already available (an example: reusable disc film for cameras). Prices would also fall, since many of these products are offered by small, fast-growing companies that don't have the market power to "fix" prices. In many cases, such low-polluting alternatives are already cheaper (cloth diaper services or nonpolluting detergents). In addition, many of the *most*-polluting products are out of reach to consumers (stretch limousines, luxury campers, motor boats). "Green" levies should be highest on luxury items.

Workers can be redeployed and retrained as companies shift to less environmentally damaging operations. There is no substitute for spending new "green" revenues on retraining. Military contracting and polluting, wasteful manufacturing are both "sunset industries." The U.S. economy is still too wasteful to compete until we reduce the two-and-a-half times as much energy we use vis-a-vis the Japanese. While they recycle over 50 percent of their "waste," we throw away 90 percent of ours. "Greening" the tax code is the best way to begin improving our position in the world. Furthermore, tax codes should be geared to discourage unhealthy behavior, like smoking, drinking, polluting and wasting resources, and to encourage useful behavior like working, saving and investing in new, cleaner more efficient enterprises. Shifting the tax code from incomes to sin taxes is a rational way to meet the new conditions of the 1990s. For example, the social cost of drug abuse alone to American society is estimated at $60 billion annually.[19]

The changing trade paradigm

The classical economic paradigm of trade still harks back to Adam Smith and his famous formula of "comparative advantage," which even today dominates economics textbooks. It was a perfectly sensible idea in the 1800s when European countries were beginning to trade with each other and capital was as immobile as labor and resources. Under such conditions—now vanished—it was logical for Portugal to export wines and the cork to bottle them to Britain, and for Britain to export textiles and buy wines abroad. Thus, "all other things equal" (a phrase indispensable to the knee-jerk formulas of economists) all countries engaging in such trade with each other would be "better off." This trade also should be "free trade," with as few barriers and encumbrances such as taxes, import fees or special rules as possible on the product or its process of manufacture. In one mighty leap this formula based on 18th century Europe, was pretty much extrapolated to cover *world* trade. Clearly, under the global financial system of the 1990s the most important change in conditions is that now capital is so mobile that trillions of dollars move around the electronic banking and trading systems every day. This means that all the textbook theorizing about trade is obsolete, since these huge financial flows dwarf trade flows between countries. At the same time, for the United States alone, up to 40 percent of our trade flows with other countries are *between* divisions joint-ventures and subsidiaries of our U.S.-based multi-national corporations. Thus, cars from the British division of a U.S. automaker are "imported" while a U.S.-based Japanese automaker may be "exporting" its cars to Europe or even back to Japan. Add to that the fact that economic theory encourages all countries to grow their economies by exporting, i.e., exploiting their "comparative advantages" whether of cheap labor, cheap land, unregulated environmental resources—and we have in the 1990s a witch's brew. Firstly, the global competition for capital heats up—as does the export-led growth rat race—since of course, not every country can run a positive trade balance.

In a system of global export competition there are only winners and losers (i.e., countries whose balance of payments worsen and must keep devaluing their currencies to continue playing the game—or lowering their wages and allowing their natural resources to be raped). The other looming problem is how *buyers* are to be found—there are many needy and hungry people in the world to be sure, but few have sufficient money to create market "demand" for all these exports. The recent failure of the 1990 Uruguay Round of GATT negotiations, was I believe, inevitable. Stalemate will continue until the "world trade" paradigm is re-thought.

Similarly, the Bush Administration has been caught with its paradigms down on trade issues. Indeed, all politicians, while urged by their economic advisors to espouse "free trade" are actually "closet protectionists" for good reasons: until some rational new rules for levelling the global playing field are promulgated they must try to conserve what little domestic "sovereignty" remains to run their economies. Thus, as Europe closed ranks around its farmers, in spite of the "free trade" rhetoric, the U.S. Administration sought its own North American Free Trade area with Canada and Mexico. The two biggest unresolved issues in "free trade" are the two most ignored by economists. *Labor*, which was supposed to be immobile and accept whatever domestic wage rates each nation customarily paid, began to move—mass migrations of people seeking higher wages in other countries will dwarf today's numbers of Mexican workers in the United States. The second issue is also ignored by conventional economics: the exploitation of the *environment* in rich and poor countries to gain "comparative advantage" for their exports. Similarly, the Japanese exploit their female labor force, as do Americans, giving their exports unfair advantage over those of Canada and Sweden where male and female wages are closer to parity. Furthermore, so far most trade agreements have been about goods exported, whereas today, one-fifth of all exports in world trade are services (which most countries' national statistics overlook or under count).

The alarms of environmentalists and labor unions over the U.S.-Mexico Free Trade agreements are just a taste of things to come. The huge differential between Mexican and U.S. wages and fears that Mexico will become a "pollution haven" for more U.S. companies, has united both constituencies. Similarly, environmentalists in both the North and South have targeted the GATT to force environmental protection criteria onto its rules. As of 1991 GATT negotiators still saw environmental protection rules as "protectionist" non-tariff barriers which could unfairly hamper "free-trade." Similarly, GATT must now deal with demands of many developing countries that would make labor as mobile as capital—and make all immigration restrictions, work rules, etc., as well as barriers to emigration, "protectionist." As of August 1991 GATT's 105 country members are still committed to abolishing rules to protect the environment which will further open rain-forests to cutting, as the Rainforest Action Network's Alert number 63, August 1991, describes.

I do *not* suggest going back to anarchy and protectionism—impossible in any case in our interdependent world. In fact, "free-trade" could help change the rules in favor of *better* worldwide standards for environmental protection and consumer and worker safety, if GATT were to incorporate such social costs and values in its calculations and ratify new indicators of development.[20] Another example was the Structural Impediments Initiative (SII) agreement signed in 1990 by George Bush and Japan's Prime Minister Toshiki Kaifu which will worsen environmental pollution and depletion and is a case in point of old paradigm approaches to trade. Such new concerns arise, as well as many others for the social and cultural impacts of trade, largely because the narrow economic frame work for talks did not take any of these broader, longer-range factors into account.

Or, take the promised revision of Japan's Large-Scale Retail Law which the United States wants abolished. Broader issues, usually ignored by economists, relate to longer-term energy efficiency and environmental quality. The United States wants the Japanese (in a small island one twenty-fifth the size of America) to adjust to our distribution scale geared to a continent. Thus, in the name of economic theories of "efficiency," the Japanese are urged to explode their appropriately scaled neighborhood retailing, pour concrete and roads over additional scarce land so that they will need to get in cars and drive twenty-five mile round trips to strip malls to shop—just like Americans do.

Purely economic calculations overlook the resulting loss of convenience, neighborhood values, the demise of the thousands of small stores and their payrolls, that give traditional towns their unique flavor. Ironically, many Americans nostalgic for this kind of quality of life which they can still find in Kyoto, mourn its loss at home as freeways and shopping malls continue to render our downtown "Main Streets" into blighted ghost towns. Many of these issues were discussed at a Kyoto conference in 1990 on Renewing the Earth sponsored by Japanese environmental groups, the Tokyo-based Center for Global Action and co-sponsored by the California-based think tank, the Elmwood Institute. Few have analyzed the environmental costs of SII: the additional losses of land, a hefty increase in fossil fuel consumption adding to pollution and increased greenhouse gases, and this inevitable blighting of urban environments with the now familiar rise in drug use, crime, and other symptoms of shattered neighborhoods and communities as we have seen in U.S. cities.

The SII debate was argued on the now familiar economic paradigm— that it would be good for Japanese consumers, lowering prices—echoed by Mr. Kaifu himself as he termed the agreement "painful, but essential" and even "promoting the quality of life in Japan." Certainly SII will promote large business interests in both countries. However, economists know little of quality-of-life factors, since they involve long term effects which cannot easily be calculated into individual prices. It is precisely these broader, longer-term calculations which *are* included in Japan's higher prices, and many are still aware of such quality-of-life factors as stable neighborhoods, cohesive community life, safe streets, and small, friendly, convenient stores which are deemed worth paying higher prices to maintain. The argument over the U.S. demand that Japan open her rice market to much cheaper U.S. rice overlooks the enormous cheap energy subsidy of U.S. rice.

Similarly, the dubious agreement that Japan will invest more money in her infrastructure and even further hype domestic consumption will only assure that the global environment will lose, since this will cause Japan's energy efficiency to fall toward the sloppy, wasteful levels of the United States. Ironically, it is this energy wastefulness which is a basic cause of the declining competitiveness of our economy, as discussed earlier. Furthermore, expecting Japan to match us in her level of imports of manufactured goods needs to take into account that Japan must import 86.7 percent of her coal, 94.8 percent of her natural gas and 99.6 percent of her oil versus the U.S. imports of 3.8 percent coal, 4.1 percent natural gas and some 40 percent of our oil.

All these new issues and questions sprouting from the SII talks and the U.S.-Mexico Free Trade debate are simply another set of symptoms of the errors of the economic paradigm. They continually focus on short-range, penny-wise benefits and ignore longer range costs passed on to other sectors of society, the environment and future generations. Using per capita averaged income and growth of the GNP to measure "progress" is becoming a tragicomic joke. In trade debates such as SII, we need to send the economists back to school to learn more sociology, cultural anthropology and ecology before we can trust their calculations as a basis for negotiation.

While many of the 80 now famous recommendations the Japanese offered the Americans to help overcome our structural impediments (that Americans lower their budget deficit, at $340 billion in 1992, improve their savings rate, and limit themselves to only one credit card, etc.) were self-serving, they also were correct in illustrating that when economists stray so broadly beyond their competence, they must expect to hear broader, interdisciplinary arguments and evidence. In fact, economic theories are falling ever further behind in mapping today's rapidly chang-ing world trade game. Economists' paradigms are still based on such vanished conditions as equilibrium, immobile capital, and formulations of trade issues within the rigid poles of free trade or protectionism. Yet, as we have seen with the SII talks, if such new Pandora's boxes of social issues are to be weighed in trade scales, the concept of protectionism itself becomes so broad as to be meaningless. If any countries' social policies can be targeted as "protectionist," then all trade debates are likely to become rife with intractable conflicts or to incur even broader social costs.

Hopefully, governments and their trade representatives will be forced by environmentalists, often in coalitions with workers and poor people, to realize that trying to level playing fields for trade by homogenizing all cultures and lifestyles, or by levelling ecosystems and exploiting land in the name of "global economic efficiency" will lead in the wrong direction. Instead, all countries need to work toward levelling the global playing field upward, by raising its ethical floor. This entails continuing work on agreements via the United Nations agencies, GATT, the G-7, the G-15 and all international treaty organizations on a latticework of standards and protocols on consumer protection, worker safety, environmental conservation and closing the excessive gap between wages and living standards. Unless trade gaps are narrowed in this future-conserving way, old economically scored GNP-based competition will continue rewarding the most exploitive companies and short sighted countries. The good news about the newly politicized trade talks is that they revealed all of these urgent future issues that lie beyond economics—and clarified the difference between money and true wealth.

Thus, in broad terms "greening the global economy" will require policy interventions at many levels with the following five levels being essential: (1) individual behavior, lifestyles and values, (2) local governments, (3) corporations and all business and private sector activities, (4) national governments, and (5) the international level. Briefly, this "greening" will involve these five levels in the following ways:

• *Individuals* As most individuals learned as a result of Earth Days 1970 and 1990, the "greening" of the economy will require that they change their buying, investing, and voting habits: by acquiring *fewer* goods that are more environmentally sound; switching to more services like self-improvement courses, adult education, retraining, etc.; and shifting more of their travel to mass transportation, bikes or smaller alternatively-powered cars. Similarly, their investments must switch to local banks and credit unions which invest in local enterprises and to socially and environmentally responsible, ethical investment vehicles.[21] Another necessity is to organize and vote at all levels of governance and to educate ourselves on key issues. Changing our behavior to recycling, reducing waste, etc., is also essential.

• *Local Governments* New ordinances must be enacted allowing multiple zoning to re-knit communities, to reduce travel, and to repeal laws which subsidize garbage hauling so the full costs are levied on local residents (thus encouraging recycling, and local and national markets for recyclables). Energy-efficiency must be built into local construction codes and pricing water, etc., at full cost is essential.

• *Corporate & Private Sector* Business of all sizes can review their products and operations to redesign them to minimize energy and materials use—as well as remove from the market inherently polluting, wasteful product lines, overpackaging, nonrecyclable components, etc. Conducting internal environmental audits with in-house task forces that report directly to the CEO will help assess the company's vulnerabilities to law suits, new regulations, citizen action groups and low ratings in such consumer buying guides as the bestselling *Shopping for a Better World*.[22] When this internal audit has been completed marketing, advertising, and public relations people can be brought in to reposition the redesigned product

The Valdez Principles

1.   Protection of the Biosphere
Minimize the release of pollutants that may cause environmental damage.

2.   Sustainable Use of Natural Resources
Conserve nonrenewable natural resources through efficient use and careful planning.

3.   Reduction and Disposal of Waste
Minimize the creation of waste, especially hazardous waste, and dispose of such materials in a safe, responsible manner.

4.   Wise Use of Energy
Make every effort to use environmentally safe and sustainable energy sources to meet operating requirements.

5.   Risk Reduction
Diminish environmental, health, and safety risks to employees and surrounding communities.

6.   Marketing of Safe Products and Services
Sell products that minimize adverse environmental impact and that are safe for consumers.

7.   Damage Compensation
Accept responsibility for any harm the company causes to the environment; conduct bio-remediation, and compensate affected parties.

8.   Disclosure
Public dissemination of incidents relating to operations that harm the environment or pose health or safety hazards.

9.   Environmental Directors and Managers
Appoint at least one board member who is qualified to represent environmental interests.

10.   Assessment and Annual Audit
Produce and publicize each year a self-evaluation of progress toward implementing the principles and meeting all applicable laws and regulations worldwide. Environmental audits will also be produced annually and distributed to the public.

For the 1990 CERES Guide to The Valdez Principles which explains the Principles in complete detail, send a self-addressed 9 x 12 envelope with $1.00 postage addressed to: CERES, 711 Atlantic Ave., Boston, MA 02111. Or contact by phone at (617) 451-0927.

PLATE 7-37

lines to take advantage of "green markets."[23] The basic assumption of all environmental audits now must accept the OECD principle that "the polluter pays." Companies can also consider signing the Valdez Principles (see Plate 7-37), thus earning them this "seal of approval" of the environmental investment community. Or companies can promulgate their own environmental principles. Early movers, such as 3M's "Pollution Prevention Pays" Program, serve as useful models. Another interesting approach to measuring is the Goodwill Theorem developed by Ellen H. Schaplowsky and Jeffrey McCord of the Intangible Assets Management Group, Inc., of New York which values a company's external goodwill, internal employee relations and other factors. Research and development programs need to be refocused for the long-term opportunities to innovate new "green" technologies.

• *National Level* National governments need to adopt scorecards of progress that correct the errors of GNP (as discussed in the previous chapter). National budget priorities need to be shifted toward increasing incentives and research and development funds for energy efficiency and renewable energy, and building a resource-based society. Transportation systems need to be balanced between public transit, buses, trains which are energy-efficient and private cars. The current enormous subsidies to the auto and highway systems need to be removed—as well as those favoring fossil and nuclear energy (about 50 times greater in the United States than for solar and renewables). Equally important, nations need to "green" their tax codes to tax environmental sins: depletion of virgin resources (severance taxes), waste, planned obsolescence and pollution emissions (as described). The new concept of "country accountability" is a recent innovation.[24]

• *International Level* National leaders are beginning to realize that in today's interdependent world, they have to spend up to half their time on international affairs, in order to have any hope of managing their domestic economies, as discussed in Chapter Three. Levelling the global playing field by raising its "ethical floor" requires rigorous leadership in forging the new agreements and protocols governing the global financial and trade system. This system itself, as pointed out earlier, has now become a crucial global "commons" along with the Earth's overcrowded electromagnetic spectrum.[25] This does not by any means imply some kind of "world government," but will be put together in many separate sectors from the ground up. For example, global agreements already govern many areas and work well without oppressing anyone or creating large bureaucracies. The world's aviation system is an extremely high-tech complex system governed by agreements reached through the

Elements of a Code of Ethics for Environmental Journalists (draft)

Journalists writing about the environment should strive to demonstrate, in their planning, research, interviewing, writing, and editing, the following qualities:

1. Respect for life (human, animal, plant, planetary)
   - Replace resources you use (sustainable development)
   - Do not do to nature what you do not want done to you (see also #3)
   - Respect redundancy and genetic diversity
   - Seek to avoid wars
   - Engage in reciprocal maintenance

2. Respect for reality (honesty)
   - Recognize that truth comes not only from experts (pluralism, respect for ideas).
   - Think globally, act locally: Pay attention to detail (see also #5)
   - Seek scientific information, not rumors

3. Respect for each other (love)
   - Give priority to spiritual things
   - Do not do to nature what you do not want nature to do to others (see also #1)
   - Optimize the development of children

4. Respect progress (reverence for the future)
   - Promote efficacy, not merely efficiency
   - Preserve the common good
   - Be optimistic

5. Respect for one's self (take responsibility for your actions)
   - Evaluate your needs rather than focusing on your wants
   - Talk, but also listen
   - Think globally, act locally (see also #2)
   - Remember that man is not only destructive but creative

This code is being developed by an international group of environmentalists and journalists who met in Florence, Italy, in March 1991, sponsored by UNICEF, the Global Forum of Spiritual and Parliamentary Leaders on Human Survival, and the Center for Foreign Journalists. For more information contact Rushworth Kidder, Institute for Global Ethics, Box 563, Camden, Maine 04843.

PLATE 7-38

International Air Traffic Association so that all passenger tickets are alike, flight schedules mesh, airports, and air traffic controllers operate with the same rules, producing an efficient, safe system unachievable without such agreements and cooperation. Similarly, the global postal system works, as does the world weather forecasting system. We can see how space cooperation is necessary since no country can afford the next stages of space research and development alone.

Most urgent are the needed new agreements over financial systems and trade. Ad hoc G-7 meetings and other such piecemeal approaches, such as today's global rules over banks regarding reserve requirements and currency fluctuation "bandwidths," are stopgap measures at best. What is needed is nothing less than a "New Bretton Woods" conference (which in 1945, set up the existing global economy, the World Bank, IMF and the GATT). The GATT was a compromise to satisfy American objections to the originally envisioned International Trade Organization (ITO) in which all countries would participate. Clearly GATT is widely viewed as unfair to developing countries and favoring the interests of the North and multi-national corporations. For example, the Uruguay Round not only broke down over the European Community's determination to continue its Common Agricultural Policy (CAP) protecting small farms, but also over the Northern countries pushing an agreement on services and "intellectual property" which the South saw as an attempt to shut them out of major areas of technological innovation, and in biotechnology, might allow their rich genetic resources to be preempted by the patenting of seeds, etc. Similarly, the World Bank and IMF need to be democratized as recommended by the London-based The Other Economic Summit. The G-7 needs to give way to a World Economic Council in which all countries can participate. Global protocols must be established on environmental sustainability, consumer and worker protection, and others on currency regimes, new reserve currencies to bolster the Eurodollar system with ECUs and yen, and expansion of Special Drawing Rights (SDRs). Most controversially, wage differentials should also be contained within "bandwidths."

Thus a level playing field can emerge that will reward—rather than punish—the most ethical companies and countries. Extreme differentials in wages between countries as well as regulatory regimes cause many short-term corporate relocation decisions—merely to take advantage of windows of opportunity that close within a few years. Many of these short-term movements of plants are highly entropic and drive excessive restructuring and disruption everywhere—often abetted by tax codes that reward these short-term relocations with fast write-offs and force local authorities to "bid" for these relocations with unrealistic "tax holidays," "export platforms," etc., Hopefully, a new generation of environmentally and globally literate journalists can interpret these activities from new-paradigm perspectives—rather than so many of today's journalists who have often been indoctrinated into the "economism" paradigm by such programs as those of the Alfred Sloan Foundation (which "teaches" journalists to be "economically literate").[26] (See Plate 7-38.)

We now turn to a fuller discussion of other elements of the emerging world order.

Chapter Seven Footnotes

1. See for example, *Green Business: Hope or Hoax?* Edited by Chistopher Plant and Judith Plant, Green Books, Schumacher Society, Bideford, Devon, UK, 1991.

2. *Shopping For a Better World*, Council on Economic Priorities, 30 Irving Place, New York, NY 10003, annual editions.

3. Report, *Fifty Most Ethical Stocks*, Franklin Research and Development, Inc., Boston, MA, 1991, 617-423-6655.

4. Council on Economic Priorities, *Better World Investment Guide*, Prentice Hall Press, New York, 1991.

5. *Business Week*, "A Bright Idea in Solar Energy," July 1, 1991, p. 79.

6. Anita Roddick, *Body and Soul: Profits with Principles*, Crown Publishing, New York, 1991.

7. *The Economist*, "Converting Nuclear Power Stations," April 7, 1990, pg. 78.

8. *New Economics*, New Economics Foundation, London, U.K., Summer 1991.

9. United Nations, *Beyond the Debt Crisis, Final Report of the International Women's Seminar*, Non-Governmental Liaison Service, available from DC-2, Room 1103, New York, NY 10017.

10. David Brooks, *An Evaluation of Our Common Future*, International Development Research Centre, Ottawa, Canada, August 1991.

11. Herman Daly, *Toward the Common Good*, Beacon, Boston. Also see *Environmental Accounting for Sustainable Development*, Yusef Ahmed, Salah E. Serafy and Ernest Lutz, eds., World Bank, Washington, DC, 1989.

12. Quoted in *World Policy Journal* is an even more alarming look at the decline of the United States, "Soul Among the Prophets," by Walter Russell Mead, World Policy Institute, New York, Summer 1991.

13. *The Economist*, "Rougher and Tougher," June 29, 1991, p. 21.

14. *The Economist*, "Political Pawns," August 10, 1991, p. 16.

15. See for example op. cit. Walter Russell Mead. In addition see *The Constant External ECU* by Jacques Riboud, St. Martin's Press, which proposes to make the ECU a stable world currency to rival gold.

16. *Business Week*, "It's the States' Turn to Play 'Raid the Pension Fund,'" July 18, 1991.

17. *The Economist,* "When GM's Robots Ran Amok," August 10, 1991, p. 64.

18. In Chapters 9 and 10 of *Politics of the Solar Age,* I dissected the "declining productivity"—a mystery to old-paradigm economists.

19. *New York Times,* "The Cost of Drug Abuse: $60 Billion a Year," December 5, 1989.

20. See for example the "Turn back the clock" arguments of Britain's Edward Goldsmith in *The Great U-Turn: De-industrializing Society,* from his influential and brilliant journal, *The Ecologist,* Bootstrap Press, New York, 1988.

21. See for example, the *Directory* of the Social Investment Forum, Boston, 1991; *The Corporate Examiner,* newsletter of the Interfaith Council on Corporate Responsibility, 475 Riverside Drive, New York, NY; *The Better World Investment Guide* (1991) and the CEP Corporate Environmental Data Clearinghouse, and the Newsletter, CEP, 30 Irving Place, New York, NY 10003.

22. *Shopping For a Better World* also from CEP.

23. "Green Marketing" is facing even more skeptical regulations and consumers as reported in "Suddenly Green Marketers are Seeing Red Flags," *Business Week,* February 25, 1991, p. 74.

An example of a state-of-the-art corporate environmental audit is found in the annual report of BFO/Origin, Utrecht, Holland, which accounts for the impact of company operations on air, water, energy, etc.

24. See for example the European Commission. While, as yet, it does not have a "green police force," it now examines all environmental complaints between its member countries and keeps data on the relative "Dirtiest Rankings" of its own Dozen Countries. The "cleanest" is Denmark and the "dirtiest" is Spain. *The Economist,* "The Dirty Dozen," July 20, 1991, p. 52.

25. See for example, "The FCC's About To Clear the Air—A Little," (where at last, the United States will be challenged by the International Telecommunications Union for its "hogging" of these common airwaves, which are used by all countries), *Business Week,* June 17, 1991, p. 38.

26. Vigilance will be required to prevent "economism" from creeping in and co-opting ecology. See for example, *Bionomics: The Inevitability of Capitalism,* by Michael Rothschild (1991) reviewed approvingly in the *Wall Street Journal,* August 19, 1991. In *The Economist,* August 17, 1991, p. 64, an Economic Focus article "A Price on the Priceless," touts obsolete economic welfare theory's ability to develop "techniques to measure environmental value" which are largely entrepreneurial "economism" rather than scientific techniques.

NOTE: *The Eco-Team Workbook,* David Gershon and Robert Gilman, Global Action Plan, West Hurley, New York, 1991, outlines a six-month plan to restore your household to ecological balance.

What the World Wants—and How to Pay for It

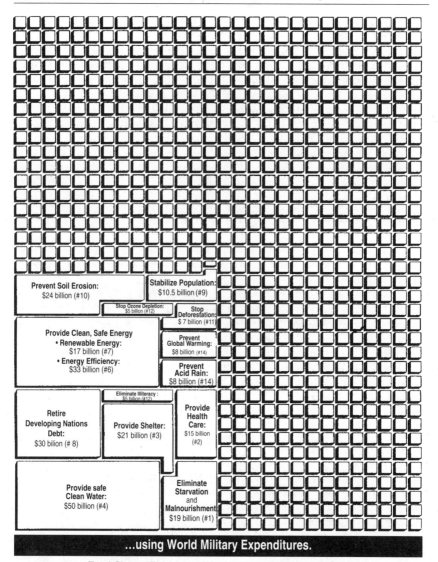

Prevent Soil Erosion:
$24 billion (#10)

Stabilize Population:
$10.5 billion (#9)

Stop Ozone Depletion:
$5 billion (#12)

Stop Deforestation:
$ 7 billion (#11)

Provide Clean, Safe Energy
• Renewable Energy:
$17 billion (#7)
• Energy Efficiency:
$33 billion (#6)

Prevent Global Warming:
$8 billion (#14)

Prevent Acid Rain:
$8 billion (#14)

Eliminate Illiteracy :
$5 billion (#12)

Retire Developing Nations Debt:
$30 bilion (# 8)

Provide Shelter:
$21 billion (#3)

Provide Health Care:
$15 billion (#2)

Provide safe Clean Water:
$50 billion (#4)

Eliminate Starvation and Malnourishment
$19 billion (#1)

...using World Military Expenditures.

Total Chart = Total Annual World Military Expenditures: $1 trillion

☐ = One-tenth of One Percent of Annual World Military Expenditures: $1 billion

The above are annual costs of various global programs for solving the major human need and environmental problems facing humanity. Each program is the amount needed to accomplish the goal for all in need in the world. Their combined total cost is approximate 25% of the world's total annual military expenditures. Footnotes and references follow. Full explanatory text is in "Doing the Right Things" ($5 postpaid from the World Game Institute, 3508 Market Street, Philadelphia, PA 19104; 215/387-0220).

PLATE 8-39

CHAPTER 8

Toward a New World Order
Visions for the 1990s

An important symbol of the realities of global interdependence has been the widespread debate about the "New World Order" whether between former Cold War protagonists in the United States and the USSR or between leaders in the Northern and Southern Hemispheres. The phrase may be a dominant metaphor for the restructurings and realignments occurring everywhere. To President George Bush, Mikhail Gorbachev and other second-wave reformers of the old Soviet Empire, "The New World Order" is primarily about the growing partnership of the two former super-powers. Neither country escaped the general loss of sovereignty inherent in the globalization process and both learned the social and economic cost of their military struggle.

The New World Order also implied a shift in the definition of "national security" from military to economic and ecological security, as well as recasting the whole debate about development. Yet the military-industrial complexes in the United States, the old Soviet empire, Western Europe and elsewhere are still deeply entrenched. These colossal global arsenals and the world's staggering $1 trillion annual expenditures on the arms trade had distorted most domestic economies, provided political patronage, pork-barrel programs and millions of jobs.

Familiar howls were heard in national legislatures when anyone made suggestions of cutbacks or conversion to civilian goods and priorities. In the United States, social problems mounted in cities, states were going broke, and the "downward mobility" of America's young "baby bust" generation were covered daily in the media, while banks, savings and loans, and insurance companies tottered. Yet instead of economic conversion of our military to shore up other sectors, the arms race went

What The World Wants

This chart seeks to make the point that what the world needs to solve the major systemic problems confronting humanity is both available and affordable. Clearly, to portray a problem as complex and large as, for example, the global food situation, with just a small part of a single graph is incomplete at best. The following explanations of the chart's various components are not intended as complete or detailed plans, but rather as very broad brush-strokes intended to give the overall direction, scope and strategy. The paper, "Doing the Right Things" goes into more detail and is available from the World Game Institute. (References listed at the end of numbered sections contain supporting documentation, further explication, and related information.)

1. **Eliminate starvation and malnourishment:** $19 billion per year total; $2 billion per year for 10 years for global famine relief—spent on international grain reserve and emergency famine relief; $10 billion per year for twenty years spent on farmer education through vastly expanded in-country extension services that teach/demonstrate sustainable agriculture, use of local fertilizer sources, pest and soil management techniques, post harvest preservation, and which provide clear market incentives for increased local production; $7 billion per year for indigenous fertilizer development. Educational resources of #10 coupled with this strategy. Closely linked with #'s 2, 2A, 2B, 4, 5, 9, 10.

2. **Provide health care:** $15 billion per year spent on providing primary health care through community health workers to all areas in the world that do not have access to health care. Closely linked with #'s 1, 3, 4, 5.

2A. **Child health care:** $2.5 billion per year spent on: a) providing Vitamin A to children who lack it in their diet, thereby preventing blindness in 250,000 children/year; b) providing oral rehydration therapy for children with severe diarrhoea; and c) immunizing 1 billion children in developing world against measles, tuberculosis, diphtheria, whooping cough, polio and tetanus, thereby preventing the death of 607 million children/year.

2B. **Special health problems:** $40 million per year for iodine addition to table salt to eliminate iodine deficiency, thereby reducing the 190 million who suffer from goiter and not adding to the 3 million who suffer from overt cretinism.

3. **Eliminate inadequate housing and homelessness:** $21 billion for ten years spent on making available materials, tools and techniques to people without adequate housing. Closely linked with #'s 1, 4, 5, 9.

4. **Provide clean and abundant water:** $50 million per year for ten years spent on water and sanitation projects—wells, pipes, water purifying systems. Closely related to #'s 1, 2, 3, 9.

5. **Eliminate illiteracy:** $4.5 billion per year for ten years; $2 billion spent on a system of 10 to 12 communication satellites and their launching; $2 billion spent on ten million televisions, satellite dish receivers, and photovoltaic/battery units for power—all placed in village schools and other needed areas throughout high literacy areas; the rest (90% of funds), spent on culturally appropriate literacy programming and maintenance of system. Closely related to #'s 1, 2, 3, 4, 9, 10, 11.

6. **Increase efficiency:** $33 billion per year for ten years spent on increasing car fleet mileage to over 50 m.p.g., plus increasing appliance, industrial processes, and household energy and materials use efficiency to state of the art. Closely linked with #'s 7, 8, 12, 13, 14.

7. **Increase renewable energy:** $20 billion per year for ten years spent on tax and other incentives for installation of renewable energy devices, graduated ten year phase-out of subsidies to fossil and nuclear fuels, research and development into more advanced renewable energy harnessing devices. Closely linked with #'s 6, 8, 11, 12, 13, 14.

8. **Debt management:** $30 billion per year for ten years spent on retiring $450 billion or more of current debt discounted to 50% face value. (Much of developing world's current debt is already discounted 10-25% face value.) Not only helps developing countries get out of debt, but helps banks stay solvent. Closely linked with #'s 1, 6, 7, 10, 11, 14.

9. **Stabilize population:** $10.5 billion per year for ten years spent on making birth control universally available. Closely linked with #'s 1, 2, 3, 4, 5.

10. **Reverse soil erosion:** $24 billion per year for ten years spent on converting one-tenth of world's most vulnerable cropland that is simultaneously most susceptible to erosion, the location of most severe erosion, and the land that is no longer able to sustain agriculture, to pasture or woodland; and conserving and regenerating topsoil on remaining lands through sustainable farming techniques. Both accomplished through a combination of government regulation and incentive programs that remove the most vulnerable lands from crop production; and by farmer education through vastly expanded in-country extension services that teach/demonstrate sustainable agriculture and soil management techniques. Closely linked to # 1.

11. **Reverse deforestation:** $7 billion per year for ten years spent on reforesting 150 million hectares needed to sustain ecological, fuelwood, and word products needs. Planted by local villagers, costs would be $400 per hectare, including seedling costs. Additional cost for legislation, financial incentives, enforcement of rainforest protection. Closely linked with # 10 and 14.

12. **Reverse ozone depletion:** $5 billion per year for twenty years spent on phasing in subsidies for CFCs, CFC taxes, incentives for further research and development. Closely linked with # 14.

13. **Stop acid rain:** $8 billion per year for ten years spent on combination of tax incentive, government regulation and direct assistance programs that place pollution control devices (electrostatic precipitators, etc.) on all industrial users of coal, increase efficiency of industrial processes, transportation, and appliances. Closely linked to #'s 6, 7, 11, 12, 13.

14. **Stop global warming:** $8 billion per year for thirty years spent on reducing carbon dioxide, methane and CFC release into atmosphere through combination of international accords, carbon taxes, increases in energy efficiency in industry, transportation, and household, decreases in fossil fuel use, increases in renewable energy use and reforestation. Closely linked with #'s 6, 7, 11, 12, 13.

References: Ho-Ping: Food for Everyone, World Game Institute, Doubleday, New York; #1, 10. State of the World's Children, UNICEF, Oxford University Press, 1990; # 2, 2A, 2B. UNICEF, Giving Children a Future: The World Summit for Children, New York, UNICEF, 1990, pp. 4-6, 10; and "Moving Towards a Global Ethic," Development Forum, p. 1, Sept./Oct. 1990; # 2, 2A, 2B. State of the World 1988, Worldwatch Institute, Washington, D.C.; # 4, 6, 7, 8, 10, 11. Energy, Earth and Everyone, World Game Institute, Doubleday, New York; # 6, 7. Soft Energy Paths, Amory Lovins, Ballinger, Boston; # 6, 7. 1990 Report on Progress Toward Population Stabilization, Population Crisis Committee, Washington, D.C.; #9. World Resources 1986, 1987, World Resources Institute, Washington, D.C.; # 12,13, 14. The Sky is the Limit, Strategies for Protecting the Ozone Layer, World Resources Institute, Washington, D.C., 1986; # 12.

PLATE 8-39b

global as military contractors and their allies in governments everywhere promoted arms sales as good "exports" and "high-tech R & D" while military strategists hunted for new enemies to justify the trade. The United States accounts for 24 percent of the world's arms exports, the USSR 41 percent, and the European NATO countries 16 percent, with 19 percent now being exported from developing countries.[1] The obscenity of these skewed priorities in a world of hunger, disease and illiteracy should be obvious. The World Game Institute (See Plate 8-39) shows that re-deploying less than one quarter of the worlds $1 trillion military expenditures could, over ten years, reverse today's worsening social and environmental problems and put all countries on the path to sustainable development.[2] The entrenchment of military-industrial sectors has hardly budged in spite of all the mounting evidence in the previous chapters, that investments in people, their health and education are the key factor in productivity. When the manufacturing productivity of the United States, USSR, United Kingdom, France, Germany, Japan, Sweden, Italy, Canada and Denmark was compared between 1962 and 1988, it was *inversely* related to the size of their military expenditures. (See Plate 6-29: Military Spending and Human Development Performance.) Thus any new world order must start with reversing the global arms trafficking and militarism, making actual reductions to arsenals beyond the token progress of the START Treaty between the United States and USSR. In spite of President Bush's welcome unilateral initiative of September 1991, ordering cuts in U.S. nuclear arsenals, much pruning remains essential in all major Cold War protagonists' military sectors. These issues are covered in depth in "Breaking the Arms Sales Addiction" by Wilham D. Hartung, *World Policy Journal*, Winter 1990-1991.

In the space of a few short years, the reality of global interdependence has restructured global geopolitics irrevocably. Leaders shorn of national sovereignty are now forced to seek partners, deal with a still dangerously anarchic world system via ad hoc alliances, and act pragmatically—even when at odds with their existing worldviews. The United States went from the Soviet-bashing, escalating military budgets and U.N.-baiting of the Reagan years to the 1990 U.N.-courting and alliance-building so as to prosecute Iraq. During the Persian Gulf War, President George Bush referred repeatedly to a New World Order for the 1990s as the rationale for U.S. policies and military action. Bush speechwriter, James Pickering, began to insert the term "new paradigm" in the President's speeches, citing (when asked for explanations) Thomas Kuhn's original usage in *The Structure of Scientific Revolutions* (1962) mentioned earlier. Mr. Bush's New World Order was widely construed as a "New Pax Americana" in global geopolitical terms, since the United States had military superiority even if its economy was weakened. Many developing countries saw Bush's vision as simply "Might is Right" in the service of a new set of Western Imperialist "crusades."

Los Angeles Times analyst Robin Wright in the June 25, 1991, edition highlighted the divergence between theory and practice in Bush's "New World Order," including: "theoretical support for partnerships and collective action; democracy; reduction of arms sales and self-determination—while, *in practice* the United States:

1. Acts unilaterally or brings in the United Nations after the fact;
2. Actively . . . promotes democracy in socialist states while tolerating slow or no change in conservative hold-outs.
3. Is negotiating new arms sales, and
4. In most flash-points, supports territorial integrity of existing states over nationalistic movements' separatist efforts."

Similar confusion over these many contradictory elements in President Bush's "New World Order" prompted the Kettering Foundation-funded National Issues Forum (which promotes civic debate over key policies) to mount a new forum for 1991-1992 on America's Role in the World around four basic choices:

1. Solo Superpower (the United States as a unilateral world actor);
2. Balancing Act in the new multi-polar world;
3. Multilateral Solution: New Rules for Mutual Security; and
4. Domestic Priorities: Refocusing on Needs Close to Home.

Whatever the judgement of history on the Gulf War there were many paradigm-breaking aspects deserving our attention. Firstly, it was a war in which mass media (particularly TV) and media polls played an unprecedented role. The Congress was in recess during the early days of the crisis in August 1990. The normal opinion-forming debates led by politicians were missing and the interpretive role was left to media and polls they commissioned. An extraordinarily simplistic national conversation emerged, with popularity polls on the President as the main barometer. Naturally, people confused and unsure of even the positions of their own congressional delegations gave the President top marks for his "handling of the crisis." By the time the Congress reconvened, media polls showed the President's position as unassailable. Not only did members of Congress avoid speaking out on the Gulf Crisis, they hardly even mentioned it during the 1990 fall election campaigns. The first big post-Cold War test of U.S. diplomacy was not even a campaign issue.

Thus did the U.S. democracy devolve into a mere "mediocracy" with active politics sinking into a TV torpor punctuated with photo opportunities and sound bites. By the time the Congress was forced into an open debate after Bush's November troop buildup, it was all too late. Americans learned to their amazement that the U.S. Senate had been almost evenly divided over the President's policies and that a third of the Congress had also been opposed to the almost predestined use of force in the Gulf. This spectacular failure of the U.S. political process was another unprecedented factor. As the bombs started falling on Baghdad in January 1991, Americans witnessed unprecedented levels of "news management" which many likened to a TV drama rather than a real war—while, throughout, the Pentagon carefully orchestrated most of the coverage, avoiding body counts and sanitizing the footage from the front.

At least one effort to democratize U.S. politics and mass media will be attempted by PBS in the 1992 elections. The brainchild of a Texas political scientist, the programs on public broadcasting stations will bring a representative "random sample" of 600 U.S. citizens into body contact with politicians running for office to try to debate and clarify some of the myriad, festering domestic and global issues so dangerously ignored in 1990, and will televise the encounter.[3] This drop in the bucket may at least open up the debate about how to democratize U.S. commercially-dominated media, which I discussed in an article in the *Columbia Journalism Review* as early as 1969.[4]

Yet there was another aspect of the Gulf War that was unprecedented in the annals of military history—this war just might have turned a profit for the United States, Britain and perhaps other members of the Western coalition. On June 12, 1991, *USA Today* headlined "Trade Surplus from War" noting that the "United States had posted its first trade surplus since 1982 in the first quarter of 1991; as billions from Gulf War allies poured into its coffers." The article went on, "The surplus is entirely due to $22.7 billion in cash received from coalition partners in the war."

Just before the Gulf War began, some economic forecasting firms predicted that a "short war" would boost the American economy and lead us out of recession. A Washington consulting group, WEFA, added that a short war "would launch a brisk recovery on the heels of an American victory." WEFA compared three scenarios—long war, short war, and stalemate—using four indicators: Gross National Product, oil prices, inflation and unemployment. Not surprisingly, a "short war" looked best. The conventional wisdom that "war is good for the economy" is widespread and contradictory. The same reasoning used to oppose military spending cuts is cited for the war in the Gulf—preserving American jobs. For many reasons, such conventional wisdom is not only obsolete, but also is part of a worrisome new trend: a U.S. policy shift toward a "mercenary" economy.

A "Conserver Society" Blueprint for Canada's Future?

Conservation Scenario	Scenario	Theme	Description
CS_0	Scenario of the status quo	"Doing more with more"	- mass-consumption society - uncontrolled growth
CS_1	Scenario of "growth with conservation"	"Doing more with less"	- increase efficiency - waste reduction - technological growth
CS_2	The high-level stable-state Scenario	"Doing the same with less"	- achievement of stability with affluence - reduction of inequalities
CS_3	The Buddhist Scenario	"Doing less with less" "Rejection of mass-consumption"	- decentralized economy - soft technology - value-change
CS_1	Scenario of the Squander Society	"Doing less with more" "Extravagance"	- dedication to mass-consumption and waste - obsolescence and self-destruction of consumer goods

Source: Conserver Society Report, 1978, Science Council of Canada

PLATE 8-40

As America loses exports, it may shift toward exporting its unquestioned security ability. America's trillions of dollars of sunk costs in our military-industrial sector (which until the end of the cold war accounted for one in six of all U.S. jobs) steers much of our national policy and Washington lobbying. The war was fought in the middle of a recession that was triggered partly by the loss of consumer confidence the war itself caused. Federal Reserve Board Chairman Alan Greenspan said in late January the United States faced "a long deep recession if the war with Iraq lasts past the middle of April." These conflicting forecasts illustrate the unreliability of economic indicators and the dangers of relying on one-dimensional statistics such as GNP.

The focus on GNP in the United States and other countries causes us to overlook vital social, cultural, political, and environmental factors. For example, the cost estimates for Desert Shield and Desert Storm overlooked vital social indicators of overall national progress, such as the U.N. Development Program's Human Development Index (HDI) now being adopted in Venezuela, Germany, France, Denmark, and Canada. As discussed, these new indexes add in data on infant mortality, military versus education budgets, and new "standard of living" measures that go beyond average money incomes per capita. If the United States does not shift to such indicators in its own policies, urgent domestic priorities— education, drugs, crime, deteriorating infrastructure, and the need to shift our economy from waste to more efficient use of energy and materials— will continue to be short-changed.

Forecasters' false optimism over the war overlooked many of these deep-seated domestic threats to our national security. They also failed to account for the costs of the war's aftermath, such as stabilizing the Mideast region, rebuilding the bomb-damaged economies and the trust of Arab populations, dealing with the Kurds, or the environmental devastation in Kuwait and the Gulf.

The new American policy of "burden-sharing" is a milestone in military financing. Even though the U.S.-led coalition was in Iraq with a U.N. mandate, the U.S.-led operation and our pro-active stance was labeled by the magazine *The Economist* as that of "rent-a-superpower." Developing countries labeled the conflict "Bush's war." In India, it destabilized the government of Chandra Shekhar. The United States will need to convince both its friends and detractors that it does *not* intend to become the world's mercenary. In today's global village, war is simply becoming less viable as an instrument of national policy. Diplomacy and creative cooperation, as well as "smarter" kinds of sanctions (which will operate as "information" quarantines or embargoes, more efficient than

Stockholm's Declaration of Principles

1) Asserts human rights, condemns apartheid, colonialism, etc.;
2) Natural resources must be safeguarded;
3) Earth's capacity to produce renewable resources must be maintained;
4) Wildlife must be safeguarded;
5) Non-renewable resources must be shared and not exhausted;
6) Pollution must not exceed environment's capacity to clean itself;
7) Damaging oceanic pollution must be prevented;
8) Development is needed to improve the environment;
9) Developing countries therefore need assistance;
10) Developing countries need reasonable prices for exports to carry out environmental management;
11) Environment policy must not hamper development;
12) Developing countries need money to develop environmental safeguards;
13) Integrated development planning is needed;
14) Rational planning should resolve conflicts between environment and development;

15) Human settlements must be planned to eliminate environmental problems;
16) Governments should plan their own appropriate population policies;
17) National Institutions must plan development of states' natural resources;
18) Science and technology must be used to improve the environment;
19) Environmental education is essential;
20) Environmental research must be promoted, particularly in developing countries;
21) States may exploit their resources as they wish but must not endanger others;
22) Compensation is due to states thus endangered;
23) Each nation must establish its own standards;
24) There must be co-operation on international issues;
25) International organizations should help to improve the environment;
26) Weapons of mass destruction must be eliminated.

Source: the UN Conference on Environment, Stockholm, 1972; available from UN Environment Programme, Nairobi, Kenya

PLATE 8-41

starving civilian populations) will carry the day. Current sanctions penalize the poor, women and children rather than elites. If a new meeting of the minds is shaping up between military actuaries, economic forecasters, and policymakers, offensive war may replace our historic defensive warfare. Such war may appear to be more "economical." New economic and conflict indicators such as those of the WEFA Group may fuel growing mercenary sentiments on the part of strategists.

Yet such a new course relies heavily on the quality of government statistics, and data quality is declining alarmingly. One poll of forecasters found that only four disagreed that the government's "economic statistical gathering system has deteriorated significantly over the past decade." It's clear that a growing GNP does not reflect growing financial health, let alone account for social and environmental costs. After eight years of GNP growth, we are faced with crisis in the savings and loan industry, trouble in banking and insurance sectors, and falling literacy rates. This domestic neglect was highlighted by even mainstream thinkers Peter G. Peterson, Chairman of the Council on Foreign Relations, and William G. Hyland, editor of *Foreign Affairs*, in an article "Shift to Domestic Concerns Urged" on page 19 of the *Washington Post*, July 19, 1991.

Dealing with economic and domestic problems is better than drifting toward a mercenary economy. Yet, so far, the issue of whether the United States is drifting toward an unprecedented new role in the world—that of a "rent-a-superpower" has hardly been noticed. Little "loyal opposition" was left in the wake of the yellow ribbons and victory parades to even ask the hard new questions in the war's aftermath. Was it really a victory—with Saddam still in power, Kuwait still an absolute monarchy, over 150,000 Iraqi dead, hundreds of thousands of casualties and stalemate still hanging over the Mideast?

Swords into plowshares

However, as Middle East combatants rush to replenish their arsenals and upgrade their weapons, it is clear that the real winners in the Gulf were the world's arms merchants.

China, in spite of glacial democratic reform, has been a leader in economic conversion of military to civilian production. It earned Worldwatch Institute's commendations for steadily reducing its military budgets over the past 15 years. China's military-industrial complex—one of the world's largest, employing over two million workers—was built in the 1960s and 1970s under Mao Zedong. Deng Xiaoping had cut troops by one million by 1985. In the past decade, China's thousands of munitions plants have developed more than 300 civilian product lines and 10,000

World Charter for Nature

United Nations Environment Programme

GENERAL PRINCIPLES

1. Nature shall be respected and its essential processes shall not be impaired.

2. The genetic viability on the earth shall not be compromised; the population levels of all life forms, wild and domesticated, must be at least sufficient for their survival, and to this end necessary habitats shall be safeguarded.

3. All areas of the earth, both land and sea, shall be subject to these principles of conservation; special protection shall be given to unique areas, to representative samples of all the different types of ecosystems and to the habitats of rare or endangered species.

4. Ecosystems and organisms, as well as the land, marine and atmospheric resources that are utilized by man, shall be managed to achieve and maintain optimum sustainable productivity, but not in such a way as to endanger the integrity of those other ecosystems or species with which they co-exist.

5. Nature shall be secured against degradation caused by warfare or other hostile activities.

Source: Public Phamplet, UNEP, New York 1991

PLATE 8-42

new products (ranging from civil airplanes, cranes, ships, autos, rail carriages, motorcycles and refrigerators to consumer electronics). Former military enterprises now supply 16.6 percent of all China's medical equipment and are now exporting many products. "Converting military technologies for civilian use is regarded as an essential part of our national economic development," notes Jin Zhude, Secretary-General of China Association for Peaceful Use of Military-Industrial Technologies, founded in 1986.[5]

Yet virtually all countries, including China, still see their "security needs" mostly in military terms, and all measure national "progress" by the growth of gross national products (GNP). As noted earlier, the two measurements are not unrelated; GNP was introduced during World War II to focus on military production. A lasting peace, let alone a new world order, will require rethinking our definitions of security, progress and development—stretching them beyond the growth of GNP.

New definitions of a new world order must include security from environmental pollution, poverty, hunger, and disease; secure work based on a well-run economy; a sound infrastructure roads, railways and public buildings; and security from crime and illegal drugs. Now is the time for debate on the ways of shifting the world's priorities and redirecting the current $1 trillion a year spent on weapons toward investments in the areas of health, education, and environmental restoration.

The means for such a shift are at hand, since it is widely recognized that global arms trafficking threatens the security of all countries. Bush has ordered a tightening of United States arms sales restrictions, and Prime Minister Brian Mulroney of Canada noted "the irony" that most of the weapons used in the Gulf were supplied by the five nations of the U.N. Security Council. In the 1991 London Economic G-7 Summit, the leaders backed a "registry" of global arms sales. Recognition of such hypocrisy may provide the impetus to implement a 1980 U.N. Commission proposal: to levy a U.N.-collected tax on global arms sales and shipments and earmark the proceeds for UNICEF and the world's children.

The same GNP accounting methods that overvalue arms production set no value on other critical concerns—such as the wellbeing of our children and of the environment on which their futures will depend. Even in a country deemed rich by GNP standards, one-fifth of all American children live in poverty, 37 million have no health insurance, and the United States now leads the world in the percentage of its people in prison.

Since the failed coup in August 1991 in the Soviet Union, it is clear that the pace of conversion from military to civilian production will quicken, since the need for this shift was vital to bolster the sagging

ECE Charter

on environmental rights and obligations. Adopted at the Experts Meeting in Oslo, Norway, 29-31 October 1990.

Reaffirming that the attainment of sustainable development on the national, regional and global levels requires fundamental changes in human values towards the environment and in patterns of behaviour and consumption as well as the establishment of necessary democratic institutions and process;

Emphasizing the importance of participation by a well informed and well educated society so as to allow the public to mobilize itself to affect political change consistent with sustainable development;

Confirming the intention to continue to improve national and international processes within the ECE region and in light of the important multisectoral dialogue among Governments and non-government sectors which was initiated for the Regional Conference on the follow-up to the Report of the World Commission on Environment and Development (WCED) in the ECE Region held in Bergen, Norway in May 1990;

Proclaim that:

FUNDAMENTAL PRINCIPLES

1. Everyone has the right to an environment adequate for his general health and well-being.

2. Everyone has the responsibility to protect and conserve the environment for the benefit of present and future generations.

3. Everyone has the right to express freely his views, to associate with others, to assemble peacefully, to publish and distribute information and to establish and maintain direct and independent contact at national and international levels on environmental issues.

ENVIRONMENTAL INFORMATION, EDUCATION AND TRAINING

4. Everyone has the right of access to adequate information relevant to the environment, including information on products and activities which could or do significantly affect the environment and on environmental protection measures. The information shall be provided in a clear way, be understandable to the public in general and be without unreasonable financial burden to the applicant.

5. Everyone has the right to receive adequate information about potential sources of accidents,including contingency planning and to be informed immediately when an emergency occurs.

6. Everyone has the right to appeal for administrative or judicial review when the requested information is not provided within a reasonable time or is withheld for any reason.

7. Everyone has the right to adequate environmental education and access to environmental training.

8. Everyone has the right to receive at regular intervals reports prepared by competent authorities on the state of the environment at local, provincial and national levels.

9. Public bodies have the responsibility and accountability to report regularly on the extent to which their activities have had a significant affect on the environment.

Source: The World Commission on Environment and Development, Geneva, Switzerland

PLATE 8-43

economy—and Mikhail Gorbachev had provided initial impetus. U.S. business exulted over the failed Soviet coup and deals already in the works (with Chevron, General Motors, IBM, as well as with such European firms as Alcatel of France, Carroll Group of the United Kingdom, Fiat of Italy and Daimler-Benz of Germany) were put on faster tracks.[6] Ironically, little progress on military conversion was visible in the United States or Europe. In 1989-91 the USSR began the conversion process by cutting military equipment orders by 30 percent. As in China, Soviet arms factories are already dual-purpose, for example, 60 percent of all streetcars, most TV sets, VCRs and washing machines are produced in military facilities. By 1991, about 600 of these enterprises (about 10 percent of the USSR's defense industry) were involved in civilian conversion.[7]

Additional ironies were the calls for help on designing the peacetime conversion requirements of the Soviets, to the American business community (still exporting 24 percent of the world's weapons). Most of the initiatives for conversion to civilian production in the United States are coming from grassroots activists, organizing business, labor, consumers and broad coalitions to develop city and state economic conversion plans in overly-dependent areas, including San Diego, St. Louis, and Tucson, as well as in states where military cuts have already caused layoffs of hundreds of thousands of workers, including Minnesota, Washington, Connecticut and Texas. Much of this activity is assisted by research from the Center for Economic Conversion and reported in their quarterly, *Positive Alternatives*.[8]

Indeed, in most parts of the world, it is grassroots activism that is the greatest force for a genuinely peaceful, just, environmentally-sane new world order. Non-Governmental Organizations (NGOs) are credited by many high-level politicians and U.N. officials for this creative pressure on their own governments. An important issue today is how *governments* who oppress their own people should be punished.

Specific planks of a comprehensive new world order are being shaped by the debate between northern and southern hemisphere countries over definitions of wealth and progress. The concept of "sustainable development" is emerging. As mentioned, it includes a longer-term view—development to meet the needs of present generations without foreclosing on the ability of succeeding generations to meet their own needs. Such a new world order was articulated last September by 71 heads of state—including President Bush, Prime Minister Mulroney, Britain's then-Prime Minister Margaret Thatcher, and other Gulf coalition leaders at the World Summit for Children. Any new order that does not focus on our children's futures is not worthy of the name.

The North American Coalition on Religion and Ecology

Proposed Principles

Therefore, we affirm that the 1992 Earth Summit should pass a draft of an Earth Charter which would include these underlying principles:

1.   All forms of life are sacred. The earth is a community, a communion of beings. We, the human beings, must acknowledge and respect that sacredness.

2.   The earth community is a complex, interdependent system, and can survive only in its integral, interconnected functioning. All the diverse parts of the system are essential to its functioning and beauty.

3.   Our relationship to the earth must be one of humility. Care for the earth must be a serious concern of every human institution, profession, program and activity.

4.   Life is a gift, given equally to all. It must be treated with respect and with due consideration of others, including future generations.

5.   Human life is part of the mystery of evolution become conscious of itself, and we stand humble before this great mystery. The beauty of the earth inspires human consciousness, imagination, and celebration.

6.   In the light of ecological interdependence, humans are obliged to repent of exploitative and destructive habits, and to live graciously with the rest of creation, experiencing the joy of being one with the whole earth community.

For more information you may contact NACRE at 5 Thomas Circle NW, Washington D.C. 20005 or at (202) 462-2591.

PLATE 8-44

Summit participants drafted an "action plan" to address the "quiet catastrophe" of 40,000 child deaths each day from malnutrition and disease, pledging to reduce this rate by one-third by the year 2000. (See Plate 4-23: Action Plan for State of the World's Children.) The goals in the plan were deemed feasible and affordable at a price tag of $2.5 billion annually (the cost of U.S. cigarette advertising each year).

Other elements of a more comprehensive new world order that merit further debate include:

- Strengthening the United Nations and supporting a permanent peacekeeping force, with treaty and border-surveillance by satellite.
- A global population credit bank to make credits available to any non-G-7 country achieving replacement fertility rates and stabilizing its population.
- A global environmental fund to make available to countries adopting environmental-protection standards credits for sustainable forms of development and "green" technologies.
- Global energy-efficiency credit and a development bank to facilitate loans, investments, joint ventures, and public infra-structure funds to promote efficient energy systems in industry, housing, agriculture, and transportation.
- Extending U.N. treaties and protocols on protection of human rights to include rights of workers and consumers, rights of political participation and rights within the family.

Alternative visions of a new world order are needed more than ever and they must include efforts to correct GNP and its narrow view of progress. More than ever new indicators are needed that remove biases toward military production.

Another rich source of alternative thinking on a "new world order" is found in the hundreds of new futures studies and research papers from all over the world. The futurist movement began in Europe and the United States in the 1960s. The World Future Society in Washington, DC, is open to both professional and lay members; and its popular magazine, *The Futurist*, and professional journal, *Futures Research Quarterly*, provide useful guides to this expanding field. Perhaps the best ongoing information monitoring useful new books and studies of key policy issues and "new world order" thinking is *Future Survey*, a monthly abstracting of all the important new books in publication.[9] Other useful sources are the Institute for World Order and its World Order Models Project (WOMP) founded by Harry B. Hollins of the World Law Fund in 1968. Professor Saul H. Mendlovitz directed a brilliant series of multi-cultural studies of "Preferred World for the 1990s," published in the

Bahá'í International Community Earth Charter

Elements for inclusion in the proposed "Earth Charter" presented to the preparatory committee of the United Nations Conference on Environment and Development (UNCED), Geneva, 5 April 1991, by the Bahá'í International Community

It is our conviction that any call to global action for environment and development must be rooted in universally accepted values and principles. Similarly, the search for solutions to the world's grave environmental and developmental problems must go beyond technical-utilitarian proposals and address the underlying causes of the crisis. Genuine solutions, in the Bahá'í view, will require a globally accepted vision for the future, based on unity and willing cooperation among nations, races, creeds and classes of the human family. Commitment to a higher moral standard, equally between the sexes and the development of consultative skills for the effective functioning of groups at all levels of society will be essential. In order to reorient individuals and societies toward a sustainable future, we must recognize the following:

•　Unity is essential if diverse peoples are to work toward a common future. The "Earth Charter" might well identify those aspects of unity which are prerequisites for the achievement of sustainable development. In the Bahá'í view, "The well-being of mankind, its peace and security, are unattainable unless and until its unity is firmly established."

•　The unrestrained exploitation of natural resources is merely a symptom of an overall sickness of the human spirit. Any solutions to the environment/development crisis must, therefore, be rooted in an approach which fosters spiritual balance and harmony within the individual, between individuals, and with the environment as a whole. Material development must serve not only the body, but the mind and spirit as well.

•　The changes required to reorient the world toward a sustainable future imply degrees of sacrifice, social integration, selfless action and unity of purpose rarely achieved in human history. These qualities have reached their highest degree of development through the power of religion. Therefore, the world's religious communities have a major role to play in inspiring these qualities in their members, releasing latent capacities of the human spirit and empowering individuals to act on behalf of the planet, its peoples, and future generations.

•　Nothing short of a world federal system, guided by universally agreed upon and enforceable laws, will allow nation states to manage cooperatively an increasingly interdependent and rapidly changing world, thereby ensuring peace and social and economic justice for all the world's peoples.

•　Development must be decentralized in order to involve communities in formulating and implementing the decisions and programs that affect their lives. Such a decentralization need not conflict with a global system and strategy, but would in fact ensure that developmental processes are adapted to the planet's rich cultural, geographic and ecological diversity.

•　Consultation must replace confrontation and domination in order to gain the cooperation of the family of nations in devising and implementing measures that will preserve the earth's ecological balance.

•　Only as women are welcomed into full partnership in all fields of human endeavor, including environment and development, will the moral and psychological climate be created in which a peaceful, harmonious and sustainable civilization can emerge and flourish.

•　The cause of universal education deserves the utmost support, for no nation can achieve success unless education is accorded all its citizens. Such an education should promote the consciousness of both the oneness of humanity and the integral connection between humankind and the world of nature. By nurturing a sense of world citizenship, education can prepare the youth of the world for the organic changes in the structure of society which the principle of oneness implies.

The Bahá'í International Community stands ready to contribute to the further elaboration and promotion of an "Earth Charter" in consultation with other interested bodies. It may be contacted at 866 UN Plaza, Suite 120, New York, NY 10017

PLATE 8-45

magazine *Alternatives*. Currently WOMP is exploring "Global Civilization: Challenges for Sovereignty, Democracy and Security."[10]

In *Reinventing the Future: Global Goals for the 21st Century*, Rushworth Kidder reports on the recommendations of thirty-five prominent global citizens convened by the *Christian Science Monitor* in 1987. The first recommendation called for refocusing measures of development away from GNP toward direct assessment of social progress. Five achievable goals for nations were highlighted: (1) an infant mortality rate of less than 25 deaths per 1,000 births; (2) a population growth rate of less than one percent per year; (3) an adult literacy rate of 85 percent; (4) life expectancy of 70 years; and (5) meaningful employment of the greatest number possible. The group stressed that development geared toward economic measures and GNP growth had failed.

Going even further, a new report by the Council of the Club of Rome, *The First Global Revolution* by Alexander King and Bertrand Schneider, points out (as this author has for two decades) that energy, not money, is the driving force in human economies. "Money," the report notes, "is simply (energy's) surrogate. There is surely a strong argument at this state of human development to devise a new economics based on the flow of energy." (Pantheon, 1991, p. 156.)

The report's other recommendations echo the growing global consensus: military to civilian conversion; clean, renewable resource based technologies; rural redevelopment initiatives; reeducation, especially of leaders and politicians; and increasing the opportunities of women.

A new debate on world order issues has been launched by Rushworth Kidder via the Institute for Global Ethics. His new monthly journal is *Insights*, from PO Box 563, 21 Elm Street, Camden, ME 04843. Another important world order modelling effort is that of Global Education Associates of New York. This small think tank run by the husband and wife team of Gerald and Patricia Mische has networked multicultural group efforts at visioning a better world in dozens of countries. Their magazine, *Breakthrough,* is an indispensable source of news of the most creative thinking *Toward a Human World Order*, which is also the title of the Mische's groundbreaking 1985 book. One of the most exciting new groups, organized in 1989, is the Student Environment Action Coalition based in Chapel Hill, NC. It has engaged about 30,000 students at 1,500 colleges and universities in taking a wholistic view that expands the environmental debate beyond the discussions of elitist environmental groups (*New York Times*, October 7, 1991). The extensive nature of these considerations is also addressed in *Social Economics: An Alternative Theory, Volume I* by Neva R. Goodwin (St. Martins's Press, NY, 1991).

Vancouver Declaration on Survival in the 21st Century

Survival of the planet has become of central and immediate concern. The present situation requires urgent measures in all sectors—scientific, cultural, economic and political, and a greater sensitization of all mankind. We must make common cause with all people on earth against a common enemy: any action that threatens balance within our environment or reduces our legacy to future generations. Today, this becomes the objective of the Vancouver Declaration on Survival.

MANKIND CONFRONTING SURVIVAL

Our planet is unstable—a constantly changing heat engine. Life appeared on its surface about four billion years ago, and developed in balance with an environment where sudden unpredictable change is the norm. The discovery, over 200 years ago, of free energy locked in fossil fuels has given humankind the power to dominate the whole planetary surface. In an unbelievably short span of time, unplanned and almost mindlessly, our species has become by far the largest factor for change on the planet.

The consequences have been drastic and unique in the history of our species:

—an accelerating increase in population growth over the past 150 years from one billion to over five billion with a current doubling time of 30-40 years;

—a comparable increase in the use of fossil fuels leading to global pollution, climate and sea-level change;

—an accelerating destruction of the habitat of life, initiating a massive and irreversible episode of mass extinction in the biosphere—the basis of the Earth's ecosystem; and

—an unimaginable expenditure of resources and human ingenuity on war and preparation for war.

And all licensed by a belief in inexhaustible resources of the planet encouraged by political and economic systems that emphasize short-term profit as a benefit, and disregard the real cost of production.

The situation facing mankind involves the collapse of any balance between our species and the rest of life on the planet. Paradoxically, at the time when we stand at the threshold of degeneration of the ecosystem and degradation of human quality of life, knowledge and science are now in a position to provide both the human creativity and the technology needed to take remedial action and to rediscover the harmony between nature and mankind. Only the social and political will is lacking.

PLATE 8-46

The upcoming U.N. Conference on Environment and Development (UNCED) scheduled in Rio de Janiero, Brazil, in June 1992, now being called the Earth Summit, will bring together the largest group of heads of state and top leaders in history. Grassroots groups and NGOs from every country are zeroing in on drafting their own versions of an Earth Charter which will be one of the outputs of the conference. UNCED is also expected to produce an Action Plan, termed Agenda 21, to address climate change, transboundary pollution, waste management, the protection of land, conservation of biological diversity, and the management of ocean, coastal and freshwater resources. It is hoped that draft treaties can actually be signed at UNCED—such an accomplishment will require unrelenting pressure by grassroots and NGO groups in reluctant countries, such as the United States. The biggest issues will involve the negotiating between North and South over an equitable sharing of the costs of pollution control measures. Naturally, Southern developing countries point out that 80 percent of these global problems were caused by industrial countries and that they must pay this "pollution debt" (much larger than any money debts owed Northern banks by developing countries). The bargaining will be hard and the South has many new "chips," including just not negotiating and continuing its own industrial development.

Certainly a different world order will be articulated in Rio de Janiero in 1992, at the *first* Earth Summit to consider new paradigms of "development" which can meet human needs without destroying our Planet's life-support systems.

How to pay for this and other needs of the New World Order? Former German Chancellor Willy Brandt proposed one method in 1980: the U.N.-collected tax on all global arms sales and shipments with the proceeds earmarked for humanitarian needs and UNICEF. A bipartisan U.S. poll in April 1991 conducted by ATIF found that 83 percent of Americans supported the arms tax proposal. In addition, 93 percent agreed that a New World Order should include the United States taking global leadership in solving the world's environmental problems.

In the past few years many countries have adopted the concept of "sustainable development." In today's Information Age, old-style "trickle-down" development can be decentralized away from megacities, and innovation can be fostered among grassroots people in rural areas. This new, "trickle-up" sustainable approach was discussed at a recent meeting in Tokyo of the GIF Research Foundation of Japan. Japan, the world's newest superpower (the world's largest international banker) is wrestling with its own role in a New World Order. Japan is now a larger world aid

Earth Summit Objectives from the United Nations Conference on Environment and Development

Rio de Janeiro, Brazil, 1-12 June 1992

The Conference is expected to produce:

- an Earth Charter that will embody basic principles which must govern the economic and environmental behavior of peoples and nations to ensure "our common future";

- Agenda 21, a blueprint for action in all major areas affecting the relationship between the environment and the economy. It will focus on the period up to the year 2000 and extend into the twenty-first century;

- the means to carry out the agenda by making available to developing countries the additional financial resources and environmentally sound technologies they require to participate fully in global environmental cooperation and to integrate environmental considerations into development policies and practices;

- agreement on strengthening institutions in order to implement these measures;

- conventions on climate change, biological diversity and, perhaps, forestry may by negotiated prior to the Conference and signed or agreed to in Brazil.

PLATE 8-47

Source: Public Brochure UNCED, 1991

donor than the United States and is taking its place in governing the World Bank and the International Monetary Fund (IMF). Overcoming its pre-World War II expansionism and role in the Pacific during the war is a challenge, as is overcoming its own inward-looking culture. Yet already there are visionary Japanese; more of their young people serve in Africa in "peace corps" roles than young Americans.

GIF's "New World Order" was seeded by Dr. Masaki Nakajima, now 86, and aims at nothing less than a "Global New Deal" to help aspiring countries of the South achieve a better life for their people. Originally, Nakajima dreamed of a Global Infrastructure Fund (GIF), with massive projects—dams, roads, railroads, and canals—historically viewed by economists as putting a country into position for the fabled "takeoff" toward economic growth. More and more, however, the social and environmental costs of such 19th century-style industrialization have become painfully visible.

The GIF Research Foundation now places its emphasis on Nakajima's vision of a "win-win" world of cooperation between North and South and the need to stop the global arms race. For example, there are ambitious plans, already partially funded by Japan's Ministry of Agriculture, to reverse the southward march of Africa's Sahara Desert into Mali and Nigeria, as well as reforestation projects and research into generating solar and renewable energy. Another GIF project is a cooperative arrangement with the Turkish government to build a "Peace Pipeline" to provide surplus water to Syria, Jordan, Kuwait, Saudi Arabia, and the Persian Gulf Emirates.

Such concrete approaches to a New World Order are seen as ways to divert military industrial complexes toward meeting civilian needs. Hopefully, they can compete with President Bush's coalition building and "burden sharing" formulas in the Persian Gulf War which were a strategic *tour de force*, but also an unprecedented and ominous shift toward a "mercenary world order."

Unlike numerous U.S. and British critics who complained that oil-scarce Japan should have supplied soldiers to the allied coalition against Saddam Hussein, many GIF participants at the recent conference noted with satisfaction that Japan's contributions to the allied effort were earmarked for a "Peace and Reconstruction Fund." Thus Japan as well as Germany, which also contributed money but no soldiers, may yet help shape the New World Order in a more positive direction by focusing on conflict resolution mechanisms short of war.

Everywhere in the world people are, in fact, changing their perceptions and values in a new awareness of their relationship to the Planet—no

Sun Day 1992

Statement of Principles and Goals

Global climate change, oil spills, air pollution, acid rain, radioactive emissions and waste, rising oil imports, and other energy-related environmental and economic problems continue to worsen, threatening major worldwide impacts. The nation's energy strategy must, therefore, begin now to shape and manage a transition to a sustainable energy future that assures a safe, clean, affordable, adequate, and independent energy supply.

National surveys confirm that the American people overwhelmingly believe that such a strategy should be based primarily on efficient energy use and renewable energy supplies, rather than on conventional fossil fuel and nuclear power energy sources.

However, national energy policy makers have thus far failed to implement such a strategy. From this failure comes the need for a national grassroots campaign for an energy policy that embodies the following principles.

First, the United States must give priority to those energy options that maximize benefits such as environmental protection, local economic development, regional self-sufficiency, and job creation, while minimizing economic, environmental, and social costs.

Second, the United States must avoid energy technologies that are particularly hazardous to human health or to the local and global environment.

Third, the United States must minimize the use of energy imports in order to avoid economic disruptions and protect national security and the economy.

Consistent with these principles, the nation's energy policy should be based on improving energy efficiency, conserving energy, and developing clean, renewable energy sources through local, state, and national initiatives. To facilitate the transition to a sustainable energy future, U.S. energy policy should strive to implement, at the minimum, the following goals, while recognizing that more aggressive targets are achievable and may ultimately prove to be necessary.

**National energy intensity (i.e., energy use per unit of Gross National Product) should be reduced by 3 percent per year, while total energy consumption should be reduced by 10 percent from today's levels by the year 2010. This can be accomplished through the implementation of existing energy-efficient technologies, such as high efficiency building designs and insulation, geothermal heat pumps, fuel cell technologies, energy efficient motors and appliances, high-output low-wattage lighting, and more fuel-efficient vehicles and alternative modes of transportation (e.g., mass transit, bicycles), as well as through recycling and common-sense energy conservation measures. (Such measures reduced projected energy demand by at least 25 percent between 1973 and 1986.)

**The environmentally responsible use of existing direct solar (e.g., photovoltaics, solar thermal, hot water and space heating), wind, hydroelectric, solar-hydrogen, biomass (e.g., wood, agricultural wastes, sewage, alcohol fuels), geothermal, and other renewable energy technologies in both centralized and small-scale applications should, in total, be tripled by the year 2010, so that they provide 25-30 percent of the U.S.'s energy supply. (These technologies now account for 8 percent of energy consumption and 13 percent of electricity generation.)

**Realizing the above goals would enable the United States to reduce emissions of carbon dioxide, the primary global-warming gas, by at least 20-25 percent by the year 2010. (Other industrialized nations such as Germany, Austria, New Zealand, Denmark, and Australia have already set goals of 20-25 percent reductions in carbon dioxide emissions by the year 2005.)

For further information, contact Public Citizen, attn: SUN DAY 1992, 215 Pennsylvania Avenue, S.E., Washington, D. C. 20003 phone: (202-546-4996); fax: (202-547-7892)

PLATE 8-48

longer as masters and exploiters, but as part of the web of all life on this fragile, beautiful Planet. From the Catholics to the many Protestant and Jewish congregations, from Native Americans to indigenous peoples all over the world, citizen's groups converged on the Earth Summit—with their own versions of Earth Charters. (See Plates)

Another example of people's vision was a bipartisan survey on The Emerging World Order released July 1991 by the Americans Talk Issues Foundation (ATIF) of Washington, DC, which found the American people ahead of their leaders in revisioning a new world order and a larger role for the United Nations in the 1990s. ATIF, founded by inventor/entrepreneur Alan F. Kay, conducts nonprofit, public interest policy surveys—a departure from conventional media and election polling. ATIF hires a bipartisan team—in the case of this Survey #16, Greenberg-Lake, Inc., a prominent pollster for the Democratic Party, and Market Strategies, Inc., a key polling firm of Republicans. While ATIF frames the questions in the surveys, the two pollsters contracted to perform the survey also "sign off" on the unbiased nature of the questions, the accuracy of the data used in framing them and the analysis in the survey report. Its results show that the American people are looking for new leadership and bold new directions in both domestic and international policy:

- Eighty percent want the United Nations to play the leading role in organizing future global responses to aggression (such as that of Saddam Hussein). Backing up this view, 88 percent support a "United Nations standing peace-keeping military force made up of units pledged by member nations." Even when such U.N. powers might clash with U.S. national sovereignty, 59 percent of the public still agree that "U.N. Resolutions should have the force of law and should rule over the actions and laws of individual countries, including the United States, where necessary to fulfill essential U.N. functions."

- Seventy-two percent support the proposal first made by the U.N.'s Brandt Commission in 1980 to "monitor and tax international arms sales with the money going to famine relief and humanitarian aid." (This question was also asked in ATIF's Survey #15 in March 1991, when it garnered 81 percent support.) In Survey #16, this Brandt proposal was retested with a range of arguments for and against it. The public was unconvinced by two of the arguments against the arms tax: (1) That this tax would fall more heavily on the United States and would hurt the American defense industry and jobs. (Fifty-four percent found this argument unconvincing, while 45 percent found it convincing.) (2) That the fund created largely with American money would be controlled by other countries, who might divert the relief to their own political purposes. (Fifty-two percent to 46 percent found this argument unconvincing.) Pragmatically, the public (by 58 percent to 40 percent) did not buy the argument that by "raising the cost of arms, the tax would limit their use around the world." Rather, the public agreed (by 54 percent to 45 percent) that "arms purchasers and merchants" should help "pay the bill for humanitarian aid needed around the world." After hearing all the arguments pro and con, support for the arms tax fund increased to 75 percent.

- The public's view of an expanded U.N. role in the new world order also expresses interest in reforming the United Nations itself to make it more participatory and democratic. Seventy-seven percent liked the idea of electing the Secretary General by popular vote in countries that hold elections. Almost 90 percent support popularizing U.N. decision rules (45 percent opting for one country-one vote, 42 percent for one person-one vote, and just 9 percent for a money-based system keyed to the amount of dues a country pays).
- Ninety-two percent (69 percent strongly) support the idea that "the United States should use its position to get other nations to join together to take action against world environmental problems." This 92 percent has held steady at the same level recorded in the ATIF #15 Survey, March 1991. In the ATIF #16 Survey this 92 percent support was maintained in the face of several arguments against such U.S. environmental initiatives. One such argument was that "other countries and governments" would develop "regulations that would hurt America's economy" and that such initiatives "are not appropriate for our society" (62 percent rejected this argument while 37 percent found it convincing).
- Eighty-seven percent agreed that "many environmental pollution problems go beyond any country's borders and can only be addressed effectively by all nations acting together."
- Seventy-eight percent agreed that global warming and ozone depletion are serious environmental threats requiring immediate action.

The survey also found the public ready to support U.S. participation in a range of non-governmental organizations concerned with world environmental problems, including: (1) 81 percent approval for an organization like the Red Cross to take the lead in cleaning up environmental disasters like Chernobyl, the Exxon Valdez oil spill or the Persian Gulf oil spills and fires; (2) 82 percent support for a bank that would finance environmental cleanups around the world and joint ventures with poorer countries to transfer environmentally-sound technologies, and (3) 80 percent would support a bank to invest in all countries to develop the use of more efficient energy systems in agriculture, industry, housing and transportation.

Lastly, while a sizeable 62 percent of Americans still believe the Gulf War was a "great victory," this represents a stunning 22 point slide from ATIF's March 1991 Survey #15. In #16, 53 percent think the country is headed on the wrong track and 61 percent say they are upset a lot or almost all the time by the President's neglect of domestic concerns. Sixty-eight percent agree that "it is extremely or very important to reduce U.S. growing use of foreign oil," 59 percent would back this concern up by supporting a five percent tax on imported oil, and 55 percent support a five cent per gallon gas tax to reduce this dependency. ATIF President Alan Kay noted, "This survey reconfirms many of our earlier findings showing the consistency of the public's views on many of these crucial issues. Now it is up to our leaders to follow them." Kay has found in surveys on global issues over the past seven years the American people were ahead of all their leaders in defining security beyond military terms.

The New York based Center for War/Peace Studies is also re-visioning the United Nations and its structure and proposes: (1) That a World Summit on Global Governance be called, similar to the San Francisco and Bretton Woods meetings of the 1940s. (2) The establishing of an Independent Commission on Global Governance. Another more official review of U.N. structure is the 1991 study, *A World in Need of Leadership: Tomorrow's United Nations* by Brian Urquhart and Erskine Childers which includes proposals for restructuring the United Nation's bureaucracy, upgrading its personnel, and bolstering the role of the Secretary General.[11]

Another proposal gathering support is that of the Foundation for Global Broadcasting of Washington, DC, for a global TV channel for citizens groups and NGOs to communicate directly with each other and the world. Agreements have already been negotiated between TV authorities in many countries to carry this "NGO Channel."

In the family of nations some are clearly taking the lead in various tasks toward building a healthy New World Order for the 21st Century. Canada, as far back as 1975, began a dialogue with all its citizens on whether Canada would continue as a Consumer Society or change its values and become instead a Conserver Society (Plate 8-40).

Sweden, in April 1991 (Plate 8-41), hosted an important meeting of world dignitaries and former heads of state convened by Prime Minister Ingvar Carlsson, which produced the innovative Stockholm Initiative on Global Security and Governance. Some of its proposals include strengthening the U.N. system and its emergency powers and monitoring of member countries commitments and treaties; and that all nations set targets of one percent of their GNPs for international development, accelerate debt forgiveness schedules, set global pollution levies, make commitments to reduce their armed forces, and allocate specific portions of their "peace dividends" to investments in human development. This report is "must" reading.[12]

Lastly, the South Commission (composed of high level dignitaries and co-chaired by Julius Nyerere of Tanzania and President Carlos Andres Perez of Venezuela) released it own report, *Challenge to the South*, in 1990 with its own bold South-South proposals described in the previous chapter. The Commission then launched the new Southern Economic Summit of the Group of Fifteen, whose first meeting in Kuala Lumpur, Malaysia, in June 1990 consolidated these initiatives. Venezuela hosted the G-15s Second Economic Summit in November 1991. *Challenge to the South* is important reading because it also augurs the new kinds of hard bargaining which can be expected between North and South in the 1990s. The South's versions of their New World Order will become central to all of the new global debates.[13]

In 1990 India's International Centre for Peace Initiatives convened forty leading statespeople and scholars, including Mother Teresa, Bishop Tutu, U.N. Secretary General Perez de Cuellar, former Costa Rican President Oscar Arias, former Japanese Foreign Minister Saburo Okita and Austrian physicist and author Fritjof Capra. The report, *The New World Order*, contains many important proposals and is edited by its convenor, Sundeep Waslekar.[14]

Africa is the continent where the failures of economic forms of "development" are stark, leading to a decade of reverses in the 1980s: famine, desertification, ecological depletion and one-party, often repressive regimes. Yet beginning in the last year of that unhappy decade, Africa, too, has seen much positive restructuring and movement toward democratic reform. In 1991, at last, the De Klerk government in South Africa began the long task of abolishing apartheid—although much remains to be done to achieve full political and economic justice for its black majority. Acting on the 1990 conference of the U.N. Economic Commission for Africa, held in Arusha, Tanzania, most African governments have agreed to some extent to "yield space to the people." "The African Charter for

Popular Participation in Development and Transformation" calls for human-centered, participatory development policies, protection of human rights and support for independent, grassroots organizations. Salim Salim, Secretary General of the Organization of African Unity (OAU) cautions that there will be more than just one model of democracy, but that African societies will be culturally diverse in a continent still "in a tribal stage" of political development.[15]

As new scorecards (such as HDI and CFI) begin to elicit a clearer accounting of the costs and benefits of investments, nations may move closer to sustainable development. As planetary citizens find and make new ways to be heard (leading their leaders), patterns of a viable new world order may become more easily recognizable. At last our children may regain their birthright, and the Earth may receive its due.

Chapter Eight Footnotes

1. *Global Arms Trade: Commerce in Advanced Military Technology and Weapons,* U.S. Congress, Office of Technology Assessment, Washington, DC 20515—documents soaring arms trade as "a major national (i.e., U.S.) policy dilemma—how to balance the use of arms exports as instruments of foreign policy, pressure by companies for greater and freer access to foreign markets and the need to stem both a dangerous worldwide arms buildup and the increasing proliferation of defense industry." For example, European firms are virtually required to export extensively in order to keep weapons costs affordable at home and to fund R & D for the next generation of weapons.

2. *Doing the Right Things* (pamphlet and chart $5 postpaid) available from World Game Institute, 3508 Market Street, Philadelphia, PA 19104.

3. *Time,* July 22, 1991, p. 27.

4. *Columbia Journalism Review,* "Access to Media: A Problem in Democracy," Hazel Henderson, Spring 1969.

5. *South,* "Bombs into Baby Carriages," June-July 1991, London, p. 33.

6. *Business Week,* September 2, 1991, p. 29.

7. *Business Week,* "Can Gorbachev Pound Missiles into Plowshares?" July 29, 1991, p. 42.

8. *Positive Alternatives,* Center for Economic Conversion, 222 View Street, Suite C, Mountain View, CA 94041, Vol. 1 #4, Summer 1991. See also, *Building a Peace Economy* by John T. Marlin and Betty Lall, Westview Press, 1991.

9. *Future Survey,* available from the World Futures Society, Washington, DC.

10. World Order Models Project (WOMP), 475 Riverside Drive, Room 460, New York, NY 10115. A book, *Global Civilization*, edited by Richard A. Falk is forthcoming in 1992.

11. Urquhart, Brian and Erskine Childers, *A World in Need of Leadership: Tomorrow's United Nations*, The Dag Hammarskjold Foundation, Uppsala, Sweden.

12. *Common Responsibility in the 1990s*, The Stockholm Initiative, Prime Ministers Office, 5-103-33, Stockholm, Sweden (free).

13. South Commission, *Challenge to the South*, Oxford University Press, London and New York, 1990.

14. *The New World Order*, ed. Sundeep Waslekar, 1991. Available from Peace Initiatives, B-704, Montana, Lokhandwala Complex, Off Four Bungalows, Andheri West, Bombay, India, 400 058. (230 pages, $22 including air mail postage, fax 91-22-262-4202).

15. *Development Forum*, "Democracy in Africa?" Ernest Hansch, July-August 1991, p. 12.

Also highly recommended:

Andrew Bard Schmookler, *The Parable of the Tribes*, University of California Press, Berkeley, 1984.

The Age of Light

Emerging Lightwave Technologies (Phototronics)

- Fiber optics — ...communications cabling, voice, data, etc.
- Optical scanners — ...supermarkets, banks, on-line computer systems
- Lasers — ...laser surgery, laser printers, laser phonographs turntables, laser bottles to see atoms, laser propulsion, Star Wars laser weapons systems, laser art

- Holography — ...computer assisted design (CAD), computer assisted manufacturing (CAM), computer integrated manufacturing (CIM), art

- Solar technologies — ...passive solar heating and cooling, Trombe walls, solar-thermal energy conversion, ocean thermal, tidal and wave power, bio-energy conversion, hydroponics, aquaculture, solar reflector "power towers," photochemical conversion (artificial and natural photosynthesis), photovoltaics, solar cell arrays for powering satellites, space based solar collectors, solar sails for deep space voyages

- Optical computers — ...use light pulses instead of electrical impulses—pushing toward the speed of light
- Multiprocessor, parallel computers and neural net computers — ...very fast architecture allows simultaneous, rather than sequential processing, speech and voice recognition, language and artificial intelligence (AI) applications
- Imaging technologies — ...TV images, liquid crystal screens, magnetic imaging diagnostics
- Biotechnologies — ...gene splicing, designing, molecular engineering, medical diagnostics, immunology, tissue culture, cloning, plant hybridization and "re-designing", and bio-remediation

- Gene machines — ...which automate the synthetic assembly of genes
- DNA sequencers — ...which "speed read" the DNA code in cells
- Tagging and tracking chemicals and genes — ...using luciferase, etc.
- Nano technologies — ...molecular "machines" to assemble, repair molecules, in many diverse ways (e.g. theories of Eric Drexler in *Engines of Creation*, 1986)

Photons (sunlight) falling on the earth supply enough energy in 10 minutes to put our entire five billion population in orbit!

PLATE 9-49

The Age of Light
Beyond the Information Age

The "Information Age" has become a ubiquitous image among futurists seeking fruitful metaphors for the ongoing restructuring of industrial societies. New images of post-industrial society proliferated in the 1970s as the restructuring of industrial societies accelerated. Alvin Toffler's *The Third Wave* (1980) depicted a globalizing human culture based on information, more appropriate use of technology, and more productive, proactive individuals outgrowing consumerism. In *Alternative Futures for America* (1970) and several other books, Robert Theobald[1] outlined what he called "the Communications Era," describing a shift toward community empowerment, automation, and greater dissemination of information.

As mentioned in Chapter Two, my own view is that information disseminated more broadly could facilitate the rise of networks of citizens that could cross-cut old power structures, facilitate learning, and initiate a widespread politics of reconceptualization, transforming our fragmented world view into an new paradigm based on planetary awareness: an Age of Light, auguring planetary cultures sustainably based on renewable resources and a deeper understanding of Nature. At a more basic level, we know from quantum physics and Planck's constant that it is *Light* (rather than matter, energy or time) that is fundamental to the Universe. Planck's equation holds that quanta of light are also quanta of *action*. The Age of Light has been augured in most religious literature, most notably in the Bible. In Genesis, God's first command was, "Let there be Light."

The Age of Light lies beyond the Information Age. The Information Age is no longer an adequate image for the present, let alone a guide to

Leading Edge Technologies Mimicking Nature

Interconnectedness Increasing

Some examples of existing successful technologies based on Nature's design: Cameras mimic the eye; Airplanes mimic birds; Radar and Antennas mimic insects

Information Technologies:

- **Artificial intelligence**...Expert systems, "hypertext," associative learning program
- **Biotechnologies**... Genetic engineering, cloning
  ...Monoclonal antibodies, interferon, insulin
  ...Gene splicing, hybridization, tissue culture
  ...Luciferase
  ...Pheromones, chemical attractants, biological pest control
  ...Protein-based catalysts, assemblers, microbes that "eat" oil spills, sulphur, etc
- **Moving beyond medicine that augments the body's defenses and healing process to cell repair and life-extension**
- **Energy technologies** ... Ocean thermal, tidal and wave generators
  ...Biomass energy conversion
  ...Dams, hydropower
  ..."Nanotechnology," molecular assemblers
  ...Synthetic photosynthesis (zinc pophyrin and ruthenium oxide), photovoltaic cells
  ...Osmosis, membrane technologies
  ...Solar arrays and sails
  ...Fusion reactors

Nature's Models

- **Human intelligence, knowledge**
  ...Human memory, language
- **DNA, RNA codes, viruses, bacteria**
  ...Human immune system
  ...Plants, wild species
  ...Viruses
  ...Fireflies
  ...Insects, microbes, fungi
  ...Amino acids
  ...Microbes
- **Human immune system, DNA, genes**
- **Oceans and other global processes**
  ...Natural decay processes, fermentation
  ...Gravity
  ...Viruses
  ...Green plants chloroplasts
  ...Living cell membranes
  ...Insect wings
  ...**The sun**

PLATE 9-50

the future. It still focuses on hardware technologies, mass production, narrow economic models of efficiency and competition, and is more an extension of industrial ideas and methods than a new stage in human development. Information is an abundant resource rather than a scarce commodity (as in economic theory) and demands new cooperative rules from local to global levels.

Information itself does not enlighten. We cannot clarify what is *mis*-information, *dis*-information, or propaganda in this media dominated, "spin-doctored" environment. Focusing on mere information has led to an overload of ever-less meaningful billions of bits of fragmented raw data and sound bites rather than the search for meaningful new patterns of knowledge.

My view of the dawning Age of Light involves a repatterning of the exploding Information Age. This requires nothing less than a paradigm shift to a holistic view of the entire human family, now inextricably linked by our globe-girdling technologies. The Earth is re-perceived as a living Planet, and the most appropriate view is organic, based on the self-organizing models of the life sciences. Biological sciences become more useful spectacles, and it is no accident that biotechnologies are becoming our most morally-ambiguous tools.

The bio-technology revolution has been in high gear since the late 1970s, when entrepreneurial biology professors began to make commercial joint ventures in genetic research and engineering, gene splicing, etc., which led to the boom on Wall Street in stock of such companies as Genentech, Inc. Ironically, most of the research that led to the bio-tech industry had been paid for by U.S. taxpayers—who were elbowed out of sharing in the huge profits from many of these deals. The most effective crusader for the public interest in this field, its ethics and hazards, has been Jeremy Rifkin, who sounded the alarm with his books *Algeny* and *Who Should Play God?*, co-authored with Ted Howard.[2] Rifkin challenged untried genetic experiments in court and fought a valiant court case to prevent corporations from "patenting" lifeforms—a battle lost in 1987, when the U.S. Supreme Court extended the original U.S. Patent Office ruling allowing limited patenting to all life forms. Thus as Rifkin points out in his *Biosphere Politics* (1991) the whole planet's genetic heritage, including DNA itself, which humans share with other species, can now be turned into private property.[3] Human genetic material can also be manipulated, combined with that of pigs, sheep and mice, as is occurring today. One inspired protest was dreamed up by Gar Smith who in 1980 began circulating mock U.S. Patent Office Applications to human parents, so that they could "patent" their own offspring—to spoof the absurd Supreme Court ruling.[4] Now the polymerase chain reaction (PCR), a method of making millions of copies of a piece of DNA quickly and reliably, has been sold by Cetus Corporation of California to Hoffman LaRoche, the Swiss multinational pharmaceutical firm. "PCR opens up whole new areas and techniques." As reported by *The Economist*, "It is the key to the biological candy store."[5]

The Age of Light will follow on from the Solar Age as humans gradually learn that it is light and action that are fundamental in the universe. The technologies of the Age of Light are already appearing. (See Plate 9-49.) Beyond electronics, these phototronic technologies are miracles of speed and miniaturization, such as the new 0.25 micron "superchip" (400 times thinner than a human hair). These superchips now on the drawing board can pack hundreds of millions of transistors—ten times today's record. In the year 2000, 0.1 micron widths will be the cutting edge, small enough to cram billions of transistors on a single chip. Even today's advance optical printing methods will have to give way to higher frequencies in the spectrum, using x-ray lithography. In 1991, San Jose, California's Cypress Semiconductor Corporation announced (*Business Week*, June 3, 1991) that it had purchased from Hampshire Instruments, Inc. of Rochester, New York, a new system that generates the x-rays, not with a room-size synchrotron (or atom smasher) that costs $30 million, but with a laser costing a modest $4 million.[6]

Another aspect of these new technologies of the Age of Light is the level of integration achieved with the biological sciences, as they shift from the "inert" classical physics worldview to the organic living system perspectives of biology and ecology. From the Plate 9-50 (Leading Edge Technologies Mimic Nature) we see striking confirmation of the continued inspiration of Nature in their design. However far out and "high tech" they all claim to be, and indeed are, they, like most technologies before them owe their inspiration to Nature. After all, Gaia, the great designer, has been optimizing these energy capture-utilization-storage systems for billions of years. Gaia is also the pre-eminent innovator and experimenter, who excels in sheer artistry as well. Further evidence that humans are still imitating Nature is the growing industrial research field of biomimetics (literally "mimicking Nature") described in the *Business Week* cover story, "The New Alchemy."[7] For example, new ceramic materials mimic the molecular structure of abalone shells to make impact resistant armor for military tanks and aircraft. As the article points out, "Nature's materials have passed the test of time." K. Eric Drexler's vision of "nanotechnology" in his 1986 book, *Engines of Creation*,[8] predicted the shape of much of this new biomimetic research, such as Argonne National Laboratories work on improving structural materials

THE AGE OF LIGHT   265

by "flirting with Creation," developing entirely new materials atom by atom using "nanophase materials" such as crystals less than 100 nanometers across—smaller than most viruses. Japan's Ministry of International Trade and Industry (MITI) has launched a 10-year program on "nanotech initiatives" which it hopes industry will fund to the tune of $100 million or more.[9]

The Age of Light is an image that reminds us that it is the light from the sun that drives the earth's processes and powers its cycles of carbon, nitrogen, hydrogen, and water and the climate "machine." It is these light-driven processes—which are then mediated by the photosynthesis of plants—that maintain conditions for us to continue our evolution beyond the Information Age. Our present technologies are already maturing from their basis in electronics and are shifting to phototronics. These new lightwave technologies include fiber optics, lasers, optical scanning, optical computing, photovoltaics, and other photoconversion processes.

As we progress in these areas we will notice how each one leads us into a deeper appreciation of Nature's technological genius; we have modeled our earlier breakthroughs, such as flight, on that of birds. Nature's light-conversion technologies, the basic of which is photosynthesis, still serve as design criteria and marvels of miniaturization, such as the chloroplast cells all green plants use to convert photons into usable glycogen, hydrocarbons and cellulose. This is still the basic production process on which all humans rely and when our photovoltaic cells can match the performance of the chloroplast, we will be on the right track. Thus the Age of Light is more than the new lightwave technologies emerging from the computer, robotics and artificial intelligence labs. The Age of Light will be characterized by our growing abilities to cooperate with and learn from Nature. The Age of Light will build on today's biotechnology, still in its exploratory, often exploitative, moral infancy.

The Age of Light will bring a new awareness and reverence for living systems and the exquisite information technology of DNA, the wisdom and coding of all living experience on this Planet. The Age of Light will go far beyond industrial, manipulative modes toward deeper interconnecting, co-creative designing with and learning from Nature, as we become a species consciously co-evolving with all life forms on this unique water Planet. The Age of Light will also be one of a time compression, as we include our holistic, intuitive, right-brain hemisphere cognition with our more analytical, left-brain functioning, and as our computers catch up in their abilities for parallel processing with the simultaneity of our own brains' synapses. The peerless design of the human brain still presents the ultimate challenge to computer designers, despite the much-vaunted progress in so-called "artificial intelligence" systems. For example, a leading designer of Cray Computer Company's efforts to create a supercomputer mimicking more closely the parallel processing ability of human brains, recently left to pursue other areas of endeavor. As we see in Plate 9-49, most leading edge technologies based on light, whether information, solar energy or biotechnologies and gene splicing also mimic nature's design, such as monoclonal antibodies, interferon and other methods based on learning from the human immune system. The "nanotechnologies" or protein-based assemblers that Eric Drexler (mentioned earlier) envisions, are designed by mimicking the functions of amino acids.

At the same time we are learning much more about our own bodies' responses to light, and how humans deprived of full-spectrum, natural light in indoor living and working conditions can suffer weakening of their endocrine and immune systems. Thus the wisest of us recognize that our Earth still has much to teach us—if we can humble ourselves and quiet our egos long enough to really listen and see, hear, smell and feel all her wonders. When we can feel this kind of attunement to the whole creation, we are transported with natural delight to the "high" that psychologist Abraham Maslow called "peak experiences." As we reintegrate our awareness in this way, we no longer crave endless consumption of goods beyond those needed for a healthy life, but seek new challenges in our societies for order, peace and justice, and to develop our spirituality. It is in this way that humans can overcome the dismal Second Law of Thermodynamics in the continual striving for learning and wisdom. We no longer blind our imagination with the dismal deterministic view of a universe winding down like a closed system. Since Prigogine, we know that the universe is full of surprises, innovation and evolutionary potential.[10] In fact, Cartesian science's search for certainty, equilibrium, predictability and control is a good definition of death. We should happily embrace the new view that uncertainty is fundamental, since it also implies that everything can change—for the better—in a twinkling of an eye! As we move on to post-Cartesian science, we can acknowledge the earlier period of the Scientific Enlightenment of Descartes and Newton, Liebniz and Galileo. Its instrumental rationality and manipulation of Nature did lead to that greatest outpouring of technological hardware and managerial virtuosity which we call the Industrial Revolution.

As we have seen, the whole process of human development is teleological and evolutionary, and therefore cannot be explained or predicted by existing reductionistic scientific paradigms. This great purposeful unfolding of human potentialities toward goals—bettering human societies, perfecting the means of production and fostering conditions of people's lives so that they might fulfill themselves—is essentially a spiritual, as well as an instrumental and materialistic endeavor.

Binding such a transcendent set of human goals and visions for the future within the so-called "laws of economics" was and is a travesty. With new perspectives and new paradigms in the 1990s we can move beyond old conceptual prisons, whether the reductionist view of the Information Age or the, so far, literal interpretations of the Solar Age. When *The Politics of the Solar Age* was first published in 1981, it was catalogued among energy books. Many who heard my lectures asked me such questions as, "What percentage of my house's heating needs could be met by solar energy?" I would always reply that this was only one level of the meaning of the Solar Age, and then proceed to remind my questioner that if the sun was not already preheating their house and the Earth, it would be about 400 degrees below zero! Thus I was referring to many other levels of the transition, from the Age of Fossil Fuels to renewable forms of energy, to the needed design revolution in our technologies and social structures, as well as to all the cultural and mythic levels of such a planetary transformation. Since then, I have focused on the evolutionary process of human development as the frontier of all these needed changes.

Human development and social organization are processes that, by definition, have goals, purposes and values—and move toward them. Thus any discipline still based on classical physics and Newton's celestial mechanics, particularly economics, cannot be overhauled or expanded enough to map the dynamics of such unfolding processes. In fact, Western science has many specific *prohibitions* against any hypothesizing about values and purpose, and most often denies the existence of teleological aspects in Nature. Thus, its methods are based on the search for certainty, fundamental laws and exactitude (what I have termed "micro-rationality" to distinguish these endeavors from the mapping of larger contexts and more holistic enquiries, which I term "macro-rationality"). A hopeful sign of today's shift to broader paradigms is the fact that the process of human development is being referred to less and less often as "economic development." The word "economic" has been dropped altogether in the new ecological definition: "sustainable development."

Meanwhile, classical science still has no theory of *process,* and development is a multi-dimensional process. Arthur M. Young in *The Reflexive Universe*[11] presents a sweeping synthesis of science and human development in his Theory of Process, based on quantum, as well as classical physics. Young, the developer of the Bell helicopter, assumes that the universe is based on freedom and that the fundamental laws that humans have discovered are constraints on this freedom, but they are secondary. As any artist or designer knows, constraints actually serve the creative process—providing the medium, conditions and context for the play of creativity. Young believes that the problem with the main body of Western science is that it limits itself to focus on the material plane, dealing with "inert" matter, i.e., molar objects, such as rocks. (These appear "inert" because the random motions of their molecules cancel each other out.) Young's Process Theory starts not from matter as fundamental, but with light, or action as fundamental (i.e., Planck's constant, as mentioned, views light as quanta of action, also as quanta of uncertainty). From this beginning point, Young assumes that processes are, by definition, purposeful and involve *individual* actions of atoms, molecules and organisms with inherent goals (rather than the statistical probabilities or averages of the classical view).

Thus, the Age of Light is metaphoric to many levels:

First, it is based on the re-membering and re-wholing of human perceptions and paradigms. Nowhere is this now more evident than in the wide understanding of the First Law of Ecology: Everything is connected to everything else. I discussed this and its complementarity with the new view in physics, citing Bell's Theorem implying a non-local universe (i.e., action and interactions occurring at a distance, with no apparent medium or linkages) in the last chapter of *The Politics of the Solar Age* (p. 391). At the same time, I proposed a Post-Cartesian Scientific Worldview (Plate 2-8), where change and uncertainty are the new constants, together with principles of redistribution and recycling of all elements, heterarchy, complementarity, interconnectedness and indeterminacy.

Secondly, this new paradigm and worldview also represents a new synthesis between Western science and religious and spiritual traditions, since it embraces purpose and meaning as fundamental to life processes. Furthermore purpose implies cognition, consciousness, heuristics, goal-seeking and visioning as central to all life, at various levels, and most pronounced in humans.

In previous ages of human history, the early gatherers and hunters learned to be competent in the material world by using and storing naturally-available photosynthesized plant energy stored in berries, seeds and trees. These early humans also invented the storage technologies—pots and woven baskets. They worshipped the Great Mother, symbol of the Earth, and as I have proposed, also symbolic of the species gene pool.

They lived in matrifocal communities and were generally (as pointed out by Riane Eisler in *The Chalice and The Blade*[12]) peace-loving, with males and females in equal partnership. In Chapter Five, I also termed this early Neolithic period the Age of the Genotype, since the species' needs came before any individual phenotype—indeed, humans at this point may not have been significantly individuated or aware of themselves.

In the Agricultural Age, humans began to learn the many ways of augmenting naturally-occurring energy and accumulated it, intensifying natural photosynthesis by farming and domesticating animals. This period ushered in what I termed in Chapter Five, the Age of the Phenotype, where the rule of the Great Mother and the values of the gene pool were eclipsed by the newly individuated phenotypes seeking their own meaning and experimenting with the natural world. This process continued right through to the Industrial Age, where humans mined out much of the planet's sixty-million year old endowment of fossilized solar energy— oil, coal and gas (laid down by plants) in an unprecedentedly brief period of less than 300 years. In spite of all the mistakes, we can only honor the impulse of individual humans to act in freedom, to test out their physical and mental skills and their increasing power to manipulate Nature. British science writer Nigel Calder portrays the positive aspects of the bio-tech revolution in *The Green Machines*.[13]

Thirdly, the dawning of the Age of Light augurs the current reintegration of ourselves into a new level of awareness of the needs of the gene pool, as we engender ever greater risks to future generations with our technologies. Thus there is also a reawakening of the values of the Great Mother and a concern to rebalance gender roles and responsibilities in a new partnership society, with cooperation and peaceful conflict resolution now clearly the *sine qua non* of our survival. Gregory Bateson's *Mind and Nature* provides a valuable synthesis.[14] Naturally, such a vast cultural change has also ushered in a new search for more comprehensive meaning to decode all of our accumulated cultural DNA in finding a new place for humans in the cosmos and new significance for the human journey on this Earth.

The Solar Age and its politics have also arrived—a decade later than I had predicted—given ghastly impetus by the 1991 Gulf War. This tragic, unnecessary conflict, which could have been avoided (as I discussed in Chapter Eight) will be viewed as the inflection point of fossil fueled industrialism. The politics of the shift to the Solar Age is fundamentally different from that of the industrial period. In *The Politics of the Solar Age*, I credited the insights of English chemist Frederick Soddy (1877-1956) who shared the Nobel Prize with Rutherford. Soddy's

Cartesian Economics (1922) could have corrected economic theory for the Solar Age,[15] but he was ridiculed by the economists of the time and had to self-publish his book. The Solar Age will be more decentralized and the transition to more democratic processes will be necessary. Hierarchical mega-governments and mega-corporations, continent-wide transport and distribution of food and goods were all predicated on cheap oil. The underlying dynamic of the Solar Age, as Soddy predicted, will be how to control energy flows in human societies most efficiently and implies a top to bottom design revolution in all societies, which is at last, beginning.

The forces and lobbies of the past—nuclear and fossil energy companies, interstate highway builders, concrete pourers, automakers and all the other industrial sectors built on waste, maximum energy use and rapidly increasing levels of entropy—are now, all over the world, locked in legislative and market combat with the emerging sectors (Plate 3-19: Restructuring Industrial Societies). The new industries which minimize entropy are based on refined, miniaturized, and more "intelligent" technologies which pinpoint end-use energy needs, re-use and recycle all resources and tackle the job of cleaning up the devastating effects of industrialism. The newest enterprises must address environmental restoration and enhancing where possible the performance of eco-systems. In 1991, one of the first "trade shows" of this budding sector of 21st century economies was convened in Florida by the Society for Ecological Restoration. Here biologists replanting sea grasses rubbed shoulders with ecologists from power companies in charge of remediation of spoiled lands and specialists in restoring ruined soils with specially designed crops or micro-organisms. Bio-remediation and desert-greening will be big business in the 21st century, a point I have been emphasizing since the 1970s. Of course, this whole scenario will depend on capturing more elegantly and efficiently some of the planet's abundant daily photon shower from the Sun. As Soddy put it in 1922, "How does man, or anything live—BY SUNSHINE!"

This will require that economics be demoted from a macro-policy tool to a micro role in keeping books between firms, based on full-cost pricing—elaborated in Part Two of *The Politics of the Solar Age*. But, as I showed, the *data* on externalities and social costs would have to be developed by more realistic disciplines: thermodynamics, biology, systems and chaos models and ecology. For example, as economic growth models disordered and destroyed ever larger ecological and biospherical systems, the analysis of this damage was taken over by such interdisciplinary teams of scientists as the U.S. National Committee on Man and the

Biosphere (MAB) and its program for evaluation of Human Dominated Systems (i.e., those significantly affected by human activities). MAB's programs, started in 1989, include in its 1991 agenda a U.S. Action Plan for Biosphere Reserves. Economists are *not* included in most of its scientific committees, since its central concerns are for ecological sustainability.[16] As I have emphasized for the past 20 years, *these* are the criteria that must form the context for all human activities and "development" goals—rather than *any* of the unscientific formulas of economic theory, still based on the outmoded "welfare" theory, Pareto Optimality (which ignores income distribution and asks absurd questions, mentioned earlier, about how much people are "willing to pay" to preserve a wilderness area from developers who can always outbid citizens, because the "development" will reward them rich profits). Allen Kneese, always one of the rare breed of honest economist (in the Soddy, Georgescu-Roegen and Daly tradition) reviews the limitations of "environmental economics" in "The Economics of Natural Resources."[17]

The dire consequences when ignorant humans trespass into "managing" natural systems is now clear, for example, adding some seven billion tons of carbon to the Earth's atmosphere each year—contributing to global warming—while at the same time cutting down between 30-50 million acres of carbon-absorbing forests. World Resources Institute of Washington, DC, offers some strategies to check this looming disaster. Tree planting is a primary strategy—one adopted all over the world by ordinary citizens. At the same time I pointed this out while serving as a member of the Advisory Council of the U.S. Congress Office of Technology Assessment in 1975, scientific committees were still arguing about whether there was a problem. In 1989, the experts and politicians caught up with citizens' movements such as Chipko and Africa's Greenbelt tree-planters, when environmental ministers from 68 countries signed the Noordwijk Declaration (in the largely below-sea level Netherlands) which called for the goal of an annual 30 million acre net increase in forest cover by the year 2000, to reduce net human carbon emissions.[18] Thus economists are learning that investments in the 1990s will have to be directed into ecological restoration and social programs—health care, education and population control—a far cry from their current investment priorities to hype GNP growth.

The Age of Light will also be a time of re-weaving the world's cultures, most of which down through history have understood our planet's total dependence on the sun. They understood and worshipped our Mother Star in myths and traditions, as well as the primal light of the universe, whether from stars or distant galaxies. As physicist David Peat notes in *The Philosophers Stone*, synchronicity is the bridge between mind and matter, and he lovingly describes the new sciences of "chaos" now inching toward mapping some parts of this wonderful universe where light, action and surprise rule, all within the constraints so well mapped by classical physics.[19] Peat envisions an era of "gentle action," where millions of more aware people in more democratic societies can act more intelligently together. As Arthur Young adds, "science is humanity's map, but myth is its compass."

The Age of Enlightenment, some 300 years ago in Europe, expressed some of these hopes and visionary designs for human potential and development. As we move beyond the Information Age to greater wisdom, we may steer through today's crises and clouds into the sunshine of the Age of Light.

Chapter Nine Footnotes

1. See for example *The Rapids of Change*, Robert Theobald, Knowledge Systems, Inc., Indianapolis, 1987.

2. Jeremy Rifkin, *Algeny*, Viking Press, New York, 1983, and *Who Shall Play God?*, co-author Ted Howard, 1977.

3. Jeremy Rifkin, *Biosphere Politics*, Crown Publishers, New York, 1991, Ch. 9, p. 65.

4. Gar Smith, *Patently Ridiculous*, 1980, PO Box 27, Berkeley, CA 94701.

5. *The Economist*, "Gene Amplification," July 27, 1991, p. 76.

6. *Business Week*, June 3, 1991.

7. *Business Week*, "The New Alchemy," July 29, 1991.

8. Eric K. Drexler, *Engines of Creation*, Doubleday, New York 1986.

9. *Business Week*, "Creating Chips an Atom at a Time," July 29, 1991, p. 54.

10. Ilya Prigogine, *From Being to Becoming*, H.H. Freeman, San Francisco, 1980.

11. Arthur M. Young, *The Reflexive Universe*, Delacorte, New York, 1976.

12. Riane Eisler, *The Chalice and the Blade*, HarperCollins, San Francisco, 1987.

13. Nigel Calder, *The Green Machines*, G.P. Putnam & Sons, New York, 1986.

14. Gregory Bateson, *Mind and Nature: A Necessary Unity*, Bantam Books, New York, 1980.

15. Hazel Henderson, *The Politics of the Solar Age*, current edition from Knowledge Systems, Indianapolis, 1988, p. 225 on Frederick Soddy.

16. *U.S. MAB Bulletin*, Vol. 15, #3, August 1991, U.S. Department of State, Washington, DC 20522-3706.

17. Allen V. Kneese, "The Economics of Natural Resources," in *Population and Resources in Western Intellectual Traditions*, a supplement of Vol. 14 (1988) Population and Development Review.

18. World Resources Institute, "Minding the Carbon Store: Weighing U.S. Forestry Strategies to Slow Global Warming" Mark C. Trexler, January 1991.

19. Another classic resource for further exploration of these understandings is the four volume *Dynamics: the Geometry of Behavior* by Ralph H. Abraham and Christopher D. Shaw, Aerial Press, Santa Cruz, 1982-1988.

Cosmic Economics

A work of art
Lies buried in the morning sand.
A sad lover seeks her necklace
Eyes scouring
The glorious, pristine beach
At sunrise.
Remembering the panic of loss
The night before
While walking this same way
Companions joined the search
That moonless hour
Scudding clouds darkening the sky

The lonely lover ponders her loss
Looking for meanings
As GAIA unfolds anew
Her morning splendor
Scurrying crabs in
Glistening pools of watery life
Diving white cranes slice
The breaking surf.

Oh! the ache
Remembering the necklace
Silver and turquoise,
Blazing sun pendant

Of the Zuni People
Fashioned by her lover's hand.
A gift of priceless beauty
From the heart.
Will the shining sand
Give back her hidden treasure?
Oh, cherished hope!
Or is the message deeper?

The giver's heart is full and pure,
Perhaps the soul who finds
The lost gem
Will feel hope and love restored
While contemplating
This sudden fortune.
Lost and Found.
Surely a bond between
Loser and Finder.
Is this the Message?

All gifts must pass
To complete the sacred
Circle of Life.
Loss and Gain are
Narrow Terms,
Eclipsed
In GAIA's cosmic economics.

The lover's search
Is rewarded with a sign:
Two majestic feathers
Lie in the sand
Discarded by a busy pelican.
Feathers of water birds
Are sacred to the Zuni People.
These gifts will now pass
From ocean to ancient
Desert Heartland.

Treasures are everywhere
For all who worship GAIA's plenitude,
Nothing is ever lost.
A part of both lovers

Now forever in this place.
When we re-member Universal Love
We rejoice
In letting all gifts pass.

GAIA does not need
To hoard her riches,
Nor do we.
Cast gladly all our gifts
Upon the water,
Sandy beaches, deserts, too,
Necklaces, bracelets,
Pots and arrowheads,
Glorious weavings, colors
Let them blend
Into the teeming
Multitudinous
Tapestries of Life
In Universal Giving.

List of Acronyms

ADF	African Development Foundation
ASATs	anti-satellite weapons systems
ATIF	Americans Talk Issues Foundation
BHN	Basic Human Needs indicator (UNEP)
BIS	Bank of International Settlements
CAP	Common Agricultural Policy
CEO	chief executive officer
CEP	Council on Economic Priorities
CFI	Country Futures Indicators
CFCs	chlorofluorocarbons
CO$_2$	carbon dioxide
DNA	deoxyribonucleic acid (chief constituent of chromosomes, responsible for transmitting genetic information)
DOD	Department of Defense
EC	European Community
ECOSOC	Economic and Social Council (U.N.)
ECU	European currency unit
EPA	Environmental Protection Agency
ESOPs	Employee Stock Ownership Plans
FAO	Food and Agricultural Organization
FDA	Food and Drug Administration
FY	fiscal year
G-7	Economic Summit countries: United States, Britain, Germany, Italy, Canada, France and Japan
G-15	Economic Summit countries: Algeria, Argentina, Brazil, Egypt, India, Indonesia, Jamaica, Malaysia, Mexico, Nigeria, Peru, Senegal, Venezuela, Yugoslavia and Zimbabwe
GATT	General Agreement on Trade and Tariffs
GDP	Gross Domestic Product
GIF	Global Infrastructure Fund
GNP	Gross National Product
GRAS	generally regarded as safe
HDI	Human Development Index (UNDP)
IBM	International Business Machines
IBRD	International Bank for Reconstruction and Development
ILO	International Labor Organization
IMF	International Monetary Fund

IPAT	(I) Impact = product of Population size (P), times per capita Affluence (A), times the damage done by Technology (T) used to supply each unit of consumption
ISEW	Index of Sustainable Economic Welfare (World Bank)
ITO	International Trade Organization
JPL	Jet Propulsion Laboratories
LETS	Local Exchange Trading Systems
MEW	Measure of Economic Welfare
MIT	Massachusetts Institute of Technology
MITI	Ministry of International Trade and Industry (Japan)
NASA	National Aeronautics and Space Administration
NCEO	National Center for Employee Ownership
NGOs	non-governmental organizations
NIEO	New International Economic Order
NNW	Net National Welfare (Japan)
NORAD	North American Aerospace Defense Command
OAU	Organization of African Unity
OCAW	Oil, Chemical and Atomic Workers Union
ODA	official development aid
OECD	Organization for Economic Cooperation and Development
OPEC	Organization of Petroleum Exporting Countries
OTA	Office of Technology Assessment
ODII	Organizing for Development Institute, Inc.
ORT	oral rehydration therapy
PBS	Public Broadcasting System
PCR	polymerase chain reaction
PPP(s)	parity purchasing power (units)
PQLI	Physical Quality of Life Indicator
R & D	research and development
SALs	structural adjustment loans
SDI	Strategic Defense Initiative, popularly called Star Wars
SDR	Special Drawing Rights
SHARE	Self-Help Association for a Regional Economy
SII	Structural Impediments Initiative
SRI	Stanford Research Institute (Ameritrust/SRI)
TOES	The Other Economic Summit
UNDP	United Nations Development Program
UNICEF	United Nations Children's Fund
UNEP	United Nations Environment Programme
UNESCO	United Nations Economic, Scientific and Cultural Organization
UNSNA	United Nations System of National Accounts
USSR	Union of Soviet Socialist Republics
WCED	World Commission on Economics and Development
WHO	World Health Organization
WMO	World Meteorological Organization
WOMP	World Order Models Project

Index

279